D0023454

AUTHENTIC LITURGICAL RENEWAL IN CONTEMPORARY PERSPECTIVE

AUTHENTIC LITURGICAL RENEWAL IN CONTEMPORARY PERSPECTIVE

Proceedings of the Sacra Liturgia
Conference held in London, 5–8 July 2016

Edited by
Uwe Michael Lang

Bloomsbury T&T Clark
An imprint of Bloomsbury Publishing Plc

B L O O M S B U R Y
LONDON · OXFORD · NEW YORK · NEW DELHI · SYDNEY

Bloomsbury T&T Clark
An imprint of Bloomsbury Publishing Plc
Imprint previously known as T&T Clark

50 Bedford Square	1385 Broadway
London	New York
WC1B 3DP	NY 10018
UK	USA

www.bloomsbury.com

BLOOMSBURY, T&T CLARK and the Diana logo are trademarks of
Bloomsbury Publishing Plc

First published 2017.

© Uwe Michael Lang and contributors, 2017

Uwe Michael Lang has asserted his right under the Copyright, Designs and Patents Act, 1988, to be identified as Author of this work.

All rights reserved. No part of this publication may be reproduced or transmitted in any form or by any means, electronic or mechanical, including photocopying, recording, or any information storage or retrieval system, without prior permission in writing from the publishers.

No responsibility for loss caused to any individual or organization acting on or refraining from action as a result of the material in this publication can be accepted by Bloomsbury or the author.

British Library Cataloguing-in-Publication Data
A catalogue record for this book is available from the British Library.

ISBN: HB: 978-0-5676-7843-0
PB: 978-0-5676-7842-3
ePDF: 978-0-5676-7844-7
ePub: 978-0-5676-7845-4

Library of Congress Cataloging-in-Publication Data
A caralog record for this book is available from the Library of Congress.

Cover image © Fr Lawrence Lew, O.P.

Typeset by Deanta Global Publishing Services, Chennai, India

Table of Contents

Notes on Contributors   vii

Preface   xi

List of Abbreviations   xii

1   Opening Remarks
     Dominique Rey   1

2   Towards an Authentic Implementation of *Sacrosanctum Concilium*
     Robert Cardinal Sarah   3

3   Liturgy and the Triune God: Rethinking Trinitarian Theology
     Helmut Hoping   21

4   The Public Nature of Catholic Liturgy
     Charbel Pazat de Lys OSB   31

5   The Ethical Character of the Mysteries: Observations
     from a Moral Theologian
     Michael P. Cullinan   53

6   Doing the World Liturgically: Stewardship of
     Creation and Care for the Poor
     David W. Fagerberg   69

7   Liturgy Beyond the Secular
     Joris Geldhof   83

8   'Especially in Mission Territories' (SC 38): New Evangelization
     and Liturgical (Reform of the) Reform
     Stephen Bullivant   97

9   The Tridentine Liturgical Reform in Historical Perspective
     Uwe Michael Lang   109

10 On the Council Floor: The Council Fathers' Debate of the
    Schema on the Sacred Liturgy
    Alcuin Reid   125

11 Sing a New Song to the Lord – Towards a Revised
    Translation of the *Liturgy of the Hours*
    Alan Hopes   145

12 *Divine Worship: The Missal* and 'the Liturgical Books Proper to the
    Anglican Tradition' (*Anglicanorum Coetibus*, Art. III)
    Andrew Burnham   155

13 The Vicissitudes of Liturgy and Architecture Shown at the
    Example of Berlin's Cathedral of St Hedwig
    Peter Stephan   171

14 Homily at the Votive Mass of Saints Peter and Paul, Apostles
    Robert Cardinal Sarah   189

15 Set Free at the Source of Our Demise: Homily at the Votive Mass of
    Our Lord Jesus Christ, Eternal High Priest
    Salvatore J. Cordileone   193

16 Homily at the Votive Mass of Blessed John Henry Newman
    Keith Newton   195

Notes on Contributors

Stephen Bullivant, who holds a DPhil from the University of Oxford (2009), is professor of theology and the sociology of religion, and director of the Benedict XVI Centre for Religion and Society, at St Mary's University, Twickenham. He has been a consulting editor for *The Catholic Herald* since 2015. His recent books include *The Trinity: How Not to Be a Heretic* (Paulist, 2015), *The Oxford Dictionary of Atheism* (with Lois Lee; OUP, 2016), and *O My Jesus: The Meaning of the Fátima Prayer* (with Luke Arredondo; Paulist, 2017).

Monsignor Andrew Burnham was one of five Anglican bishops who announced their resignations in November 2010, following the publication of *Anglicanorum Coetibus*, and their intention to join the proposed Personal Ordinariate in England and Wales. He was received into full communion with the Catholic Church, ordained as a Catholic priest and appointed a prelate of honour in 2011. He has since served as an assistant to the ordinary in the Personal Ordinariate of Our Lady of Walsingham and as parish priest of East Hendred Catholic Parish. Among his publications is the book *Heaven and Earth in Little Space: The Re-enchantment of Liturgy* (Canterbury Press, 2010). He was also the compiler and editor, with Fr Aidan Nichols OP, of *The Customary of Our Lady of Walsingham* (Canterbury Press, 2012). Serving on the Interdicasterial Commission *Anglicanae Traditiones*, he has been instrumental in the producing of *Divine Worship: Occasional Services*, 2014 and *Divine Worship: The Missal*, 2015.

Archbishop Salvatore J. Cordileone, who holds a doctorate in Canon Law from the Pontifical Gregorian University in Rome, was appointed to the see of San Francisco by Pope Benedict XVI in 2012. He chairs the United States Conference of Catholic Bishops' Subcommittee for the Promotion and Defense of Marriage and sits on the Committee for Canonical Affairs. He is a member of the Board of Trustees of the Catholic University of America, the Governing Board of the International Theological Institute, and has served on the Interdicasterial Commission *Anglicanae Traditiones*. Together with Fr Samuel Weber OSB, he established the Benedict XVI Institute for Sacred Music and Divine Worship, based at Saint Patrick's University and Seminary in Menlo Park, California.

Father Michael P. Cullinan is a priest of the Archdiocese of Westminster. Having completed a PhD in numerical analysis at Cambridge University, his first career was as a mathematician. After academic posts at the University of Salford and Dublin City University, he entered Allen Hall Seminary in 1988, was ordained a priest in 1995 and then served in the parishes of Holy Trinity, Brook Green, and St James's Spanish Place. In 2000 he went to Rome for further studies, gaining an STL in moral theology from the Angelicum in 2002 and defending his doctorate at the Alfonsianum in 2005.

His thesis was subsequently published in the series *Tesi Accademia Alfonsiana*. He has spoken at the Society of Biblical Literature International Meeting and lectured at the International Theological Institute in Austria. He was recently appointed as director of the Higher Institute of Religious Sciences at Maryvale, Birmingham, where he has been director of the theology programme since April 2009.

David W. Fagerberg is professor in the Department of Theology at the University of Notre Dame. He holds an MDiv from Luther Northwestern Seminary; an MA from St John's University, Collegeville; an STM from Yale Divinity School; and MA, MPhil and PhD from Yale University. His work has explored how the Church's *lex credendi* (law of belief) is founded upon the Church's *lex orandi* (law of prayer). He has published articles on liturgical theology in various academic journals and dictionaries of theology, and is the author of *What is Liturgical Theology?* (Liturgical Press, 1992), *The Size of Chesterton's Catholicism* (University of Notre Dame Press, 1998), *Theologia Prima* (Hillenbrand Books, 2003), *Chesterton is Everywhere* (Emmaus Press, 2013), *On Liturgical Asceticism* (Catholic University of America Press, 2013) and *Consecrating the World: On Mundane Liturgical Theology* (Angelico Press, 2016).

Joris Geldhof, PhD (KU Leuven), is professor of liturgical studies and sacramental theology at the Faculty of Theology and Religious Studies, Catholic University of Leuven, Belgium. He is the chair of the Liturgical Institute, coordinator of the Research Unit of Pastoral and Empirical Theology and editor-in-chief of the bilingual journal *Questions Liturgiques/Studies in Liturgy*. His major areas of interest and expertise are liturgical theology, the Eucharist and questions pertaining to Christian sacramentality in a secularized world. He is the editor of *Mediating Mysteries, Understanding Liturgies: On Bridging the Gap Between Liturgy and Systematic Theology* (Peeters, 2015); *Ritual Participation and Interreligious Dialogue: Boundaries, Transgressions, Innovations* (Bloomsbury, 2015); and *Approaching the Threshold of Mystery: Liturgical Worlds and Theological Spaces* (Pustet, 2015). In August 2015 he was elected president-elect of Societas Liturgica.

Bishop Alan Hopes studied theology at King's College, London, and Warminster Theological College. He was ordained for ministry in the Church of England in 1968 and served as an Anglican priest until 1994 when he was received into the Catholic Church. He was ordained a Catholic priest in 1995 in the Archdiocese of Westminster, and he was chosen by Pope John Paul II as an auxiliary bishop in the same diocese in 2003. In 2010 he became the episcopal delegate of the Catholic Bishops' Conference of England and Wales for the implementation of Pope Benedict XVI's Apostolic Constitution *Anglicanorum Coetibus*. In 2013 Pope Francis made him the fourth bishop of East Anglia. Bishop Hopes is the chairman of the Committee for Liturgy of the Catholic Bishops' Conference of England and Wales and he has been involved in the work of the International Commission for English in the Liturgy since 2004.

Helmut Hoping is professor of dogmatic theology and liturgy at the University of Freiburg in Breisgau, Germany. He completed his doctorate at the University of Tübingen in 1989, followed by the *Habilitation* in 1995. From 1991 to 1992 he was visiting researcher at the Catholic University of America in Washington, DC. From 1996 to 2000 he was professor of dogmatic theology at the University of Lucerne, Switzerland, and in Spring 2004 he taught as visiting professor at Boston College. Among his publications are *Einführung in die Christologie* (Wissenschaftliche Buchgesellschaft, 3rd edition 2014) and *Mein Leib für euch gegeben: Geschichte und Theologie der Eucharistie* (Herder, 2nd edition 2015; English translation in preparation).

Father Uwe Michael Lang, MagTheol (Vienna), STL (Leuven), DPhil (Oxford), a native of Nuremberg, Germany, is a priest of the Oratory of St Philip Neri in London, where he serves as parish priest, and a lecturer in Church history at Heythrop College, University of London. He is an associate staff member at the Maryvale Institute, Birmingham, and was on the visiting faculty of the Liturgical Institute in Mundelein, Illinois in 2014. He is a board member of the Society for Catholic Liturgy and the editor of *Antiphon: A Journal for Liturgical Renewal*. He was a staff member of Congregation for Divine Worship and the Discipline of the Sacraments (2008–12) and consultor to the Office for the Liturgical Celebrations of the Supreme Pontiff (2008–13). Among his publications are *Turning Towards the Lord: Orientation in Liturgical Prayer* (Ignatius Press, 2nd edition, 2009), *The Voice of the Church at Prayer: Reflections on Liturgy and Language* (Ignatius Press, 2012) and *Signs of the Holy One: Liturgy, Ritual and Expression of the Sacred* (Ignatius Press, 2015).

Monsignor Keith Newton served as a priest and bishop in the Church of England, most recently as bishop of Richborough in the Province of Canterbury from 2002 until 2010, before being received into full communion with the Catholic Church. He was ordained to the sacred priesthood in 2011 and appointed by Pope Benedict XVI as the first ordinary of the Personal Ordinariate of Our Lady of Walsingham. Subsequently, he was elevated to the rank of protonotary apostolic.

Dom Charbel Pazat de Lys OSB, born in Madrid, with both Spanish and French citizenship, began his monastic life in Le Barroux (France) in 1985 and took his solemn vows in 1988. He was ordained to the priesthood in 1994. In the monastery he has had various offices, including assistant master of novices, teacher of liturgy, master of students and master of ceremonies. In 2002 he completed a Licence in Sacred Liturgy at the Pontifical Liturgical Institute of Sant'Anselmo in Rome. He is in charge of the *Editions Ste Madeleine*. He has contributed to several of the colloquia organized by CIEL (Centre international d'études liturgiques) and was one of the invited speakers at the 2001 liturgical conference convened by Joseph Cardinal Ratzinger at the Abbey of Fontgombault.

Dom Alcuin Reid is a monk of the Monastère Saint-Benoît in the Diocese of Fréjus-Toulon, France. After studies in Theology and in Education in Melbourne, Australia, he was awarded a PhD from King's College, University of London, for a thesis on twentieth-century liturgical reform (2002), which was subsequently published as *The Organic Development of the Liturgy*, with a preface by Joseph Cardinal Ratzinger (Ignatius Press, 2005). He has lectured internationally and has published extensively in the field of liturgical studies. He has recently edited the *T&T Clark Companion to*

Liturgy (Bloomsbury, 2016) and the proceedings of the *Sacra Liturgia USA* conference in New York in 2015, *Liturgy in the Twenty First Century: Contemporary Issues and Perspectives* (Bloomsbury, 2016). He is currently working on *Continuity or Rupture? A Study of the Second Vatican Council's Reform of the Liturgy*. He coordinates the ongoing *Sacra Liturgia* initiatives and organizes its annual summer school in France.

Bishop Dominique Rey was appointed to the see of Fréjus-Toulon in southern France by Pope John Paul II in 2000 and is a leading figure in the French episcopate. He was a member of the Synod on Evangelisation in 2012. Bishop Rey convened the *Adoratio* conference at the Pontifical Salesian University in Rome in 2011 as well as the *Sacra Liturgia* conference at the Pontifical University of the Holy Cross in Rome in 2013.

Robert Cardinal Sarah was archbishop of Conakry in his native country, Guinea, from 1979 to 2001. Called to Rome by St John Paul II in 2001, he has served as the secretary of the Congregation for the Evangelisation of the Peoples and as the president of the Pontifical Council *Cor Unum*. Pope Benedict XVI appoined him cardinal in 2010, and in November 2014 Pope Francis appointed him prefect of the Congregation for Divine Worship and Discipline of the Sacraments. His popular and insightful 2015 book-length interview *Dieu ou rien* has been translated into many languages, including English (*God or Nothing*, Ignatius Press, 2015). His latest book is *The Power of Silence: Against the Dictatorship of Noise* (Ignatius Press, 2017).

Peter Stephan studied ancient history, Church history and Christian archaeology in Freiburg, Heidelberg and Würzburg from 1982 to 1990. After his master degree, he pursued doctoral studies in art history and classical archaeology. In 1996 he completed his doctorate on Tiepolo's frescoes in the Würzburg Residenz. In 2006 followed his *Habilitation* on the three-dimensionality of facades early modern architecture. In 2011 he became an adjunct professor of art history at the University of Freiburg, and since 2013 he has been professor for architectural theory at the Fachhochschule Potsdam. He also has numerous teaching commitments in Germany and in other countries. His research focuses on architectural history, as well as political and religious iconography. A major interest of his is interaction of architecture and art history with theology.

Preface

This book contains the proceedings of the *Sacra Liturgia UK* conference, held at Imperial College, London, with liturgical celebrations at the Church of the Oratory, Brompton Road, and the Church of Our Lady of the Assumption and St Gregory, Warwick Street, from 5 to 8 July 2016.

The *Sacra Liturgia* initiative, which is inspired by the Second Vatican Council's insistence that the Church's public worship, especially the Eucharistic sacrifice, is the 'source and summit (*fons et culmen*) of the whole Christian life',[1] began with a conference in Rome in June 2013 and was continued with a conference in New York City in June 2015.[2] At the time of writing, a fourth *Sacra Liturgia* conference is being planned in Milan for June 2017. This series of successful events has shown our time to be particularly receptive to the study and debate of liturgical questions. The responses to the pastoral proposal made by Robert Cardinal Sarah at the London conference regarding the priest's direction of prayer during the Liturgy of the Eucharist were not confined to the ecclesiastical sphere, but also reached the secular media.[3] The discussion on the liturgy is clearly of interest to a wider public, not least because it touches upon a variety of historical, cultural and artistic matters.

This volume will no doubt contribute to this lively conversation. It offers different perspectives and covers a variety of topics, but it is forged into a whole by the authors' shared concern for authentic liturgical renewal, which is essential for the life and mission of the Catholic Church today.

Uwe Michael Lang
The Epiphany of the Lord 2017

---

[1] Second Vatican Council, Dogmatic Constitution on the Church *Lumen Gentium* (21 November 1964), no. 11, and Constitution on the Sacred Liturgy *Sacrosanctum Concilium* (4 December 1963), no. 10.

[2] The proceedings of both conferences have been published: *The Sacred Liturgy: Source and Summit of the Life and Mission of the Church*, ed. Alcuin Reid (San Francisco: Ignatius Press, 2014), and *Liturgy in the Twenty-First Century: Contemporary Issues and Perspectives*, ed. Alcuin Reid (London and New York: Bloomsbury, 2016).

[3] See Christopher Howse, 'Sacred Mysteries: Eastward Ho! A Surprise from an African Cardinal', in *The Daily Telegraph*, 13 July 2016, and 'Hearts, Minds and Souls', in *The Economist*, 30 July 2016.

List of Abbreviations

PG   J.-P. Migne (ed.), *Patrologiae cursus completus… Series graeca* (166 vols.; Paris: J.-P. Migne, 1857–83)

PL   J.-P. Migne (ed.), *Patrologiae cursus completus… Series latina* (221 vols.; Paris: J.-P. Migne, 1844–65)

CChrSL   Corpus Christianorum. Series Latina (Turnhout: Brepols, 1953–)

CSEL   Corpus Scriptorum Ecclesiasticorum Latinorum (Vienna: Geroldi, then Tempksy, 1866–)

Opening Remarks

Dominique Rey

It is with great joy that I open this third international *Sacra Liturgia* conference here in London, following on from two very rich and successful conferences in Rome (2013) and New York (2015).

To His Eminence, Vincent Cardinal Nichols, for his kind words of welcome of *Sacra Liturgia* to the Archdiocese of Westminster, I express my gratitude in a spirit of fraternal communion.

It is a great privilege to have celebrated our opening Vespers in the beautiful church of the Fathers of the London Oratory. I am profoundly grateful to the Provost and to the Fathers for their liturgical hospitality during these days. So too I am grateful for the invitation Monsignor Keith Newton, Ordinary of the Personal Ordinariate of Our Lady of Walshingham, has extended to us to participate in the Pontifical Mass in the *Divine Worship* use, which will close this conference on Friday.

I thank the organizing team for their vision and for their hard work in putting together this conference and enabling us to consider once again, and in new ways, the essential role of liturgical formation and celebration in the life and mission of the Church. And I thank the many generous benefactors and sponsors who have made it possible for us to meet here today: may God bless and reward each one of you.

It is for me personally, as I am sure it is for each one of us present, a privilege and a joy to welcome His Eminence, Robert Cardinal Sarah, prefect of the Congregation for Divine Worship and the Discipline of the Sacraments. Your Eminence, I thank you for honouring us by your presence and for agreeing to give the opening address this evening and to celebrate the Holy Sacrifice of the Mass for us.

I thank also His Excellency, Archbishop Salvatore Cordileone, for his presence – both last year in New York City and now here in London. Archbishop Cordileone will also offer Holy Mass for us and will present the concluding reflections on Friday. Thank you, Your Excellency.

So too I thank all those men and women who will address us in the coming days, and whose scholarship and liturgical work is an apostolate of the first importance in the Church today. We look forward to learning from your insights.

My brothers and sisters, we meet here in London during the Extraordinary Jubilee of Mercy. In announcing this jubilee, our Holy Father, Pope Francis, stated: 'I am confident that the whole Church, which is in such need of mercy for we are sinners, will be able to find in this Jubilee the joy of rediscovering and rendering fruitful God's mercy, with which we are all called to give comfort to every man and every woman of our time.'[1]

My friends, where do we encounter the mercy and love of Almighty God if not first in the sacred liturgy? Perhaps we forget that it is in the liturgical rite of Baptism that original and actual sin is remitted, and that it is through this liturgical act that we are given the life of Christ for the first time. Perhaps we forget that the sacrament of the Most Blessed Eucharist is not only the fruit of Christ's saving sacrifice on the Cross given for us, but that over the centuries the Church has fittingly celebrated this ultimate mercy of Almighty God with liturgical symbols and rites of a beauty and dignity that befits the ultimate triumph of God's mercy that is the passion, death and resurrection of our Lord Jesus Christ. Perhaps, too, we forget that the sacrament of penance – of confession – where, when necessary, our baptismal dignity is restored, is also a liturgical rite – one which our Holy Father has rightly called us to rediscover and to celebrate with renewed fervour during this jubilee year.

We first encounter the love and mercy of God in the sacred liturgy. And from that saving and healing encounter we are empowered and sent as missionaries into a world that so often does not even know it needs His love and mercy.

My brothers and sisters, let us not forget this: we rightly concern ourselves in these days about questions of liturgical formation and celebration. And the reason we do so is to enable each of us here present, and those for whose formation we as priests or parents or teachers are responsible, to experience more profoundly the saving love and mercy of Jesus Christ. Sound liturgical formation and correct and worthy liturgical celebration are essential if the Church's life and mission are to flourish in the twenty-first century. Let us keep this in mind most especially in this jubilee year of mercy.

Our work in these days may seem academic or theoretical. But we must build liturgical renewal upon solid foundations. Therefore, as we study together in these days, as we pray together in Catholic unity in three distinct uses of the Roman rite, as we meet each other and share our concerns, let us remember that the sacred liturgy is truly 'the summit toward which the activity of the Church is directed; at the same time it is the font from which all her power flows',[2] and that therefore our work is crucial for the life and mission of the Church in our day.

---

[1] Pope Francis, *Homily at Penitential Celebration in the Vatican Basilica* (13 March 2015).
[2] Second Vatican Council, Constitution on the Sacred Liturgy *Sacrosanctum Concilium* (4 December 1963), no. 10.

Towards an Authentic Implementation of *Sacrosanctum Concilium*

Robert Cardinal Sarah

In the first place I wish to express my thanks to His Eminence, Vincent Cardinal Nichols, for his welcome to the Archdiocese of Westminster and for his kind words of greeting. So too I wish to thank His Excellency Dominique Rey, bishop of Fréjus-Toulon, for his invitation to be present at this, the third international *Sacra Liturgia* conference, and to present the opening address this evening. Your Excellency, I congratulate you on this international initiative to promote the study of the importance of liturgical formation and celebration in the life and mission of the Church.

I am very happy to be here with you all today. I thank each of you for your presence, which reflects your appreciation of the importance of what the then cardinal Ratzinger once called 'the question of the liturgy' today, at the beginning of the twenty-first century. This is a great sign of hope for the Church.

1 Introduction

In his message dated 18 February 2014 to the symposium celebrating the fiftieth anniversary of the Second Vatican Council's Constitution on the Sacred Liturgy, *Sacrosanctum Concilium*, the Holy Father, Pope Francis, observed that the marking of fifty years since the promulgation of the constitution should push us 'to revive the commitment to accept and implement [the] teaching [of *Sacrosanctum Concilium*] in an ever fuller way'. The Holy Father continued:

> It is necessary to unite a renewed willingness to go forward along the path indicated by the Council Fathers, as there remains much to be done for a correct and complete assimilation of the Constitution on the Sacred Liturgy on the part of the baptized and ecclesial communities. I refer, in particular, to the commitment

to a solid and organic liturgical initiation and formation, both of lay faithful as well as clergy and consecrated persons.[1]

The Holy Father is correct: we have much to do if we are to realize the vision of the fathers of the Second Vatican Council for the liturgical life of the Church. We have very much to do if today, some fifty years after the council concluded, we are to achieve 'a correct and complete assimilation of the Constitution on the Sacred Liturgy'.

In this address I wish to place before you some considerations on how the Western Church might move towards a more faithful implementation of *Sacrosanctum Concilium*. In doing so I propose to ask what the fathers of the Second Vatican Council intended in the liturgical reform. Then I would like to consider how their intentions were implemented following the council. Finally, I would like to put before you some suggestions for the liturgical life of the Church today, so that our liturgical practice might more faithfully reflect the intentions of the council fathers.

2 What is the Sacred Liturgy?

But first we must consider a preliminary question: what is the sacred liturgy? Because if we do not understand the nature of Catholic liturgy, as distinct from the rites of other Christian communities and of other religions, we cannot hope to understand the Second Vatican Council's Constitution on the Sacred Liturgy, or to move towards a more faithful implementation of it.

In his Motu Proprio *Tra le sollecitudini* (22 November 1903), Pope St Pius X taught that 'the holy mysteries' and 'the public and solemn prayer of the Church', that is, the sacred liturgy, are the 'foremost and indispensable fount' for acquiring 'the true Christian spirit'.[2] St Pius X therefore called for a real and fruitful participation in the Church's liturgical rites by all. As we know, this teaching and this exhortation would be repeated by article 14 of *Sacrosanctum Concilium*.[3]

Pope Pius XI raised his voice to the same end some twenty-five years later in his Apostolic Constitution *Divini Cultus* (20 December 1928), teaching that 'the liturgy is indeed a sacred thing, since by it we are raised to God and united to Him, thereby professing our faith and our deep obligation to Him for the benefits we have received and the help of which we stand in constant need'.[4]

Pope Pius XII devoted an Encyclical Letter, *Mediator Dei* (20 November 1947), to the sacred liturgy, in which he taught that

> the sacred liturgy is ... the public worship which our Redeemer as Head of the Church renders to the Father, as well as the worship which the community of the

---

[1] Pope Francis, *Message to the Participants of the Roman Symposium on* Sacrosanctum Concilium (18 February 2014).

[2] St Pius X, Motu Proprio on the Restoration of Sacred Music *Tra le sollecitudini* (22 November 1903).

[3] References to the Second Vatican Council's Constitution on the Sacred Liturgy *Sacrosanctum Concilium* (4 December 1963) will be made in the body of the paper, with the abbreviation SC followed by the paragraph number.

[4] Pius XI, Apostolic Constitution on Divine Worship *Divini Cultus* (20 December 1928).

faithful renders to its Founder, and through Him to the heavenly Father. It is, in short, the worship rendered by the Mystical Body of Christ in the entirety of its Head and members.[5]

The pope taught that the 'nature and the object of the sacred liturgy' is that 'it aims at uniting our souls with Christ and sanctifying them through the divine Redeemer in order that Christ be honoured and, through Him and in Him, the most Holy Trinity'.[6]

The Second Vatican Council taught that through the liturgy 'the work of our redemption is accomplished' (SC 2), and that the liturgy

> is considered as an exercise of the priestly office of Jesus Christ. In the liturgy the sanctification of the man is signified by signs perceptible to the senses, and is effected in a way which corresponds with each of these signs; in the liturgy the whole public worship is performed by the Mystical Body of Jesus Christ, that is, by the Head and His members.
>
> From this it follows that every liturgical celebration, because it is an action of Christ the priest and of His Body which is the Church, is a sacred action surpassing all others; no other action of the Church can equal its efficacy by the same title and to the same degree. (SC 7)

Following on from this, *Sacrosanctum Concilium* taught that the liturgy

> is the summit toward which the activity of the Church is directed; at the same time it is the font from which all her power flows. For the aim and object of apostolic works is that all who are made sons of God by faith and baptism should come together to praise God in the midst of His Church, to take part in the sacrifice, and to eat the Lord's supper. (SC 10)

It would be possible to continue this exposition of the magisterium's teaching on the nature of the sacred liturgy with the teaching of the post-conciliar popes and of the *Catechism of the Catholic Church*. But for the moment let us stop at the council. Because it is very clear, I think, that the Church teaches that Catholic liturgy is the singularly privileged locus of Christ's saving action in our world today, by means of real participation in which we receive his grace and strength, which is so necessary for our perseverance and growth in the Christian life. It is the divinely instituted place where we come to fulfil our duty of offering sacrifice to God, of offering the one true sacrifice. It is where we realize our profound need to worship Almighty God. Catholic liturgy is something sacred, something that is holy by its very nature. Catholic liturgy is no ordinary human gathering.

I wish to underline a very important fact here: God, not man, is at the centre of Catholic liturgy. We come to worship him. The liturgy is not about you and me; it is not where we celebrate our own identity or achievements or exalt or promote our own culture and local religious customs. The liturgy is first and foremost about God and what he has done for us. In his divine providence Almighty God founded the Church and instituted the sacred liturgy by means of which we are able to offer him true

---

[5]   Pius XII, Encyclical on the Sacred Liturgy *Mediator Dei* (20 November 1947), no. 20.
[6]   Ibid., no. 171.

worship in accordance with the New Covenant established by Christ. In doing this, in entering into the demands of the sacred rites developed in the tradition of the Church, we are given our true identity and meaning as sons and daughters of the Father.

It is essential that we understand this specificity of Catholic worship, for in recent decades we have seen many liturgical celebrations where people, personalities and human achievements have been too prominent, almost to the exclusion of God. As Cardinal Ratzinger once wrote: 'If the liturgy appears first of all as the workshop for our activity, then what is essential is being forgotten: God. For the liturgy is not about us, but about God. Forgetting about God is the most imminent danger of our age.'[7]

We must be utterly clear about the nature of Catholic worship if we are to read the Second Vatican Council's Constitution on the Sacred Liturgy correctly and if we are to implement it faithfully. For the fathers of the council were formed in the magisterial teachings of the twentieth-century popes that I have cited. St John XXIII did not call an ecumenical council to undermine these teachings, which he himself promoted. The council fathers did not arrive in Rome in October 1962 with the intention of producing an anthropocentric liturgy. Rather, the pope and the council fathers sought to find ways in which Christ's faithful could draw ever more deeply from the 'foremost and indispensable fount' so as to acquire 'the true Christian spirit' for their own salvation and for that of all men and women of their day.

3 What Did the Fathers of the Second Vatican Council Intend?

We must explore the intentions of the fathers of the council in more detail, particularly if we seek to be more faithful to their intentions today. What did they intend to bring about through the Constitution on the Sacred Liturgy? Let us begin with the very first article of *Sacrosanctum Concilium*, which states:

> This sacred Council has several aims in view: it desires to impart an ever increasing vigour to the Christian life of the faithful; to adapt more suitably to the needs of our own times those institutions which are subject to change; to foster whatever can promote union among all who believe in Christ; to strengthen whatever can help to call the whole of mankind into the household of the Church. (SC 1)

Let us remember that, when the council opened, liturgical reform had been a feature of the past decade and that the fathers were very familiar with these reforms. They were not considering these questions theoretically, without any context. They expected to continue the work already begun and to consider the 'altiora principia', the higher or fundamental principles of liturgical reform, spoken of by St John XXIII in his Motu Proprio *Rubricarum Instructum* of 25 July 1960.[8]

---

[7] Joseph Ratzinger, 'The Organic Development of the Liturgy', in *Theology of the Liturgy*, Collected Works, 11 (San Francisco: Ignatius Press, 2014), 589–94 (originally published in 2005), at 593.

[8] John XXIII, Apostolic Letter Issued *Motu Proprio* Approving the New Roman Breviary and Missal *Rubricarum Instructum* (25 July 1960).

Hence, the opening article of the constitution gives four reasons for undertaking a liturgical reform. The first, 'to impart an ever increasing vigour to the Christian life of the faithful', is the constant concern of the Church's pastors in every age.

The second, 'to adapt more suitably to the needs of our own times those institutions which are subject to change', may cause us to pause and reflect, particularly given the zeitgeist of the 1960s. But in truth, if it is read with that hermeneutic of continuity with which most certainly the council fathers intended it, this means that the council desired liturgical development where possible so as to facilitate an increased vigour to Christian life. The council fathers did not want to change things simply for the sake of change!

So too, the third reason, 'to foster whatever can promote union among all who believe in Christ', might cause us to pause lest we think that the fathers wished to make of the sacred liturgy an ecumenical tool, to render it a means to an end. But can this be the case? Certainly, after the council, some may have tried to do this. But the fathers themselves knew that this was not possible. Unity in worship before the altar of sacrifice is the desired *end* of ecumenical endeavour. The liturgy is not a means to promote good will or cooperation in apostolic works. No, here the council fathers are saying that they believe that liturgical reform can be part of a momentum which can help people to achieve that Catholic unity without which full communion in worship is not possible.

The same motivation is found in the fourth reason given for liturgical reform: 'to strengthen whatever can help to call the whole of mankind into the household of the Church'. Here, though, we move beyond our separated Christian brothers and sisters and consider 'the whole of mankind'. The Church's mission is to every man and woman! The fathers of the council believed this and hoped that more fruitful participation in the liturgy would facilitate a renewal in the Church's missionary activity.

Let me give one example. For many years before the council, in missionary countries and also in the more developed ones, there had been much discussion about the possibility of increasing the use of the vernacular languages in the liturgy, principally for the readings from Sacred Scripture, also for some of the other parts of the first part of the Mass (which we now call the 'Liturgy of the Word') and for liturgical singing. The Holy See had already given many permissions for the use of the vernacular in the administration of the sacraments. This is the context in which the fathers of the council spoke of the possible positive ecumenical or missionary effects of liturgical reform. It is true that the vernacular has a positive place in the liturgy. The fathers were seeking this, not authorizing the protestantization of the sacred liturgy or agreeing to it being subjected to a false inculturation.

I am an African. Let me say clearly: the liturgy is not the place to promote my culture. Rather, it is the place where my culture is baptized, where my culture is taken up into the divine. Through the Church's liturgy (which missionaries have carried throughout the world) God speaks to us, he changes us and enables us to partake in his divine life. When people become Christian, when they enter into full communion with the Catholic Church, they receive something more, something which changes them. Certainly, cultures and other Christians bring gifts with them into the Church – the liturgy of the Ordinariates of former Anglicans now in full communion with the

Catholic Church is a beautiful example of this. But they bring these gifts with humility, and the Church in her maternal wisdom makes use of them as she judges appropriate.

Nevertheless, it seems incumbent to be very clear on what we mean by inculturation. If we truly understand the meaning of the term as an insight into the mystery of Jesus Christ, then we have the key to inculturation, which is not a quest nor a claim for the legitimacy of Africanization nor Latin Americanization nor Asianization in substitution of a Westernization of Christianity. Inculturation is neither a canonization of a local culture nor a settling into this culture at the risk of making it absolute. Inculturation is an irruption and an epiphany of the Lord in the depths of our being. And the irruption of the Lord in our life causes a disruption, a detachment opening the way to a path according to new orientations that are creating elements of a new culture, vehicle of the Good News for man and his dignity as a son of God. When the Gospel enters into our life, it disrupts it, it transforms it. It gives it a new direction, new moral and ethical orientations. It turns the heart of man towards God and neighbour to love and serve them absolutely and without design. When Jesus enters into a life, he transfigures it, he deifies it by the radiant light of his face, just as when St Paul was on the road to Damascus (see Acts 9.5-6).

Just as by his Incarnation the Word of God became like men in all things, except sin (Heb. 4.15), so the Gospel assumes all human and cultural values, but refuses to take shape in the structures of sin. This means that the more individual and collective sins abound in a human or ecclesial community, the less room there exists for inculturation. On the contrary, the more a Christian community shines with holiness and radiates evangelical values, the more it is likely to inculturate the Christian message. The inculturation of the faith is the challenge of sanctity. It verifies the degree of holiness, the level of the Gospel's penetration, and the deep faith in Jesus Christ in a Christian community. Inculturation, therefore, is not religious folklore.

It is not essentially realized in the use of local languages, instruments and Latin American music, African dances or African or Asian rituals and symbols in the liturgy and the sacraments. Inculturation is God who descends into the life, into the moral behaviour, into the cultures and into the customs of men in order to free them from sin and in order to introduce them into the life of the Trinity. Certainly the faith has need of a culture so as to be communicated. This is why St John Paul II affirmed that a faith that does not become culture is a faith that is dying: 'Properly applied, inculturation must be guided by two principles: "compatibility with the gospel and communion with the universal Church".'[9]

I have spent some time considering the first article of the constitution because it is very important that we do read *Sacrosanctum Concilium* in its context, as a document that intended to promote legitimate development (such as the increased use of the vernacular) in continuity with the nature, teaching and mission of the Church in the modern world. We must not read into it things which it does not say. The fathers did not intend a revolution, but an evolution, a moderate reform.

The intentions of the council fathers are very clear from other key passages. Article 14 is one of the most important of the whole constitution:

---

[9] John Paul II, Encyclical Letter on the Permanent Validity of the Church's Missionary Mandate *Redemptoris Missio* (7 December 1990), no. 54.

Mother Church earnestly desires that all the faithful should be led to that fully conscious and active participation in liturgical celebrations which is demanded by the very nature of the liturgy. Such participation by the Christian people as 'a chosen race, a royal priesthood, a holy nation, a redeemed people' (1 Pet. 2.9; cf. 2.4-5), is their right and duty by reason of their Baptism.

In the restoration and promotion of the sacred liturgy, this full and active participation by all the people is the aim to be considered before all else; for it is the primary and indispensable source from which the faithful are to derive the true Christian spirit; and therefore pastors of souls must zealously strive to achieve it, by means of the necessary instruction, in all their pastoral work.

Yet it would be futile to entertain any hopes of realizing this unless the pastors themselves, in the first place, become thoroughly imbued with the spirit and power of the liturgy, and undertake to give instruction about it. A prime need, therefore, is that attention be directed, first of all, to the liturgical instruction of the clergy. (SC 14)

We hear the voice of the pre-conciliar popes here, seeking a real and fruitful participation in the liturgy, and in order to bring that about, the insistence that a thorough instruction or formation in the liturgy is urgently necessary. The fathers show a realism here that was perhaps forgotten afterwards. Let us listen again to those words of the council and ponder their importance: 'It would be futile to entertain any hopes of realizing this (active participation) unless the pastors themselves, in the first place, become thoroughly imbued with the spirit and power of the liturgy, and undertake to give instruction about it.'

At the beginning of article 21 we also hear the fathers' intentions very clearly: 'In order that the Christian people may more certainly derive an abundance of graces from the sacred liturgy, holy Mother Church desires to undertake with great care a general restoration of the liturgy itself (ut populus christianus in sacra Liturgia abundantiam gratiarum securius assequatur ...)' (SC 21). When we study Latin we learn that the word 'ut' signifies a clear purpose that follows in the same clause. What did the council fathers intend? That the Christian people may more certainly derive an abundance of graces from the sacred liturgy. How did they propose to do this? By undertaking with great care a general restoration of the liturgy itself ('ipsius Liturgiae generalem instaurationem sedulo curare cupit'). Please note that the fathers speak of a 'restoration', not a revolution!

One of the clearest and most beautiful expressions of the intentions of the fathers of the council is found at the beginning of the second chapter of the constitution, which considers the mystery of the Most Holy Eucharist:

The Church ... earnestly desires that Christ's faithful, when present at this mystery of faith, should not be there as strangers or silent spectators; on the contrary, through a good understanding of the rites and prayers they should take part in the sacred action conscious of what they are doing, with devotion and full collaboration. They should be instructed by God's word and be nourished at the table of the Lord's body; they should give thanks to God; by offering the Immaculate Victim, not only through the hands of the priest, but also with him, they should learn also to offer themselves; through Christ the Mediator they should be drawn day by day into ever more perfect union with God and with each other, so that finally God may be all in all. (SC 48)

My brothers and sisters, this is what the council fathers intended. Yes, certainly, they discussed and voted on specific ways of achieving their intentions. But let us be very clear: the ritual reforms proposed in the constitution such as the restoration of the prayer of the faithful at Mass (SC 53), the extension of concelebration (SC 57) or some of its policies such as the simplification desired by SC 34 and 50, are all subordinate to the fundamental intentions of the council fathers I have just outlined. They are means to an end, and it is the end that we must achieve.

If we are to move towards a more authentic implementation of *Sacrosanctum Concilium,* it is these goals, these ends, which we must keep before us first and foremost. It may be that, if we study them with fresh eyes and with the benefit of the experience of the past five decades, we shall see some specific ritual reforms and certain liturgical policies in a different light. If, today, so as to 'impart an ever increasing vigour to the Christian life of the faithful' and 'help to call the whole of mankind into the household of the Church', some of these need to be reconsidered, let us ask the Lord to give us the love and the humility and wisdom so to do.

4　What Has Happened Following the Promulgation of *Sacrosanctum Concilium?*

I raise this possibility of looking again at the constitution and at the reform that followed its promulgation, because I do not think that we can honestly read even the first article of *Sacrosanctum Concilium* today and be content that we have achieved its aims. My brothers and sisters, where are the faithful of whom the council fathers spoke? Many of the faithful are now unfaithful: they do not come to the liturgy at all. To use the words of St John Paul II:

> Forgetfulness of God led to the abandonment of man. It is therefore no wonder that in this context a vast field has opened for the unrestrained development of nihilism in philosophy, of relativism in values and morality, and of pragmatism – and even a cynical hedonism – in daily life. European culture gives the impression of 'silent apostasy' on the part of people who have all that they need and who live as if God does not exist.[10]

Where is the unity the council hoped to achieve? We have not yet reached it. Have we made real progress in calling the whole of mankind into the household of the Church? I do not think so. And yet we have done very much to the liturgy!

In my forty-seven years of life as a priest and after more than thirty-six years of episcopal ministry I can attest that many Catholic communities and individuals live and pray the liturgy as reformed following the council with fervour and joy, deriving

---

[10]　John Paul II, Post-Synodal Apostolic Exhortation on Jesus Christ Alive in His Church the Source of Hope for Europe *Ecclesia in Europa* (28 June 2003), no. 9.

from it many, if not all, of the goods that the council fathers desired. This is a great fruit of the council. But from my experience I also know – now also through my service as prefect of the Congregation for Divine Worship and the Discipline of the Sacraments – that there are many distortions of the liturgy throughout the Church today, and there are many situations that could be improved so that the aims of the council can be achieved. Before I reflect on some possible improvements, let us consider what happened following the promulgation of the Constitution on the Sacred Liturgy.

In the sixteenth century the pope entrusted the liturgical reform desired by the Council of Trent to a special commission that worked to prepare revised editions of the liturgical books that were eventually promulgated by the pope. This is a perfectly normal procedure and it was the one adopted by Bl. Paul VI in 1964 when he established the *Consilium ad exsequendam Constitutionem de Sacra Liturgia*. We know much about this commission because of the published memoirs of its secretary, the later archbishop Annibale Bugnini.[11]

The work of this commission to implement the constitution was certainly subject to influences, ideologies and new proposals that were not present in *Sacrosanctum Concilium*. For example, it is true that the council did not propose the introduction of new Eucharistic prayers, but that this idea came up and was accepted, and that new prayers were authoritatively promulgated by the pope. It is true, also, as Archbishop Bugnini himself makes clear in retrospect, that some prayers and rites were constructed or revised according to the spirit of the times, particularly according to ecumenical sensitivities. Whether or not too much was done, or whether what was done truly helped to achieve the aims of the constitution, or whether they in fact hindered them, are questions we need to study. I am very happy that today scholars are considering these matters in depth. Nevertheless it is an important fact that Bl. Paul VI judged the reforms proposed by the commission to be suitable and that he promulgated them. With his apostolic authority he established them as normative and ensured their liceity and validity.

But while the official work of reform was taking place some very serious misinterpretations of the liturgy emerged and took root in different places throughout the world. These abuses of the sacred liturgy grew up because of an erroneous understanding of the council, resulting in liturgical celebrations that were subjective and which were more focused on the individual community's desires than on the sacrificial worship of Almighty God. My predecessor as prefect of the Congregation for Divine Worship, Francis Cardinal Arinze, once called this sort of thing 'the *do-it-yourself Mass*'. St John Paul II even found it necessary to write the following in his Encyclical Letter *Ecclesia de Eucharistia*:

> The Magisterium's commitment to proclaiming the Eucharistic mystery has been matched by interior growth within the Christian community. Certainly *the liturgical reform inaugurated by the Council* has greatly contributed to a more conscious, active and fruitful participation in the Holy Sacrifice of the Altar on the part of the faithful. In many places, *adoration of the Blessed Sacrament* is also

---

[11] Annibale Bugnini, *The Reform of the Liturgy: 1948-1975*, trans. Matthew J. O'Connell (Collegeville, MN: Liturgical Press, 1990).

an important daily practice and becomes an inexhaustible source of holiness. The devout participation of the faithful in the Eucharistic procession on the Solemnity of the Body and Blood of Christ is a grace from the Lord which yearly brings joy to those who take part in it.

Other positive signs of Eucharistic faith and love might also be mentioned.

Unfortunately, alongside these lights, *there are also shadows*. In some places the practice of Eucharistic adoration has been almost completely abandoned. In various parts of the Church abuses have occurred, leading to confusion with regard to sound faith and Catholic doctrine concerning this wonderful sacrament. At times one encounters an extremely reductive understanding of the Eucharistic mystery. Stripped of its sacrificial meaning, it is celebrated as if it were simply a fraternal banquet. Furthermore, the necessity of the ministerial priesthood, grounded in apostolic succession, is at times obscured and the sacramental nature of the Eucharist is reduced to its mere effectiveness as a form of proclamation. This has led here and there to ecumenical initiatives which, albeit well-intentioned, indulge in Eucharistic practices contrary to the discipline by which the Church expresses her faith. How can we not express profound grief at all this? The Eucharist is too great a gift to tolerate ambiguity and depreciation.

It is my hope that the present Encyclical Letter will effectively help to banish the dark clouds of unacceptable doctrine and practice, so that the Eucharist will continue to shine forth in all its radiant mystery.[12]

As well as abusive practices, there was an adverse reaction to the officially promulgated reforms. Some people found that they had gone too far too quickly, or even thought that the official reforms could be doctrinally suspect. One remembers the controversy that emerged in 1969 with the letter sent to Paul VI by Cardinals Ottaviani and Bacci expressing very serious concerns, after which the pope judged it appropriate to make certain doctrinal precisions. These questions, too, need to be studied carefully.

But there was also a pastoral reality here: whether for good reasons or not, some people could not, or would not, participate in the reformed rites. They stayed away, or only participated in the unreformed liturgy where they could find it, even when its celebration was not authorized. In this way the liturgy became an expression of divisions within the Church, rather than one of Catholic unity. The council did not intend that the liturgy should divide us one from another! St John Paul II worked to heal this division, aided by Cardinal Ratzinger who, as Pope Benedict XVI, sought to facilitate the necessary internal reconciliation in the Church by establishing in his Motu Proprio *Summorum Pontificum*[13] that the older form of the Roman rite is to be available without restriction to those individuals and groups who wish to draw from its riches. In God's Providence it is now possible to celebrate our Catholic unity while respecting, and even rejoicing in, a legitimate diversity of ritual practice.

---

[12] John Paul II, Encyclical on the Eucharist and its Relationship to the Church *Ecclesia de Eucharistia* (17 April 2003), no. 10.
[13] Benedict XVI, Apostolic Letter Given *Motu Proprio* on the Use of the Roman Liturgy Prior to the Reform of 1970 *Summorum Pontificum* (7 July 2007).

Finally, I would like to note that amidst the work of reform and translation that took place after the council (and we know that some of this work was done too quickly, meaning that today we have to revise the translations to render them more faithful to the original Latin), there was perhaps not enough attention paid to what the council fathers said was essential if the fruitful participation in the liturgy that they desired was to be achieved: that the clergy 'become thoroughly imbued with the spirit and power of the liturgy, and undertake to give instruction about it'. We know that a building with weak foundations is at risk of damage or even of collapse.

We may have built a very new, modern liturgy in the vernacular, but if we have not laid the correct foundations – if our seminarians and clergy are not 'thoroughly imbued with the spirit and power of the liturgy' as the council required – then they themselves cannot form the people entrusted to their care. We need to take the words of the council itself very seriously: it would be 'futile' to hope for a liturgical renewal without a thorough liturgical formation. Without this essential formation clergy could even damage peoples' faith in the Eucharistic mystery.

I do not wish to be thought of as being unduly pessimistic, and I say again: there are many, many faithful lay men and women, many clergy and religious for whom the liturgy as reformed after the council is a source of much spiritual and apostolic fruit, and for that I thank Almighty God. But, even from my brief analysis here, I think you will agree that we can do better so that the sacred liturgy truly becomes the source and summit of the life and mission of the Church now, at the beginning of the twenty-first century, as the fathers of the council so earnestly desired.

Anyway, this is what Pope Francis asks us to do: 'It is necessary to unite a renewed willingness to go forward along the path indicated by the Council Fathers, as there remains much to be done for a correct and complete assimilation of the Constitution on the Sacred Liturgy on the part of the baptized and ecclesial communities. I refer, in particular, to the commitment to a solid and organic liturgical initiation and formation, both of lay faithful as well as clergy and consecrated persons.'[14]

5 How Should We Move Towards a More Authentic Implementation of *Sacrosanctum Concilium* today?

In the light of the fundamental desires of the council fathers and of the different situations that we have seen arise following the council, I would like to present some practical considerations on how we can implement *Sacrosanctum Concilium* more faithfully today. Even though I serve as the prefect of the Congregation for Divine Worship, I do so in all humility as a priest and a bishop in the hope that they will promote mature reflection and scholarship and good liturgical practice throughout the Church.

It will come as no surprise if I say that first of all we must examine the quality and depth of our liturgical formation, of how we imbue our clergy, religious and lay faithful with the spirit and power of the liturgy. Too often we assume that our candidates for ordination to the priesthood or the permanent diaconate 'know' enough about the

[14] Pope Francis, *Message to the Participants of the Roman Symposium on* Sacrosanctum Concilium.

liturgy. But the council was not insisting on knowledge here, though, of course, the constitution stressed the importance of liturgical studies (see SC 15-17). No, the liturgical formation that is primary and essential is more one of immersion in the liturgy, in the deep mystery of God our loving Father. It is a question of living the liturgy in all its richness, so that having drunk deeply from its fount we always have a thirst for its delights, its order and beauty, its silence and contemplation, its exultation and adoration, its ability to connect us intimately with God who is at work in and through the Church's sacred rites.

That is why those 'in formation' for pastoral ministry should live the liturgy as fully as is possible in their seminaries or houses of formation. Candidates for the permanent diaconate should have an immersion in an intense liturgical life over a prolonged period also. And, I would add, that the full and rich celebration of the Extraordinary Form of the Roman rite, the *usus antiquior*, should be an important part of liturgical formation for clergy, for how can we begin to comprehend or celebrate the Ordinary Form with a hermeneutic of continuity if we have never experienced the beauty of the liturgical tradition which the fathers of the council themselves knew and which has produced so many saints over the centuries? A wise openness to the mystery of the Church and her rich, centuries-old tradition, and a humble docility to what the Holy Spirit says to the churches today are real signs that we belong to Jesus Christ. 'And he said to them, "Therefore every scribe who has been trained for the kingdom of heaven is like a householder who brings out of his treasure what is new and what is old"' (Mt. 13.52).

If we attend to this, if our new priests and deacons truly thirst for the liturgy, they will themselves be able to form those entrusted to their care – even if the liturgical circumstances and possibilities of their ecclesial mission are more modest than those of the seminary or of a cathedral. I am aware of many priests in such circumstances who form their people in the spirit and power of the liturgy, and whose parishes are examples of great liturgical beauty. We should remember that dignified simplicity is not the same as reductive minimalism or a negligent and vulgar style. As our Holy Father, Pope Francis, teaches in his Apostolic Exhortation *Evangelii Gaudium*: 'The Church evangelizes and is herself evangelized through the beauty of the liturgy, which is both a celebration of the task of evangelization and the source of her renewed self-giving.'[15]

Secondly, I think that it is very important that we are clear about the nature of liturgical participation, of the *participatio actuosa* for which the council called. There has been a lot of confusion here over recent decades. The Constitution on the Sacred Liturgy states: 'The Church ... earnestly desires that Christ's faithful, when present at this mystery of faith, should not be there as strangers or silent spectators; on the contrary, through a good understanding of the rites and prayers they should take part in the sacred action conscious of what they are doing, with devotion and full collaboration' (SC 48). The council sees participation as primarily internal, coming about 'through a good understanding of the rites and prayers'. The inner life, the life immersed in God and intimately inhabited by God is the indispensable condition for a successful and fruitful participation in the holy mysteries that we celebrate in the liturgy. The

---

[15] Pope Francis, Apostolic Exhortation on the Proclamation of the Gospel in Today's World *Evangelii Gaudium* (24 November 2013), no. 24.

Eucharistic celebration must be essentially lived internally. It is within us that God wants to meet us. The fathers called for the faithful to sing, to respond to the priest, to assume liturgical ministries that are rightfully theirs, certainly, but it insists that all should be 'conscious of what they are doing, with devotion and full collaboration'.

If we understand the priority of internalizing our liturgical participation we will avoid the noisy and dangerous liturgical activism that has been too prominent in recent decades. We do not go to the liturgy so as to perform, to do things for others to see: we go to be connected with Christ's action through an internalization of the external liturgical rites, prayers, signs and symbols. It may be that we priests whose vocation is to minister liturgically need to remember this more than others! But we also need to form others, particularly our children and young people, in the true meaning of liturgical participation, in the true way to pray the liturgy.

Thirdly, I have spoken of the fact that some of the reforms introduced following the council may have been put together according to the spirit of the times and that there has been an increasing amount of critical study by faithful sons and daughters of the Church asking whether what was in fact produced truly implemented the aims of the constitution, or whether in reality they went beyond them. This discussion sometimes takes place under the title of a 'reform of the reform', and I am aware that Father Thomas Kocik presented a learned study on this question at the *Sacra Liturgia* conference in New York one year ago.[16]

I do not think that we can dismiss the possibility or the desirability of an official reform of the liturgical reform, because its proponents make some important claims in their attempt to be faithful to the council's insistence in article 23 of the Constitution on the Sacred Liturgy 'that sound tradition ... be retained, and yet the way remain open to legitimate progress'. It must begin with a careful theological, historical, pastoral study and 'there must be no innovations unless the good of the Church genuinely and certainly requires them; and care must be taken that any new forms adopted should in some way grow organically from forms already existing' (SC 23).

Indeed, I can say that when I was received in audience by the Holy Father last April, Pope Francis asked me to study the question of a reform of a reform and the way in which the two forms of the Roman rite could enrich each other. This will be a long and delicate work and I ask for your patience and prayers. But if we are to implement *Sacrosanctum Concilium* more faithfully, if we are to achieve what the council desired, this is a serious question which must be carefully studied and acted on with the necessary clarity and prudence in prayer and total submission to God.

We priests, we bishops bear a great responsibility. How our good example builds up good liturgical practice; how our carelessness, our routine or wrongdoing harms the Church and her sacred liturgy!

We priests must be worshippers first and foremost. Our people can see the difference between a priest who celebrates with faith and one who celebrates in a hurry, frequently looking at his watch, almost so as to say that he wants to get back to his pastoral work or to other engagements or to go to view his television as quickly as possible! Fathers, we

---

[16] See Thomas M. Kocik, 'The Reform of the Reform', in *Liturgy in the Twenty-First Century: Contemporary Issues and Perspectives*, ed. Alcuin Reid (London and New York: Bloomsbury, 2016), 19–50.

can do no more important thing than celebrate the sacred mysteries: let us beware of the temptation of liturgical sloth or lukewarmness, because it is a temptation of the devil.

We must remember that we are not the authors of the liturgy; we are its humble ministers, subject to its discipline and laws. We are also responsible to form those who assist us in liturgical ministries in both the spirit and power of the liturgy and indeed its regulations. Sometimes I have seen priests step aside to allow extraordinary ministers distribute Holy Communion: this is wrong; it is a denial of the priestly ministry as well as a clericalization of the laity. When this happens it is a sign that formation has gone very wrong, and that it needs to be corrected. 'Then, taking the five loaves ... gave them to his disciples to set before the people. ... Those who ate of the loaves were five thousand men' (Mk. 6.30-44; Mt. 14.18-21).

I have also seen priests, and bishops, vested to celebrate Holy Mass, take out telephones and cameras and use them in the sacred liturgy. This is a terrible indictment of what they believe to be the mission they assume when they put on the liturgical vestments, which clothe and transform us as an *alter Christus*; and much more, as *ipse Christus*, as Christ himself. To do this is a sacrilege. No bishop, priest or deacon vested for liturgical ministry or present in the sanctuary should be taking photographs, even at large-scale concelebrated Masses. That priests sadly often do this at such Masses, or talk with each other and sit casually, is a sign, I think, that we need urgently to rethink the appropriateness of these immense concelebrations, especially if they lead priests into this sort of scandalous behaviour that is so unworthy of the mystery being celebrated, or if the sheer size of these concelebrations leads to a risk of the profanation of the Blessed Sacrament.

It is equally a scandal and profanation for the lay faithful to take photographs during the celebration of the Holy Eucharist. They should participate through prayer and not by spending their time taking photos!

I want to make an appeal to all priests. You may have read my article in *L'Osservatore Romano* in June 2015 or my interview with the journal *Famille Chrétienne* in May 2016.[17] On both occasions I said that I believe it is very important that we return as soon as possible to a common orientation, of priests and the faithful turned together in the same direction – Eastwards or at least towards the apse – to the Lord who comes, in those parts of the liturgical rites when we are addressing God. This practice is permitted by current liturgical legislation. It is perfectly legitimate in the modern rite. Indeed, I think it is a very important step in ensuring that in our celebrations the Lord is truly at the centre.

And so, dear Fathers, I humbly and fraternally ask you to implement this practice wherever possible, with prudence and with the necessary catechesis, certainly, but also with a pastor's confidence that this is something good for the Church, something good for our people. Your own pastoral judgement will determine how and when this is possible, but perhaps beginning this on the first Sunday of Advent this year, when

---

17   Robert Cardinal Sarah, 'Silenziosa azione del cuore', *L'Osservatore Romano*, 12 June 2015, 6, and 'Comment remettre Dieu au cœur de la liturgie', *Famille Chrétienne*, 23 May 2016, 32.

we attend the Lord who 'will come and … will not delay,'[18] may be a very good time to do this. Dear Fathers, we should listen again to the lament of God proclaimed by the prophet Jeremiah: 'They have turned their backs to me and not their faces' (Jer. 2.27). Let *us* turn again towards the Lord! Since the day of his Baptism, the Christian knows only one direction: the Orient. As St Ambrose explained to the newly baptized: 'You entered to confront your adversary, whom you were to renounce to his face. You turned towards the East (*ad orientem*), for one who renounces the devil turns towards Christ and fixes his gaze directly on him.'[19]

I very humbly and fraternally would like to appeal also to my brother bishops: please lead your priests and people towards the Lord in this way, particularly at large celebrations in your dioceses and in your cathedrals. Please form your seminarians in the reality that we are not called to the priesthood to be at the centre of liturgical worship ourselves, but to lead Christ's faithful to him as fellow worshippers united in the one same act of adoration. Please facilitate this simple but profound reform in your dioceses, your cathedrals, your parishes and your seminaries.

We bishops have a great responsibility, and one day we shall have to answer to the Lord for our stewardship. We are the owners of nothing! Nothing belongs to us! As St Paul teaches, we are merely 'the servants of Christ and the stewards of the mysteries of God. Now it is of course required of stewards that they be found trustworthy' (1 Cor. 4.1-2). We are responsible for ensuring that the sacred realities of the liturgy are respected in our dioceses and that our priests and deacons not only observe the liturgical laws, but know the spirit and power of the liturgy from which they emerge. I was very encouraged to read the presentation on 'The Bishop: Governor, Promoter and Guardian of the Liturgical Life of the Diocese' made to the 2013 *Sacra Liturgia* conference in Rome by Archbishop Alexander Sample of Portland, Oregon, in the United States, and I fraternally encourage my brother bishops to study his considerations carefully.[20]

All liturgical ministers should make an examination of conscience periodically. For this I recommend the second part of the Apostolic Exhortation *Sacramentum Caritatis* of Benedict XVI, 'The Eucharist, a Mystery to be Celebrated'.[21] It is ten years since this exhortation was published as the collegial fruit of the 2005 Synod of Bishops. How much progress have we made in that time? What more do we need to do? We must ask ourselves these questions before the Lord, each of us according to our responsibility, and then do what we can and what we must to achieve the vision outlined by Pope Benedict.

At this point I repeat what I have said elsewhere, that Pope Francis has asked me to continue the extraordinary liturgical work Pope Benedict began.[22] Just because we

---

[18] *The Roman Missal: Renewed by Decree of the Most Holy Second Ecumenical Council of the Vatican, Promulgated by Authority of Pope Paul VI and Revised at the Direction of Pope John Paul II*, English translation according to the third typical edition (Totowa, NJ: Catholic Book Publishing, 2011), First Week of Advent, Wednesday, Entrance Antiphon.

[19] Ambrose of Milan, *De mysteriis*, 2, 7 (CSEL 73,91).

[20] See Alexander K. Sample, 'The Bishop: Governor, Promoter and Guardian of the Liturgical Life of the Diocese', in *The Sacred Liturgy: Source and Summit of the Life and Mission of the Church*, ed. Alcuin Reid (San Francisco: Ignatius Press, 2014), 255–71.

[21] Benedict XVI, Post-Synodal Apostolic Exhortation on the Eucharist as the Source and Summit of the Church's Life and Mission *Sacramentum Caritatis* (22 February 2007), nos. 34–69.

[22] See my 'Message', in *Liturgy in the Twenty-First Century: Contemporary Issues and Perspectives*, ed. Alcuin Reid (London and New York: Bloomsbury, 2016), xv–xvii.

have a new pope does not mean that his predecessor's vision is now invalid. On the contrary, as we know, our Holy Father Pope Francis has the greatest respect for the liturgical vision and measures Pope Emeritus Benedict XVI implemented in utter fidelity to the intentions and aims of the council fathers.

Before I conclude, please permit me to mention some other small ways that can also contribute to a more faithful implementation of *Sacrosanctum Concilium*. One is that we must sing the liturgy, we must sing the liturgical texts, respecting the liturgical traditions of the Church and rejoicing in the treasury of sacred music that is ours, most especially that music proper to the Roman rite, Gregorian chant. We must sing sacred liturgical music not merely religious music, or worse, profane songs.

We must get the right balance between the vernacular languages and the use of Latin in the liturgy. The council never intended for the Roman rite to be exclusively celebrated in the vernacular. But it did intend to allow its increased use, particularly for the readings. Today it should be possible, especially with modern means of printing, to facilitate comprehension by all when Latin is used, perhaps for the Liturgy of the Eucharist, and of course this is particularly appropriate at international gatherings where the local vernacular is not understood by many. And naturally, when the vernacular is used, it must be a faithful translation of the original Latin, as Pope Francis recently affirmed to me.

We must ensure that adoration is at the heart of our liturgical celebrations. The heart of our liturgy is the adoration of God. Too often we do not move from celebration to adoration, but if we do not do that I worry that we may not have always participated in the liturgy fully, internally. Two bodily dispositions are helpful, indeed indispensable here. The first is silence. If I am never silent, if the liturgy gives me no space for silent prayer and contemplation, how can I adore Christ, how can I connect with him in my heart and soul? Silence is very important, and not only before and after the liturgy. It is the foundation of any deep spiritual life.

So too kneeling at the consecration (unless I am sick) is essential. In the West this is an act of bodily adoration that humbles us before our Lord and God. It is itself an act of prayer. Where kneeling and genuflection have disappeared from the liturgy, they need to be restored, in particular for our reception of our Blessed Lord in Holy Communion. Dear Fathers, where possible and with the pastoral prudence of which I spoke earlier, form your people in this beautiful act of worship and love. Let us kneel in adoration and love before the Eucharistic Lord once again! 'Man is not fully man unless he falls on his knees before God to adore Him, to contemplate his dazzling sanctity and let himself be remodelled in his image and likeness.'[23]

In speaking of the reception of Holy Communion kneeling I would like to recall the July 2002 letter of the Congregation of Divine Worship and Discipline of the Sacraments, which clarifies that 'any refusal of Holy Communion to a member of the faithful on the basis of his or her kneeling posture [is] a grave violation of one of the most basic rights of the Christian faithful.'[24]

---

[23] Robert Cardinal Sarah, *On the Road to Niniveh: Journey to Conversion* (Nairobi: Pauline Publications Africa 2012), 199.

[24] Congregation for Divine Worship and the Discipline of the Sacraments, 'Litterae Congregationis', in *Notitiae* 38 (2002), 582–4, at 583.

Correctly vesting all the liturgical ministers in the sanctuary, including lectors, is also very important if such ministries are to be considered authentic and if they are to be exercised with the decorum due to the sacred liturgy – also if the ministers themselves are to show the correct reverence for God and for the mysteries they minister.

These are some suggestions: I am sure that many others could be made. I put them before you as possible ways of moving towards 'the right way of celebrating the liturgy inwardly and outwardly', which was of course the desire expressed by Cardinal Ratzinger at the beginning of his great work, *The Spirit of the Liturgy*.[25] I encourage you to do all that you can to realize this goal, which is utterly consistent with that of the Second Vatican Council's Constitution on the Sacred Liturgy.

6 Conclusion

I began this address with a consideration of the teachings of the twentieth-century popes on the sacred liturgy. The first of them, St Pius X, had the personal motto: *instaurare omnia in Christo* – to restore all things in Christ. I suggest that we take these words and make them our own standard as we seek to work towards a more faithful implementation of *Sacrosanctum Concilium*, for if when we come to the sacred liturgy we enter into the mentality of Christ, if we put on Christ as we put on our baptismal robe or the vestments proper to our liturgical ministry, we cannot go far astray.

It is sadly true that in the decades since the Second Vatican Council, 'alongside [the] lights, *there are also shadows*' in the Church's liturgical life, as St John Paul II said in *Ecclesia de Eucharistia*.[26] And it is our duty to address the causes of this. But it is a source of great hope and joy that today, as the twenty-first century proceeds, many faithful Catholics are convinced of the importance of the liturgy in the life of the Church and dedicate themselves to the liturgical apostolate, to what may be broadly called a new liturgical movement.

My brothers and sisters, I thank you for your commitment to the sacred liturgy. I encourage you and bless you in all your endeavours, great or small, to bring about 'the right way of celebrating the liturgy inwardly and outwardly'. Persevere in this apostolate: the Church and the world needs you!

---

[25] Joseph Ratzinger, 'The Spirit of the Liturgy', in *Theology of the Liturgy*, Collected Works, 11 (San Francisco: Ignatius Press, 2014), 3–150 (originally published in 2000), 4.

[26] John Paul II, *Ecclesia de Eucharistia*, no. 10 (emphasis in the original).

3

Liturgy and the Triune God: Rethinking Trinitarian Theology

Helmut Hoping

1 Introduction: The Relationship of Liturgy and Theology

Aidan Kavanagh (1929–2006), Alexander Schmemann (1921–83) and others have attributed the status of *prima theologia* to liturgy rather than the *intellectus fidei*[1] because first priority is not speaking *about God*, but speaking *to God*. The 'entirety of the relation to God'[2] concentrates on doxology; thus, doxology is the shared root of liturgy and theology.[3] According to Eph. 1.4-7, God chose us to the praise of his glory with which he has blessed us in his beloved Son. The theological significance of liturgy originates in praising God, which is prior to any speaking about God. The Constitution on the Sacred Liturgy *Sacrosanctum Concilium* demands to teach theology, especially dogmatics, in such a way that its connection to liturgy becomes apparent. Nevertheless, until today, theology is done to a large extent independently from liturgy. This applies also and in particular to Trinitarian theology.

Catherine Mowry LaCugna (1952–97) has asked: 'Can Liturgy ever again become a Source for Theology?'[4] Despite a slightly feminist tendency of her book *God for Us: The Trinity and Christian Life*,[5] LaCugna correctly emphasizes the inherent connection of

[1] See Aidan Kavanagh, *On Liturgical Theology: The Hale Memorial Lectures of Seabury-Western Theological Seminary, 1981* (New York: Pueblo Pub. Co., 1984); Alexander Schmemann, *Introduction to Liturgical Theology* (New York: St. Vladimir's Seminary Press, 1986); *Liturgy and Tradition: Theological Reflections of Alexander Schmemann*, ed. Thomas Fisch (Crestwood, NY: St. Vladimir's Seminary Press, 1990); David W. Fagerberg, *What is Liturgical Theology? A Study in Methodology* (Collegeville, MN: Liturgical Press, 1992); Kevin W. Irwin, *Context and Text: Method in Liturgical Theology* (Collegeville, MN: Liturgical Press, 1994).

[2] Gerhard Ebeling, *Dogmatik des christlichen Glaubens*, vol. 1 (Tübingen: Mohr, 1979), 208.

[3] On doxology see Geoffrey Wainwright, *Doxology: The Praise of God in Worship, Doctrine and Life. A Systematic Theology*, 2nd edn (London: Epworth Press, 1982).

[4] See Catherine Mowry LaCugna, 'Can Liturgy ever again become a Source for Theology?', *Studia Liturgica* 19 (1989): 1–13.

[5] Catherine Mowry LaCugna, *God for Us: The Trinity and Christian Life* (New York: HarperSanFrancisco, 1991). See also LaCugna, 'The Baptismal Formula, Feminist Objections and Trinitarian Theology', *Journal of Ecumenical Studies* 26 (1989): 235–50. Notice that LaCugna defends the baptismal formula 'In the name of the Father and the Son and the Holy Spirit'. But it is necessary to recognize the ambivalence of the word *Father* in a patriarchal context.

liturgy and theology, for there is no human answer to the mystery of the triune God as revealed in Christ that is more authentic than the living language of prayer, including praise as well as thanksgiving and supplication. All theology arises from speaking to God; and it is to this relationship that it always has to refer back to.[6] The subject of theology is not God *qua* God without reference to God's relationship to us, but the mystery of God in his revelation.[7] LaCugna refers to Leo Scheffcyzk, who said that the Trinitarian mystery is not a *mysterium logicum*, but a *mysterium salutis*, worthy of adoration.[8]

It is not accidental that Trinitarian formulas in the New Testament were originally liturgical texts, and that confession of God as the triune God has its *Sitz im Leben* in the liturgy of the Christian initiation, with the Eucharist as its objective. At the same time, the Eucharist is the central place for an encounter with the triune God. That is why there is an inherent connection between the Eucharist and the Trinity. We owe significant studies of a Trinitarian theology of the Eucharist to Jean Corbon (1924–2001)[9] and Edward J. Kilmartin SJ (1923–94).[10] The theology of the *Deus Trinitas* has to reconnect again to the praying of Jesus Christ and his Church. In the following, I want to illustrate this in three parts.

2 Our Lord: The Teacher of Prayer and His Divine Adoration

Jesus's prayers that were handed down in the Gospels (Mt. 26.36-46; Mk 14.32-42; Lk. 22.39-46; see also Jn 12.27), as well as his last words on the cross (Mt. 27.46; Mk 15.34; Lk. 23.46; Jn 19.30) show him as a man of prayer. His prayer practice was influenced on the one hand by God's unity and unicity proclaimed in the *Sh^ema Israel* (Deut. 6.5) and on the other hand by the instruction of God's unconditional love (Mk 12.28-30). However, according to its form, the *Sh^ema Israel* is not a prayer addressed to God, but a proclamation and instruction of God.[11] Nevertheless, its position in Jewish liturgy is as central as it is in Christian doxology. The addressee of Jesus's prayer was the Holy One, whom he calls *abba* (Mk 14.36), father, and who is described as the one God, as ὁ θεός, in the New Testament.

Jesus conveyed to the early Church the faith in the one God (Rom. 3.29-30), and it is this faith that in the New Testament also shapes the faith in Christ (1 Cor. 8.6). The Jewish idiolect of Jesus's prayers is also underlined in the farewell prayer that was passed on by John (Jn 17). At the beginning, Jesus thanks his Father in heaven,

---

[6] See LaCugna, *God for Us*, 321.

[7] See LaCugna, 'Can Liturgy ever again become a Source for Theology?', 4.

[8] See Leo Scheffcyzk, 'Lehramtliche Formulierung und Dogmengeschichte der Trinität', in *Mysterium Salutis: Grundriß heilsgeschichtlicher Dogmatik*, vol. 2, ed. Johannes Feiner and Magnus Löhrer (Einsiedeln – Zürich – Cologne: Benzinger, 1967), 146–217, at 187.

[9] See Jean Corbon, *Liturgie aus dem Urquell* (Einsiedeln: Johannes Verlag, 1981).

[10] See Edward J. Kilmartin SJ, *Christian Liturgy: Theology and Practice*, vol. 1 (Kansas City: Sheed & Ward, 1988).

[11] See Jakob J. Petuchowski, 'Höre Israel', in *Jüdische Liturgie: Geschichte – Struktur – Wesen*, Quaestiones Disputatae, 86, ed. Hans Herman Henrix (Freiburg – Basel – Vienna: Herder, 1979), 66–76.

who gave him the authority to give eternal life to men (Jn 17.1-5). It resumes with the supplication to glorify the Son. This request is reminiscent of the ending of the Jewish prayer called *And the Redeemer shall come to Zion*.[12] It is one of the final prayers of the Jewish morning services. By recourse to the *kedusha* (Isa. 6.3)[13] and the Song of Moses (Exod. 15.18) the *shekinah* of the Holy One of Israel whom the people of his covenant await as their redeemer to Zion (Isa. 59.20), is praised in heaven and on earth.[14]

It was only a matter of time for his disciples to notice that Jesus lived in an – until then – unknown intimate unity with the God of Israel; and that he even went into his death trusting in him. However, the disciples comprehended the unfathomable depth of this unity only when meeting him who was crucified and had risen again. Therefore, the prayer of Jesus is not merely about his prayer during his earthly life. According to the Letter to the Hebrews, which is decisive for Christian theology of prayer, Christ, who is 'merciful and faithful … in the service of God' (Heb. 2.17), 'has passed through the heavens' (Heb. 4.14-16) in his *transitus* from death to life, and is now forever our high priest with God. The Letter to the Hebrews also testifies Jesus's perseverance in his prayer disposition, which was characterized by his inalienable trust in the Holy One even in the face of death. Jesus offered up supplications, with loud cries and tears, to the God of life who was able to save him from death (Heb. 5.7-10).[15]

As the risen and exalted Lord, Christ is the heavenly liturgist who has initiated the worship for God's messianic people by his *transitus*. The risen Lord performs as 'minister in the holy places' his ritual duties (Heb. 8.1-6). His duties are based on the offering of his body that has been perfected and that has sanctified us once and for all: Christ 'through the eternal Spirit offered himself without blemish to God' (Heb. 9.14). The Book of Revelation perceives the sacrificed lamb that offered itself to God and lives now for ever (Rev. 5), as the centre of the heavenly liturgy – which is realized in the earthly liturgy by Christ's self-realization through the spirit. The origin of Christian liturgy is the risen Lord performing his duty as high priest.

The renowned biblical scholar Raymond E. Brown (1928-98), author of the two-volume work *The Death of the Messiah*,[16] supports in his article 'Does the New Testament call Jesus God?' (1965) the following hypothesis: In all passages that call Jesus either unambiguously (Jn 1.1; 1.18; 20.28; Heb. 1.8-9) or at least with a certain exegetical probability (Rom. 9.5; Tit. 2.13; 2 Pet. 1.1) θεός, this title originates in liturgical prayer.[17] Brown justifies his thesis not only with the doxological setting of the relevant texts,[18] but also by referring to Pliny the Younger (61/62–113/115): in his *Epistulae* to the emperor Trajan, Pliny reports that Christians in Asia Minor call on

---

[12] See *Sidur Sefat Emet*, mit deutscher Übersetzung von Rabbiner Dr S. Bamberger (Basel: Goldschmidt, 1999), 62–3.

[13] That is why the closing prayer is also called *Kedusha de-Sidra*.

[14] Whether the prayer existed in the form as we know it today already in Jesus's time is of no relevance for my argument, as Jesus was familiar with the *kedusha* as well as with the Song of Moses and the concept of God's *shekinah*.

[15] For the pagan world Jesus' pleading prayer in the face of death was a similar provocation as his suffering and appalling death on the cross. See Origen, *Contra Celsum* II.9.24.

[16] See Raymond E. Brown, *The Death of the Messiah*, 2 vols. (London: Geoffrey Chapman, 1994).

[17] See Raymond E. Brown, 'Does the New Testament call Jesus God?', *Theological Studies* 26 (1965): 545–73.

[18] See Ibid., 570.

their Lord in hymns as God.[19] The opening chapter of the Gospel of John, the hymn of Christ in the Letter to the Philippians (Phil. 2.6-11) as well as the hymn in the Letter to the Colossians (Col. 1.12-20) emphasize the reliability of this report. The hymns that were passed on in the Pauline epistles do not explicitly denominate Christ as God, but they praise his divinity.

It is certainly remarkable that in the New Testament only the risen Lord or the pre-existing Word is called θεός, as Brown points out, either in third person (Heb. 1.8-9; Rom. 9.5) or in direct address as, for example, in the confession of Thomas (Jn 20.28). A προσκύνεσις (falling on one's knees) is mentioned not only in association with the risen and exalted Lord (Mt. 28.9; 28.17; Lk. 24.52; Rev. 5.7-14), but also in relation to the earthly Jesus (Mt. 14.33). Here, it is important to take into account that *proskynesis* can also refer to a gesture of adoration.[20] Worship of Christ in the sense of λατρεία is indicated in Lk. 24.52, as for Luke a *proskynesis* in terms of adoration is allowed before God only. Unlike Mark and especially Matthew, Luke avoids the verb προσκυνεῖν in connection with the earthly Jesus. Though the ritual of a liturgical *proskynesis* cannot be proved for the time of the New Testament, already in the early Church there have been prayers (acclamations and hymns) that were addressed to Christ. However, the adoration of Christ was always directed towards the glorification of the Father.[21]

For Christian doxology the phrase διὰ Ἰησοῦ Χριστοῦ is decisive. We find its classical wording in Heb. 13.15: 'Through (*dia*) him [Jesus Christ] then let us continually offer up a sacrifice of praise to God, that is, the fruit of lips that acknowledge his name.' In the Letter to the Hebrews, Christ's motion towards the Father – which is imitated in the liturgical action by the Christian congregation – is understood as a priestly service. Christ does not just teach how to pray (Mt. 6.5-13; Lk. 11.1-13), but is also an example of self-sacrifice to God (Eph. 5.2) and a mediator of our prayers to God (Rom. 1.8). He does not just take side with the praying congregation. As a divine mediator of salvation (2 Pet. 3.18), as the lamb who was slain and lives (Rev. 5.12-13), he will be glorified and praised, as the Father is. Therefore, hymns of the early Church such as *Hosanna to the Son of David* or *Marana tha* (1 Cor. 16.22) are part of Christian liturgy as well as more formal prayers addressed to Christ. The liturgical prayer to Christ developed from the acclamation and divine adoration of Christ.

3 The Addressee of the Eucharist, the Prayer to Christ and the Holy Spirit

In 1925, Josef Andreas Jungmann (1889–1975) published a study on Jesus's position in liturgical prayer.[22] The main result of his study is that liturgical prayer was addressed through Christ to God, the Father until well into the fourth century. Only the

---

[19] See Pliny the Younger, *Epistulae* 10.96.7.
[20] See Gerhard Lohfink, 'Gab es im Gottesdienst der neutestamentlichen Gemeinden eine Anbetung Christi?', *Biblische Zeitschrift* 18 (1974): 161–79, at 164.
[21] See ibid., 177.
[22] See Josef Andreas Jungmann, *Die Stellung Christi im liturgischen Gebet*, 2nd edn (1925; repr., Münster: Aschendorff, 1962).

demarcation from Arianism did eventually lead to a liturgical prayer that was addressed to Christ. For a long time, Jungmann's thesis was considered as *sententia communis*. By now, however, it is generally agreed upon that the prayer to Christ is much older than Jungmann assumed.[23] In his study, Jungmann concentrated on presidential prayers, but with this he excluded other forms of liturgical prayers such as the hymn to Christ.

An earlier example from the second century is the hymn *Phos hilaron* addressed to Christ. Basil of Caesarea (c. 330–79) quotes the hymn in his tract *De Spiritu Sancto* (375) in order to defend the new form of doxology that was introduced by him. He went from the mediator-doxology *Glory be to the Father through the Son in the Holy Spirit* to the doxology *Glory be to the Father with the Son and the Holy Spirit*. To a large extent, the mediator-doxology got lost as a consequence of the councils of Nicaea (325) and Constantinople (381). The τριαδικὴ πίστις, though, which expressed the new form of doxology, was not supposed to question the monotheism of the Christian belief. Christians do not worship three Gods, but the one God that exists as Father, Son and Spirit. To this effect, the paratactic doxology is to be understood as *Glory to the Father and to the Son and to the Holy Spirit*.

Even if single Eucharistic prayers have Christ as their addressee, as does the Greek Anaphora of St Gregory or the Anaphora of Addai and Mari, the great majority of Eucharistic prayers are addressed to God the Father. In the Roman rite, the Eucharistic prayer and, with only a few exceptions, all presidential prayers are addressed to God. Therefore, the traditional Roman closing prayer reads *per Dominum Iesum Christum*. The exalted Lord is the chief speaker of the *Ecclesia orans*.[24] The Holy Spirit connects the *Ecclesia orans* with the person of Christ, who is head of the Church. He enables liturgical *anaclesis* (invocation) in the Father's salutation. Because it is the Spirit of the Son who calls in the heart of the person at prayer: 'Abba! Father!' (Gal. 4.6). The Communion Antiphon of the Solemnity of the Most Holy Trinity captures this beautifully: 'Quoniam autem estis filii, misit Deus Spiritum Filii sui in corda vestra clamantem: Abba, Pater' (Since you are children of God, God has sent into your hearts the Spirit of his Son, the Spirit, who cries out: Abba, Father).[25] The few presidential prayers addressed to Christ that are listed in the *Roman Missal* are the Collect for 24 December, the Collect and the Prayer after Communion for the Solemnity of Corpus Christi, the Prayer after Communion for the Feast of the Exaltation of the Holy Cross (14 September), as well as for the votive Mass of the Holy Cross. The presidential prayers that are addressed to Christ are not considered to be an anomaly; because Christ is the divine mediator of salvation, he is also praised and glorified together with

---

[23] See Albert Gerhards, 'Zu wem beten? Die These Josef Andreas Jungmanns (+ 1975) über den Adressaten des eucharistischen Hochgebets im Licht der neueren Forschung', *Liturgisches Jahrbuch* 32 (1982): 219–30, at 224–8; Brian Spinks, 'Trinitarian Theology and the Eucharistic Prayer', *Studia Liturgica* 27 (1996): 209–24, at 220–1.

[24] See Reinhard Messner, *Einführung in die Liturgiewissenschaft* (Paderborn – Munich – Vienna – Zürich: Schöningh, 2001), 232.

[25] *Missale Romanum ex decreto Sacrosancti Oecumenici Concilii Vaticani II instauratum auctoritate Pauli PP. VI promulgatum Ioannis Pauli PP. II cura recognitum*, editio typica tertia (Vatican City: Typis Vaticanis, 2002), 488; *The Roman Missal: Renewed by Decree of the Most Holy Second Ecumenical Council of the Vatican, Promulgated by Authority of Pope Paul VI and Revised at the Direction of Pope John Paul II*, English translation according to the third typical edition (Totowa, NJ: Catholic Book Publishing, 2011), 352.

the Father and the Spirit. The principle of ὁμοτιμία as formulated by Basil of Cesarea holds both for the Son and the Spirit. That is why the Roman rite also includes prayers that are addressed to the Spirit, as for example the sequence of Pentecost. However, the strong focus of the Roman Mass on the Father is striking. Therefore, Hans Urs von Balthasar (1905–88) talked about a so-called 'patrocentric worship'.[26]

Nevertheless, the patrocentric character of the Roman Mass is still defined by the bipolarity of theocentricism and christocentricism that is constitutional for Christian prayer. The *Catechism of the Catholic Church* defines the Eucharist as 'thanksgiving and praise to the Father', 'the sacrificial memorial of Christ and his Body' and 'the presence of Christ by the power of his word and of his Spirit'.[27] Hence, the *Ecclesia orans* prays not only *ad Patrem* but also *ad Christum*.[28] For, according to the Second Vatican Council, the liturgy is 'considered as an exercise of the priestly office of Jesus Christ'.[29] It is the exalted Lord who carries all liturgical acting as primary subject. Without Christ, our high priest before God who is interceding for us, there is no Christian liturgy. Edward J. Kilmartin says about Christ's position in the liturgy: 'The personal presence of Christ in the Church results from the initiative of the risen Lord. ... Christ brings himself and his saving work to appearance in the temporal-spatial conditions of the liturgy in order that the assembly might be incorporated into his *transitus* to the father.'[30] This incorporation, though, does not occur without the Holy Spirit, who is given to us.[31] Jean Corbon refers to the eternal liturgy as breaking through into the earthly liturgy.[32] The Holy Spirit is the *water of life* that springs from the *throne of God* and from the *Lamb*. 'The eternal liturgy is the mystery of the earthly liturgy.'[33] To pray in a Christian manner thus means praying Trinitarian, in communion with the triune God – a communion that we are incorporated into by being baptized, sealed with the gift of the Holy Spirit, and by participating in the celebration of the Eucharist. In order to pray Trinitarian, the movement of God's revelation in his Son through the Spirit has to be followed.[34] This movement is clearly expressed in the Roman rite.

The one God has reconciled himself with us through his Messiah so that we can call with the Spirit, through whom 'God's love has been poured into our hearts' (Rom. 5.5), on our Father in prayer, as Jesus did (Rom. 8.15). So the basic structure of Christian liturgy since the early Church is constituted in praying to the Father through Christ, our true high priest with God, and in unity with the Holy Spirit (*ad Patrem per Christum in unitate Spiritus Sancti*). This traditional patrocentric character of the Eucharistic prayer in the Roman rite is partially criticized, as for example by the Anglican liturgist Bryan

---

[26] Hans Urs von Balthasar, *Herrlichkeit: Eine theologische Ästhetik*, vol. 1, 3rd edn (1961; repr., Einsiedeln-Trier: Johannes Verlag, 1988), 553.

[27] *Catechism of the Catholic Church*, 2nd edn (Washington, DC: United States Catholic Conference, 2000), no. 1358.

[28] See Joseph Ratzinger, *The Spirit of the Liturgy*, trans. John Saward (San Francisco: Ignatius Press, 2000), 75–6.

[29] Second Vatican Council, Constitution on the Sacred Liturgy *Sacrosanctum Concilium* (4 December 1963), no. 7.

[30] Kilmartin, *Christian Liturgy*, 189.

[31] See ibid., 350–1.

[32] See Corbon, *Liturgie aus dem Urquell*, 58.

[33] Ibid., 190.

[34] See Julie Kirchberg, 'Stellt das trinitarische Gebet den christlichen Monotheismus in Frage?', *Kirche und Israel* 7 (1992): 61–73, at 71.

D. Spinks.[35] It is correct that in the *Canon Romanus* the Holy Spirit rather remains in the background. That holds true for the epiclesis of the consecration, which is not an explicit Spirit-epiclesis, in contrast to the new Eucharistic prayers of the Missal of Paul VI.

The prerequisite of Christian liturgy is the Paschal Mystery of Christ, who is in his person none other than God's consubstantial Word. With his life delivered from death, Christ belongs to the identity of the living God for all eternity.[36] The prayer *ad Christum* befits the position Christ took in the life of the triune God, owing to the divine and human nature of the Son. At the same time the prayers addressed to Christ, the *Kyrie* or the second part of the *Gloria* for example, emphasize the eschatological dimension of the mass. The prospect of Christ's Parousia at the end of time is a constitutive part of the Eucharistic liturgy, as is the anamnesis of Christ's Parousia in his incarnation. In the Missal of Paul VI, the eschatological dimension of the Eucharistic liturgy was reinforced by the acclamation connected to the *Mysterium fidei*, which, in the *Novus Ordo*, follows the consecration.

The Gospel procession, accompanied by the Alleluia, stages Christ's epiphany in his word, it testifies the Good News of our eschatological Sovereign (Rev. 19.6-7), who is praised by the congregation with the *Laus tibi Christe*. By jointly participating (*koinonia*) in the Eucharistic bread and the chalice of salvation, we are being incorporated into the life delivered from death that Christ laid down for us on the cross.

The account of the institution of the Eucharist assures that the celebration of the Eucharist today is still based on the original event of its foundation. According to their literary form, the *Verba Testamenti* are a quote. Their purpose, however, is much more than merely the recollection of an incident from the past. The *Verba Testamenti* 'This is my Body … this is my Blood' spoken, according to Catholic doctrine, by the priest *in persona Christi* over bread and wine, are more than the narrative of the Eucharist's account of institution. Just as at the Last Supper, the *Verba* identify the gifts of bread and wine with Christ's Body and Blood.

The Spirit-epiclesis, asking God the Father to send down the Spirit on the sacrifices that we offer so that he may change our gifts into the reality of Christ's Body and Blood, stresses the pneumatological dimension of the Eucharistic liturgy. In the new Eucharistic prayers of the Roman rite, the epiclesis precedes the *Verba Testamenti*. The epiclesis is the core of the Eucharistic liturgy. Corbon calls it the attempt to put the inexpressible of the transsubstantiation into words.[37] By means of the epiclesis, Christ's words spoken by the priest become the consecration, and God's Spirit changes the gifts of bread and wine into Christ's Body and Blood.[38]

As a symbol of Christ, the altar represents the 'eccentric middle' of the gathered congregation.[39] It also represents the opened heaven and thus emphasizes the eschatological dimension of the Eucharistic liturgy that is visibly made manifest in the

---

[35] See Spinks, 'Trinitarian Theology and the Eucharistic Prayer', 220–4.
[36] See Ratzinger, *The Spirit of the Liturgy*, 57.
[37] See Corbon, *Liturgie aus dem Urquell*, 85.
[38] See ibid. 120.
[39] See Reinhard Messner, 'Gebetsrichtung, Altar und die exzentrische Mitte der Gemeinde', in *Communio-Räume: Auf der Suche nach der angemessenen Raumgestalt katholischer Liturgie*, ed. Albert Gerhards, Thomas Sternberg and Walter Zahner (Regensburg: Schnell & Steiner, 2003), 27–36.

traditional orientation of prayer. It corresponds to the orientation of the congregation to the altar for the remembrance of the Paschal Mystery to reassure itself time and again about their exalted Lord in liturgical prayer, to refer to him who is simultaneously guide as well as essential content of the Church's prayer in anamneses and acclamations.

It is important to consider that the Risen-Crucified, who is present in the celebration of the Eucharist, is not yet the Messiah for all. Rather, he still has a future ahead in his messiahship. As the completion of God's kingdom still remains to be concluded, the promise connected to Jesus's messiahship is not yet entirely fulfilled. The eschatological prospect is always to be kept in mind, which follows Jesus's words over the chalice at the Last Supper with His disciples, and which the majority of exegetes considers to be part of Jesus's *ipsissima verba*: 'Truly, I say to you, I will not drink again of the fruit of the vine until that day when I drink it new in the kingdom of God.' (Mk 14.25)

The Communion, where Christ gives himself with his life, sacrificed for many and forever delivered from death, is a foretaste of 'the marriage supper of the Lamb' (Rev. 19.9). Christ's Body and Blood are received as *pledge* and *promise* for the eternal communion with the triune God.[40] Receiving Christ's Body and Blood means being grasped and embraced by the person of the divine Logos in the power of the Spirit, of the Father's consubstantial Word that appeared in our flesh. Through Christ and his *transitus* from death to life we are drawn into the triune life of the one God.

4 The Hermeneutics of the Trinity and the Liturgy of the Church

Pope Alexander II (1061–73) reportedly said that no Sunday was to be dedicated to the Trinity – as, indeed, on every Sunday we celebrate the memory of the mystery of salvation of the divine Trinity. But around the turn of the millennium, a feast for the Holy Trinity emerged.[41] Only three hundred years later the feast was established for the entire Roman Church.[42] Liturgists call it a 'feast of ideas', even though the triune God is not a theological idea, but the centre of the Christian faith.

In his book *The Art of Praying* (1957; *Vorschule des Betens* [1943]), Romano Guardini writes on the question of prayer and the triune God:

> Man is only one person – the one which he expresses by the word *I*. In God, however, there are three who speak thus. Triple is the face of His being. Triple the way in which His life is master of itself. ... [The one God] has revealed Himself to us and ... has told us His name. Our prayer must go out to Him as He has declared Himself to us – as the *triune* God. Thus Christian prayer is communion with the Trinity.[43]

---

[40] See Geoffrey Wainwright, 'Grundlagen des christlichen Gottesdienstes: Systematisch-theologische Grundlegung', in *Handbuch der Liturgik*, ed. Hans-Christoph Schmidt-Lauber and Karl-Heinrich Bieritz (Göttingen: Vandenhoeck & Ruprecht, 1995), 72–95, at 83.

[41] See Peter Browe, 'Zur Geschichte des Dreifaltigkeitsfestes', *Archiv für Liturgiewissenschaft* 1 (1950): 65–81.

[42] Trinity Sunday was established in 1334 by Pope John XXII.

[43] Romano Guardini, *The Art of Praying: The Principles and Methods of Christian Prayer*, trans. Prince Leopold of Loewenstein-Wertheim (Manchester, NH: Sophia Institute, 1995), 86 and 88.

Four years earlier, Guardini wrote in *The World and the Person* (1965; *Welt und Person* [1939]):

> To become a Christian means to enter into the existentiality of Christ. The one who is reborn says 'Thou' to the Father, as he is given a share in Christ's pronouncing of His 'Thou'. In the ultimate and definitive sense the Christian does not say 'Thou' to Christ. He does not confront Him, but goes with him, 'follows Him'. He enters into Christ and carries out the movement with Him. Together with Christ, he says 'Thou' to the Father and says 'I' of himself. ... But it is the Spirit who brings man into the intimacy of the personal relation. He inserts him in Christ and so summons him to become his true self. He sets him before the Father and so enables him to speak the essential 'Thou'.[44]

The prayer addressed to Christ must not compromise the faith in God's unicity.[45] The prayer to Christ is only legitimate if he is addressed not as a kind of *second God* but as the true icon of the Father, with the ὁμοούσιος being strictly understood according to incarnational doctrine and image theology. Even the elaborate Christology of the Gospel of John contains a theocentric foundation. In the Fourth Gospel Christ says: 'Whoever has seen me has seen the Father' (Jn 14.9). If the divine persons of the Trinity are understood as distinct, self-conscious subjects, each with their own unique freedom, in prayer the unity of the triple divine threatens to break up, as God gives himself as Father through the Son and in the Holy Spirit. However, God's immanent Trinity must not be dissolved into an economical Trinity.[46] Immanent and economical Trinity are not indistinctively identical. Rather, the immanent personal distinction within God is the ontological precondition for the economical Trinity. In the revelation of the one God, ontology and phenomenology are not opposites. God is triune from all eternity because he is the origin without an origin, the first to exist, who proceeds from the self-creation of divine life from eternity as the Father's image as well as the Spirit who reveals this life.

The Pseudo-Athanasian Creed *Quicumque* records that Father, Son and Spirit are all omnipotent. At the same time there are not three Almighty in God but only one.[47] The same is also taught by Augustine in his treatise *De Trinitate*.[48] The formula of faith agreed upon at the 11th Council of Toledo (675) stressed, in accordance with Augustine, the interdicition of pluralism regarding the divine being. The formula does allow for the Father, Son and Spirit to be called almighty, whereas talking about the three Almighty is

---

[44] Romano Guardini, *The World and the Person*, trans. Stella Lange (Chicago: Regnery, 1965), 156–7.

[45] See Albert Gerhards, 'Zur Frage der Gebetsanrede im Zeitalter des jüdisch-christlichen Dialogs', *Trierer Theologische Zeitschrift* 102 (1993): 245–57.

[46] I see a tendency for this understanding with Thomas Freyer, 'Vergessener Monotheismus? Zur gegenwärtigen Trinitätslehre', in *Jahrbuch Politische Theologie, vol. 4: Monotheismus*, ed. Jürgen Manemann (Münster: Lit-Verlag, 2002), 93–103.

[47] See *Enchiridion symbolorum definitionum et declarationum de rebus fidei et morum*, ed. Heinrich Denzinger and Peter Hünermann, 43rd edn (San Francisco: Ignatius Press, 2012), no. 75.

[48] See Augustine, *De Trinitate*, VIII.Prooem.1 (CChrSL 50,268): 'Quod uero ad se dicuntur singuli non dici pluraliter tres sed unum ipsam trinitatem sicut *deus pater, deus filius, deus spiritus sanctus*; et bonus pater, bonus filius, bonus spiritus sanctus; et *omnipotens pater, omnipotens filius, omnipotens spiritus sanctus*; nec tamen tres dii aut tres boni aut tres omnipotentes, sed *unus deus*, bonus, omnipotens, ipsa trinitas, et quidquid aliud non ad inuicem relatiue sed ad se singuli dicuntur'.

perceived as a threat to God's unity.[49] However, if God's freedom, like his omnipotence, is part of his nature, how is it possible then to talk of a *plural* of divine freedoms, as some theologians do, and state at the same time that God's nature exists in *singular* only?[50] If one wants to attribute a conscious life to the one God in analogy to the subjectivity of our conscious life, which our notion of God naturally tends to do, this is only possible if a single divine self-consciousness is presupposed. Bernard Lonergan (1904–84) argues that, provided God's unity is interpreted as referring to his consciousness, one can only talk of a single divine consciousness and three bearers of it.[51]

On the one hand, the prayer addressed to Christ belongs to the foundation of the Eucharist and will exist as long as there are Christians. On the other hand, a Trinitarian liturgical theology has to make the *proprium christianum* accessible in such a way that it is not directed against God's unity and unicity. It is also important to always keep in mind that the liturgical prayer of the Church is based upon the underlying pattern of the *ad Patrem per Iesum Christum in Spiritu Sancto*, as it is expressed in the presidential prayers. This pattern follows the demand of Canon 21 of the Synod of Hippo Regius (393) that reads: 'Et cum altari assistitur, semper ad Patrem dirigatur oratio.'[52] The traditional orientation of prayer, the sacred direction, mirrors the patrocentric character of the Eucharist and the expectation of the Parousia of Christ. The narrow concept of the liturgical space after the Second Vatican Council has darkened this understanding of liturgy.

Augustine, who facilitated the breakthrough of the *Patrem dirigatur oratio* principle, was present at the Synod of Hippo Regius as a presbyter. When in the points made above the confession to the *Deus Trinitas* was repeatedly mentioned, then this was an allusion to the well-known prayer of Augustine formulated at the end of his great treatise *De Trinitate*:

> But when we shall come to You, these 'many things' which we say 'and fall short' shall cease; and You as One shall remain, You who are all in all [cf. *1 Corinthians* 15:28]; and without ceasing we shall say one thing, praising You in the one, we who have also been made one in You.
>
> O Lord, the One God (*domine deus une*), God the Trinity (*deus trinitas*), whatever I have said in these books as coming from You, may they acknowledge who are Yours; but if anything as coming from myself, may You and they who are Yours forgive me. Amen.[53]

Mutatis mutandis, this plea applies for every attempt to uncover the *mysterium trinitatis* for the human mind, the *mysterium* that we are drawn into anew time and again by the liturgy and the true priest of the new covenant, be it *sub specie doctrinae* or *sub specie celebrandi*.

---

[49] See Denzinger-Hünermann, *Enchiridion symbolorum*, no. 530.

[50] See ibid., no. 529.

[51] See Bernard Lonergan, *De Deo trino: Pars systematica seu Divinarum personarum conceptio analogica* (Rome: Apud Aedes Universitatis Gregorianae, 1957), 175; Thomas Schärtl, *Theo-Grammatik: Zur Logik der Rede vom trinitarischen Gott* (Regensburg: Pustet, 2003), 536.

[52] *Sacrorum conciliorum nova et amplissima collectio* III, ed. Giovanni Domenico Mansi (Florence: A. Zatta, 1759), 884.

[53] Augustine, *De Trinitate*, XV, xxviii, 51 (CChrSL 50A,535); English translation: *Augustine: On the Trinity, Books 8-15*, ed. Gareth B. Matthews, trans. Stephen McKenna, Cambridge Texts in the History of Philosophy Author (Cambridge: Cambridge University Press, 2002), 224.

4

The Public Nature of Catholic Liturgy

Charbel Pazat de Lys OSB

1 Introduction

First of all, I must ask for your forgiveness for my audacity in addressing you in a language that is unfamiliar to me. May the Spirit of Pentecost give you the grace to understand me, and ensure that I merit only slight and acceptable ridicule.

Moved, perhaps by the same boldness, I propose to invite your attention to a difficult theme: the public character, the public nature of Catholic liturgy. At first, the theme may appear abstract, quite detached from daily practical considerations. Also, it is a hotly debated topic. Therefore, I will limit our subject.

Before, however, delineating our subject, I must confide in you that speaking publicly on the liturgy is somewhat like the novice surgeon who is effecting an open heart surgery on his mother. The liturgy is truly the heart of our Holy Mother Church. Not having the leisure to be able to consult all the available literature on this subject, I am not going to offer a thesis but rather a personal point of view about a contentious subject that today is at the base of many liturgical problems. May the holy angels help me to remain humble, realistic and spiritual.

We will attempt to present certain elements in order to respond to the following three questions: What does the 'public character' of liturgy mean? What are the difficulties and practical consequences of this today? How can we favour a just conscience of this reality?

2 What Does the 'Public Nature' of the Liturgy Mean?

Let us begin by citing a classic definition of liturgy: the ensemble of signs perceptible to the senses, which efficiently bring about public worship and the sanctification of the Church.[1] Even if one lacks a profound knowledge, it is universally admitted that liturgy

---

[1] See Cipriano Vagaggini OSB, *Initiation théologique à la liturgie*, vol. 1, trans. Philippe Rouillard (Paris: Société Liturgie, 1959), 28.

has something of a public character. The original Greek word is tied to a public service, something done in favour of the people, principally worship.[2]

Once this foundation is laid, we must discover what lies beneath the word 'public'. We are not speaking abstractly when using the word public, but rather joining it to the word liturgy, and not just to the word worship. In other words, Catholic liturgy is a public act not only finalized towards worship (adoration, thanksgiving, reparation, supplication) but also towards sanctification.

The term 'public' can be understood with four principle meanings: practical, sociological, institutional and Christological. We will see how all these meanings can refer to the liturgy. Only the last, however, the Christological meaning, can correspond fully to the liturgy.

2.1 The practical sense

The first definition of the word 'public' that I have called practical is nothing more than a description. This indicates situations where a certain 'public' is gathered, a physical or virtual meeting of people for an event. This applies legitimately to liturgy in a descriptive sense. For example, the famous text that launched the Liturgical Movement of the twentieth century, the Motu Proprio of Pope St Pius X *Tra le Sollecitudini*, uses the description of liturgy as 'a public and solemn worship'.[3]

This practical or descriptive meaning of the term is in itself the least important because it does not enter into the heart of the matter at hand, even if it is generally true that liturgy is better celebrated with the participation of as many Christians as needed. Having said this, this practical meaning cannot be applied to certain liturgical acts like the sacrament of penance, which is of a public nature, but this does not mean that what happens in the confessional would be open to the public.

The antonym for this word is 'solitary'. For example, if a bishop pontificated without the assembly, one could say that in this case, 'it was a solemn and solitary act of worship'. A journalist and not a theologian would describe it in this manner!

2.2 Sociological sense

The second meaning of 'public' can be called sociological. In this case, 'public' is the underlying idea of many expressions that indicates people coming together in common, in order to pray, or in order to form a community or prayer group, etc. One hears of the community's celebration, of the celebrating assembly, etc. One finds many forms of this kind of description.

---

[2] *Catechism of the Catholic Church*, 2nd edn (Washington, DC: United States Catholic Conference, 2000), no. 1070: 'In the New Testament the word "liturgy" refers not only to the celebration of divine worship but also to the proclamation of the Gospel and to active charity. In all of these situations it is a question of the service of God and neighbour. In a liturgical celebration the Church is servant in the image of her Lord, the one "*leitourgos*"; she shares in Christ's priesthood (worship), which is both prophetic (proclamation) and kingly (service of charity).'

[3] Pius X, Motu Proprio on the Restoration of Sacred Music *Tra le sollecitudini* (22 November 1903).

In fact, it is not false to apply to the liturgy this sociological sense of a 'community coming together', in the measure that, effectively, a group comes together for a purpose. While it is not false, it is insufficient for it to avoid ambiguity and for it to give the full sense of the meaning of 'public worship'. Besides, the sociological sense cannot be applied to all cases of 'public worship', like the sacrament of penance.

This term reveals its ambiguity when, for example, one uses the following passage of St Matthew as the basis for the liturgical assembly, 'Again I say to you, if two of you agree on earth about anything they ask, it will be done for them by my Father in heaven. For where two or three are gathered in my name, there am I in the midst of them' (Mt. 18.19-20). If properly understood, this passage could not be more true. Yet, in order to understand this passage well, one cannot omit the following: Jesus points to 'two of you' from among the disciples whom he has just given the power to bind and to loosen, and he says 'in my name' and not in the name of members of a group. Thus, the efficacy of prayer comes from the *sequela Christi* and from the mission received, and not from the fact that some persons form a group.[4]

Let us be more precise with our vocabulary: by the sociological sense of the word 'public' we want to speak of a group, of an assembly, in opposition to the traditional terms of a 'constituted' or 'perfect society'.[5] Consequently, in the usage of the term that I am trying to determine here, the difference is found in that when we speak of a group, it is to be looked at in a functional manner, it comes together to do something. However, a society is ontological, constituted of people who are an entity that has come together. The group comes after the person, but the society comes before. The group receives its identity from the people who compose it, while the society gives its identity to the people who make it up.

To finish speaking about the term 'public' in the sociological sense of a 'group', one can mention its antithesis: the individual. For example, three hundred young people reciting the rosary together or singing a hymn of praise would not make it liturgical, but a sort of public worship as opposed to a mere 'individual act of worship' done by multiple persons reciting or singing each on their own.[6] In these two instances, one can speak of common or individual prayer, but not of a liturgy in the proper sense of the term; at best it can be called a 'para-liturgy'.

2.3 The Institutional Sense

When we understand the term 'public' in an institutional sense, we no longer speak of the action of a mere group or assembly, but of a truly stable society in the proper sense.

---

[4] This does not rescind from the fact that being two or three *disciples* gathered *in the name of Christ* provides effectively a special manner of identification with him in his Trinitarian relationships, giving therefore a specific character to this prayer.

[5] We need to be attentive to the meaning of the words in different contexts, because society, group and community are sometimes used as equivalents. Here we use the word 'society' with a stronger meaning. By 'perfect societies' we mean those societies having by themselves the means to reach their end, as the Church and the State; the family is also a constituted society, but an imperfect one, needing other societies to reach its own ends.

[6] See Congregation for the Divine Worship and Discipline of Sacraments, *Directory on Popular Piety and the Liturgy: Principles and Orientations* (17 December 2001), no. 7: 'public or private expressions of Christian piety which, although not part of the Liturgy, are considered to be in harmony with the spirit, norms, and rhythms of the Liturgy'.

The Second Vatican Council says: 'Religious communities are a requirement of the social nature both of man and of religion itself.'[7]

In this sense, sanctification and public worship are done in the name of society. This means that it is no longer just a question of common prayer in the name of someone, rather each one or certain persons pray in the name of all, of all those who make part of this society. Pope Pius XI underlines this sense, noting that

> the human race has always felt the need of a priesthood: of men, that is, who have the official charge to be mediators between God and humanity ... men set aside to offer to God public prayers and sacrifices in the name of human society. For human society as such is bound to offer to God public and social worship. ... In fact, priests are to be found among all peoples whose customs are known, except those compelled by violence to act against the most sacred laws of human nature.[8]

We have just heard the terms 'official charge' and 'mediators'. One quickly perceives that in order to speak in the name of all, something that ties everyone together in a stable manner must exist, and the person who speaks in the name of all is a representative of this connection. In order for this connection to be stable, it requires an institution; one could substitute 'public worship' with 'institutional worship'.

This is, yet, not the sense that applies to liturgy, even if it comes close and allows us to arrive closer, because if there exists an instituted society with an official mission and with mediators, inevitably a code of law must underlie it. From this fact, a juridical notion of liturgy becomes necessary inasmuch as it is 'public worship and sanctification'. This is why Canon Law affirms: 'Such worship takes place when it is carried out in the name of the Church by persons legitimately designated and through acts approved by the authority of the Church.'[9]

It is not scandalous to speak of a juridical notion of the liturgy; it is even necessary in order to provide a foundation for certain of its most mystical aspects. Those most opposed to any 'legal aspect' in liturgy can meditate on the biblical foundations of the juridical part of human reality, most notably, as conveyed by the expression 'in the name of' and its equivalents. These are found a hundred times in Sacred Scripture, for example in the Gospel of St John: 'I have come in my Father's name, and you do not receive me; if another comes in his own name, him you will receive' (Jn 5.43).

We have not the leisure to study this subject any further; however, it should be said that this institutional dimension of a stably constituted society, already valid on the natural order, is elevated to the supernatural and theological order once it is applied to

---

[7]   Second Vatican Council, Declaration on Religious Freedom *Dignitatis Humanae* (7 December 1965), no. 4. For the reasons explained in fn. 6, the Latin '*communitates*' is translated as 'societies', in order to avoid confusion.

[8]   Pius XI, Encyclical on the Catholic Priesthood *Ad Catholici Sacerdotii* (20 December 1935), no. 8.

[9]   *Code of Canon Law* (1983), can. 834 §2. See John M. Huels, *Liturgy and Law: Liturgical Law in the System of Roman Catholic Canon Law* (Montréal: Wilson et Lafleur, 2006), 65-6: 'Thus, there are three elements to a juridic understanding of the liturgy. 1) The liturgy is the *public* worship of God ... the officially recognized worship of the Church. ... 2) The liturgy is celebrated by legitimately designated persons who act in the name of the Church. All the faithful, sharing in the common priesthood (cf. c. 836), are fundamentally deputed for the celebration of the liturgy in virtue of their baptism. ... 3) The liturgy consists of acts approved by the authority of the Church.'

liturgy. It is strictly tied in with the biblical notion of the Church as the People of God.[10] St Thomas Aquinas seems to hold as a fact this meaning of the word 'public' when he says that 'common worship ... is offered by ministers impersonating the whole Church (*in persona totius Ecclesiae*). For even as he would be guilty of falsehood who would, in the name of another person, proffer things that are not committed to him, so too does a man incur the guilt of falsehood who, on the part of the Church, gives worship to God contrary to the manner established by the Church or divine authority, and according to ecclesiastical custom.'[11] We have here in some words the idea of 'juridical personhood', the idea of an official charge and that of authenticity.

This allows us to situate ourselves in relation to the problem of the sacrament of confession. It carries a public dimension in the institutional sense, because pardon is given to us in the name of the Church that receives it from the power of the keys and from whom the mission comes. Yet, this does not say everything.

The antithesis of this institutional sense of 'public worship' would be 'private worship', in other words that which is done in one's own name. This in itself is not pejorative, but it simply does not belong to liturgy and lacks no value for it, inasmuch as Pope Pius XII explains this in his famous allocution to the Assisi Liturgical Congress of 1956:

> Public worship is not ... the whole Church. It does not exhaust the field of her activities. Alongside public worship ... there is still place for the private worship, which the individual pays to God in the secret of his heart or expresses by his exterior acts. ... The Church not only tolerates this kind of worship, but gives it full recognition and approval, without however raising it in any way to the primary position of liturgical worship.[12]

As we previously stated, personal prayer or with family, praise with a group, etc. are private forms of worship that have their place and value without becoming part of the liturgy.

2.4 The Christological Sense

Finally, the word 'public' can be understood in a Christological sense or, we can say, it is the fullest sense of the term, which recapitulates and surpasses preceding meanings. In other words, it is an official worship of the sanctification of an institutional society, yet a very special one, for it is the Church. The unity of the

---

[10] Second Vatican Council, Dogmatic Constitution on the Church *Lumen Gentium* (21 November 1964), no. 9: 'God, however, does not make men holy and save them merely as individuals, without bond or link between one another. Rather has it pleased Him to bring men together as one people, a people which acknowledges Him in truth and serves Him in holiness. He therefore chose the race of Israel as a people unto Himself. With it He set up a Covenant. ... Christ instituted this New Covenant, the New Testament, that is to say, in His Blood ... making them one, not according to the flesh but in the Spirit. This was to be the new People of God.'

[11] St Thomas Aquinas, *Summa Theologiae* II-II, a.93, a.1, resp.

[12] Pius XII, Allocution to the Participants of the International Congress of Pastoral Liturgy *Vous Nous Avez* (23 September 1956). An English translation of the original French text is available on http://www.ccwatershed.org/media/pdfs/13/07/30/12-10-32_0.pdf (accessed 2 January 2017).

members of this society is more than institutional: it is divine in the persons of Christ as the Head and the Holy Spirit as the source of unity.[13] Also, the greater part of the most eminently active members of this society are not of this world, a society that follows an eschatological end,[14] beyond time, lacking a common measure with any other sort of human society.

Thus, here the term 'public' acquires a unique fullness and profundity that takes nothing legitimately away from the other lesser meanings that we have seen. On the contrary, the Christological sense perfects them in a supreme way under these two complementary aspects of the theology of the Covenant, that is, that the Church celebrates the liturgy inasmuch as the Body of Christ and the Spouse[15] of the Lamb.[16]

We cannot go any further into detail in order to explain these already well-known aspects, but it was necessary to bring them up to clarify the complete definition of liturgy as given in the *Catechism*, that follows both Pope Pius XII and Vatican II: 'The liturgy then is rightly seen as an exercise of the priestly office of Jesus Christ. It involves the presentation of man's sanctification under the guise of signs perceptible by the senses and its accomplishment in ways appropriate to each of these signs. In it full public worship is performed by the Mystical Body of Jesus Christ, that is, by the Head and his members.'[17]

The Christological sense of the term 'public' lacks any true antithesis, because sanctification and the integral worship of the Mystical Body of Christ are strictly universal inasmuch as they always involve the whole of the Church – militant, suffering and triumphant. We have already seen this when speaking about confession. They are never individual acts because they are never just the worship or the sanctification of an individual, independent from others, but they involve as such the whole social and Mystical Body; even in the sacrament of confession, which rightly restores the penitent's configuration to Jesus Christ. Nevertheless, the liturgy is completely personal in the way it totally involves each person as a member of Christ, as it is obvious in the

---

[13] *Lumen Gentium*, no. 13: 'For this too God sent the Spirit of His Son as Lord and Life-giver. He it is who brings together the whole Church and each and every one of those who believe, and who is the well-spring of their unity.'

[14] Ibid., no. 48: 'The Church ... will attain its full perfection only in the glory of heaven, when there will come the time of the restoration of all things. At that time the human race as well as the entire world, which is intimately related to man and attains to its end through him, will be perfectly re-established in Christ.'

[15] Ibid., no. 7: 'By communicating His Spirit, Christ made His brothers, called together from all nations, mystically the components of His own Body. In that Body the life of Christ is poured into the believers who, through the sacraments, are united in a hidden and real way to Christ who suffered and was glorified.'

[16] Ibid., no. 6: 'The Church ... is described as the spotless spouse of the spotless Lamb, whom Christ "loved and for whom He delivered Himself up that He might sanctify her".'

[17] *Catechism of the Catholic Church*, no. 1070, quoting Second Vatican Council, Constitution on the Sacred Liturgy *Sacrosanctum Concilium* (4 December 1963), no. 7, based on Pius XII, Encyclical on the Sacred Liturgy *Mediator Dei* (20 November 1947), no. 20: 'The sacred liturgy is, consequently, the public worship which our Redeemer as Head of the Church renders to the Father, as well as the worship which the community of the faithful renders to its Founder, and through Him to the heavenly Father. It is, in short, the worship rendered by the Mystical Body of Christ in the entirety of its Head and members.'

confessional. The same can be said about the sacrament of marriage, and the Holy Father recently reminded us of its public nature.[18]

Thus the fullest sense of the term 'public' applied to liturgy expands with new meaning all the other used expressions: collective, communal, assembly, meeting and gathering.

If we want to briefly summarize the four full meanings of the term 'public', one must simply note that at each level it indicates a certain degree of bond between persons. First, and practically, this connection is purely circumstantial: persons are merely present physically or virtually. Secondly, on the sociological level, the bond comes from choice of persons to be present or absent somewhere to do something together. Thirdly, on the institutional level, whether persons are present or absent, and whether they have chosen or not, they share a common connection of belonging that allows certain members to act in the name of all under some sort of conditions. Fourthly, on the deepest level, the Christological, the bond consists in that together they make up the one and only Body of Jesus Christ, to which they are configured in order to enter with him into the everlasting Covenant with the Father and in the Spirit.

2.5 A Slowly Acquired Synthesis

The Church took a while to acquire all these notions, as seen through a certain amount of polemics where authors of great knowledge and good will seem to have trouble in finding a balanced point of view.

A typical and well-known case was the debate begun in 1913 by Father Jean-Joseph Navatel in an article with the heading: 'The liturgical apostolate and personal piety'.[19] The Jesuit rightly blamed certain authors of the Liturgical Movement, especially Dom Maurice Festugière, of using contemptuous language against personal piety and devotions. Unfortunately, he also was guilty of expressing an absolutely bleak conception of liturgy, reducing it 'to the purely sensible and decorative aspect' of worship. Among those he called 'innovators' were many who underlined the irreplaceable importance of the liturgy in the life of the Christian, following very closely the efforts begun by St Pius X. It is not certain, however, that everyone possessed a very precise or accurate concept about the public nature of liturgy, oftentimes reducing liturgy to its sociological meaning of common activity.

Twenty-four years after this debate – there were others, for example, the exchange with Jacques Maritain about the superiority of meditative prayer over liturgy – the Encyclical *Mediator Dei* of Pius XII allowed the Christological sense of 'integral public

---

[18] See Pope Francis, Apostolic Exhortation on Love in the Family *Amoris Laetitia* (19 March 2016), no. 121: 'The spouses, "in virtue of the sacrament, are invested with a true and proper mission, so that, starting with the simple ordinary things of life they can make visible the love with which Christ loves his Church and continues to give his life for her"'. Ibid., no. 131: 'It is nonetheless true that choosing to give marriage a visible form in society by undertaking certain commitments shows how important it is. … This is much more meaningful than a mere spontaneous association for mutual gratification, which would turn marriage into a purely private affair. As a social institution, marriage protects and shapes a shared commitment to deeper growth in love and commitment to one another, for the good of society as a whole. … Its essence derives from our human nature and social character.'

[19] Jean-Joseph Navatel, 'L'apostolat liturgique e la piété personnelle', *Etudes* 50 (1913): 449–76.

worship', as we have defined it, to take root, thus avoiding the exaggerations of that which was called 'public piety' (liturgical piety) as opposed to 'subjective piety' (the practice of non-liturgical devotions). Let me cite from the encyclical:

> It is an unquestionable fact that the work of our redemption is continued, and that its fruits are imparted to us, during the celebration of the liturgy, notable in the august sacrifice of the altar. ... Sacraments and sacrifice do, then, possess that 'objective' power to make us really and personally sharers in the divine life of Jesus Christ. Not from any ability of our own, but by the power of God, are they endowed with the capacity to unite the piety of members with that of the head, and to make this, in a sense, the action of the whole community. From these profound considerations some are led to conclude that all Christian piety must be centred in the mystery of the Mystical Body of Christ, with no regard for what is 'personal' or 'subjective', as they would have it. As a result, they feel that all other religious exercises not directly connected with the sacred liturgy, and performed outside public worship should be omitted. ...
>
> Very truly, the sacraments and the sacrifice of the altar, being Christ's own actions, must be held to be capable in themselves of conveying and dispensing grace from the divine Head to the members of the Mystical Body. But if they are to produce their proper effect, it is absolutely necessary that our hearts be properly disposed to receive them. ... But observe that these members are alive, endowed and equipped with an intelligence and will of their own. It follows that they are strictly required to put their own lips to the fountain, imbibe and absorb for themselves the life-giving water, and rid themselves personally of anything that might hinder its nutritive effect in their souls.[20]

These clarifications have unfortunately not prevented a number of undercurrents, notably, those along the lines of a piety that is willed to be sociological, festive, anti-individualist, anti-juridical and anti-institutional. Especially during the fifteen years after the Second Vatican Council, these undercurrents carried a set of social demands tainted in a colour that had nothing to do with that of a cardinal's garb. It was a charming age when the members of parish teams – styled 'base communities' – would call one another 'comrade', as I personally experienced in the archives of a certain diocese, and when it was not rare that praying the rosary meant a quick dismissal from the seminary. Unfortunately, at the same time a great void appeared in liturgical formation, lacking in its fullest sense as 'public worship and sanctification', as we have seen.

These extreme positions, even if dominant in many places, have clearly not affected the very doctrine of the Church. Meanwhile, a number of countries, especially in South America and, without doubt, in Africa, remain profoundly attached to popular piety. Throughout many years and with different interventions by the magisterium, most notably in 2001 with the *Directory on Popular Piety and the Liturgy*, that we have already cited, the bar was globally raised to a more balanced level.

After this evidently too schematic summary, it seems natural to put forth the following question: have we, today, truly assimilated, understood, even among

---

[20] Pius XII, *Mediator Dei*, nos. 29 and 31.

seminarians and the Christian people, the necessity of a profound and just vision about the public nature of the liturgy, for our union with Christ and with Christians? Thus, we arrive at our second question.

3 What are Today's Difficulties and Practical Consequences?

Throughout the first part of our presentation, we noted that the 'public nature of the liturgy' is based on the natural and supernatural bonds uniting Christians in a special way. So if we want to get an idea of the difficulties and the practical consequences of the public nature of the liturgy, we must assess the identity and the strength of these bonds; and for that, we must look at their foundation, whereupon they depend.

The main bonds are: the fact of belonging to creation, of which man is the centre; the social nature of the human being; the new common identity that has created our baptismal configuration to Jesus Christ; our common participation in the Trinitarian life; our interdependence as members of the Church instituted as one Mystical Body of Christ; our authentic mission of sanctification and official worship through fixed sacramental acts by which the Church offers itself as the Bride to her Lord.

Thus we see that these bonds are forged with a number of fundamental realities, with the main ones being creation, nature, the body, sacramentality, identity, filiation, society, institution and law. Maybe all this seems something that is far away in the background, but looking more closely at some of these basic facts will help us understand where the weak points of these bonds are found and how to remedy them.

Allow me to clarify that if we are led to mention, in what is following, some current problems, it is not in a spirit of nostalgia and sterile lamentation – as if everything was necessarily better before – which has nothing to do with what we are speaking about. We just want to know how to do better in the future.

3.1 Creation and Nature

I remember that, in an exchange during the liturgical conference at Fontgombault in July 2001 (*Journées Liturgiques de Fontgombault*), the then cardinal Ratzinger had observed that we should restore a position of honour to the theology of creation, without which redemption becomes meaningless. Since then the Encyclical *Laudato Si'*[21] has worked in this direction. In relation to our subject: what is important in the theology of creation? There are especially two things: the initiative of God and the wisdom of God.

---

[21] Pope Francis, Encyclical on Care for our Common Home *Laudato Si'* (24 May 2015), nos. 75–6: 'A spirituality which forgets God as all-powerful and Creator is not acceptable. ... The best way to restore men and women to their rightful place ... is to speak once more of the figure of a Father who creates and who alone owns the world. Otherwise, human beings will always try to impose their own laws and interests on reality. In the Judaeo-Christian tradition, the word "creation" has a broader meaning than "nature", for it has to do with God's loving plan in which every creature has its own value and significance.'

First, it is God's initiative that creates. This is from the simple fact that God, a personal being, is the cause of everything, whereas today many imagine that things are the children of chaos, of evolution, of emanation, of immanence. Whatever the theories, they refuse the origin of the world and its development as coming from a free choice exercised with wisdom by Someone,[22] and they deny that this Someone governs. What is then denied is a personal and sovereign intelligence that governs all, a reason, a *logos*, in the heart of every creature, and it is that which connects them with God and with one another in fundamental and radical ways. This is not the mathematical determinism of blind fate, but of a loving design, of a deliberated act of freedom that gives each being a meaning, a dynamic and a place in the grand concert of creation. In other words, it is God's supreme sovereignty that even before he is worshipped as the Redeemer, he is already worshipped as the Creator, as we see from the beginning with Cain and Abel (see Gen. 4.3-7).

What are the consequences for the public nature of the liturgy? First, that all creation as a whole must worship God; then, that neither the individual nor society is at the origin of this worship or of their sanctification, that is to say, of this very special bond between the creature and Creator. If it is true that it was not us who loved God first, but rather that it was he who loved us first (see 1 Jn 4.10), then it is true that we have not invented ourselves as capable of being able to love; and thus are incapable of sanctifying ourselves and giving worship to God. It is our Creator who determined our ability to pray, how to be able to pray and how to integrate into worship all creatures put at the service of man by respecting their proper place and finality.[23] St John Paul II taught that 'not only has God given the earth to man, who must use it with respect for the original good purpose for which it was given to him, but man too is God's gift to man. He must therefore respect the natural and moral structure with which he has been endowed.'[24]

Does this seem too abstract? To be more concrete, let us think about the institution of the Sabbath and then of Sunday as a day given to men in order to render to God the worship due to him: this comes from a true understanding of creation.[25] Consider then the mere fact that material things such as incense, oil, water and many others can really serve a spiritual worship, while in our age we tend to confuse the spiritual with the conceptual, and to accuse of magic or of superstition the use of material things in our relationship with God. Consider also the liturgical orientation that puts us in connection with all creation in its deepest sense.

---

[22] Ibid., no. 77: '"By the word of the Lord the heavens were made" (Ps. 33.6). This tells us that the world came about as the result of a decision, not from chaos or chance, and this exalts it all the more. The creating word expresses a free choice. The universe did not emerge as the result of arbitrary omnipotence, a show of force or a desire for self-assertion. ... Every creature is thus the object of the Father's tenderness, who gives it its place in the world'.

[23] Rom. 8.19-22: 'For the creation waits with eager longing for the revealing of the sons of God; for the creation was subjected to futility, not of its own will but by the will of him who subjected it in hope; because the creation itself will be set free from its bondage to decay and obtain the glorious liberty of the children of God. We know that the whole creation has been groaning in travail together until now.'

[24] St John Paul II, Encyclical in the Hundredth Anniversary of *Rerum Novarum Centesimus Annus* (1 May 1991), no. 38.

[25] Pope Francis, *Laudato Si'*, no. 237: 'Sunday, like the Jewish Sabbath, is meant to be a day which heals our relationships with God, with ourselves, with others and with the world. ... It also proclaims "man's eternal rest in God". See also *Catechism of the Catholic Church*, no. 2175.

Let us illustrate all this with a bad example. A few years ago an Italian diocese organized an architectural competition to build churches. It was a competition where most participants were not Christians. One of them nearly won with the project of a church made up of huge superimposed independent halls facing each other in every direction, with a kind of centre, also an independent hall, where the celebration was supposed to take place. The ceremony would then be broadcast through the internet to other parts of the building. Beyond all practical considerations, we are witnessing a dramatic misunderstanding of creation and liturgy. The public dimension of the liturgy implies, above all, full acceptance of reality, of all reality, so that worship can take place, the worship of a social body, and also of the Mystical Body of him who recapitulates in himself all creation, including our brothers, the angels: 'For he has made known to us in all wisdom and insight the mystery of his will, according to his purpose which he set forth in Christ as a plan for the fullness of time, to unite all things in him, things in heaven and things on earth.'[26]

Closely related to creation is the reality of nature: let us pragmatically define it as the stability of order within the being of people and things, with interior laws that guide it towards its end. 'Nature', says St Thomas Aquinas, 'is nothing but a certain kind of art, i.e. the divine art impressed upon things, by which these things are moved to a determinate end. It is as if the shipbuilder were able to give to timbers that by which they would move themselves to take the form of a ship.'[27] It is therefore a matter, as Pope Francis wrote, of recognizing the 'message contained in the structures of nature itself',[28] for, as Benedict XVI says, 'Man does not create himself. He is intellect and will, but he is also nature ... a nature that he must respect and that he cannot manipulate at will.'[29] Thus, nature constitutes the very solid hook of the link that unites us because we take part in all its laws.

But is seems quite clear that our contemporaries have enormous trouble with this understanding of nature. Romano Guardini already noted that human beings 'no longer have the sense ... that nature is a valid norm'.[30] What would he say were he to see the genetic and other sorts of manipulation of our times! Not only do some find it difficult to accept the fact of creation, but also that this comprises universal norms and hence unconditional limits. The consequences for our subject are very extensive.

Indeed, the notion that all of humanity is subject to unalienable natural laws that ground and condition our public worship has not always been pleasing. For example, in their preoccupation for inculturation some have often forgotten the simple fact that the diversity of cultures does not take away from common human nature, with the universal demands that Pius XII described in *Mediator Dei*: 'Three characteristics of which Our predecessor Pius X spoke should adorn all liturgical services: sacredness,

---

[26] Eph. 1.9-10. See *Laudato Si'*, no. 100: 'The creatures of this world no longer appear to us under merely natural guise because the risen One is mysteriously holding them to himself and directing them towards fullness as their end. The very flowers of the field and the birds which his human eyes contemplated and admired are now imbued with his radiant presence'.

[27] St Thomas Aquinas, *In Octo Libros Physicorum Aristotelis Expositio*, lib. II, lectio 14; cited in *Laudato Si'*, no. 80.

[28] *Laudato Si'*, no. 117.

[29] Benedict XVI, Address to the Bundestag in Berlin (22 September 2011); cited in *Laudato Si'*, no. 155.

[30] Romano Guardini, *Das Ende der Neuzeit*, 9th edn (Würzburg: Werkbund Verlag, 1965); cited in *Laudato Si'*, no. 115.

which abhors any profane influence; nobility, which true and genuine arts should serve and foster; and universality, which, while safeguarding local and legitimate custom, reveals the catholic unity of the Church.'[31] These three characteristics arise as a consequence of this public dimension of the liturgy.

Finally, it is a matter of being aware of the constants of human reality, including those relative to its social dimension. Among the most important practical consequences, there is the fact that these constants of nature will contribute to determining the laws of organic development of the liturgy. The Second Vatican Council was well aware of this when it asked that 'any new forms adopted in some way grow organically from forms already existing.'[32] This, in fact, requires a certain number of conditions that come not so much from great theological theories as simply from nature.

In order that someone be able to receive from the liturgy every spiritual benefit that the Lord wishes to offer him, it is not enough that the sacramental rite by which grace is given be 'technically' properly developed, or 'valid' according to the theological sense of the term. There could be valid sacraments celebrated in conditions very unfavourable for the disposition of him who receives – such as a Mass celebrated in great haste. Therefore, besides respecting the theological conditions of the sacramental rites, it is also necessary to respect the human conditions that will create the dispositions for the reception of that which the sacrament provides, and hence will impose the rules in order for development to be organic and vital.

On another occasion[33] I tried to explore the main human conditions of organic development, but allow me to mention only the one factor of our nature that is least taken into account: time, not the laughable 'real time' of your smartphones, but the time that 'does not respect that which is done without it' ('Le temps ne respecte pas ce qui se fait sans lui'). When one wants to make the liturgy evolve, one is tempted to seek to emancipate oneself by means of an almost magical incantation: formation, information. But there it is: when speaking about the liturgy, what is to be formed are not only men or groups of men, but entire civilizations, for 'the liturgy itself generates culture and shapes them'.[34] Now, peoples and civilizations are not computers: there is no 'update' button. Moreover, let us note that to inform is not to form: the same distance separates the two words as the distance between reading the *Catechism* and becoming saints! Father (later Cardinal) Ferdinando Antonelli said: 'This is something which cannot be achieved in a few months or years. When the masses have to be re-educated, one has to think in terms of generations.'[35]

We could also think of many other constants of human nature to take into account for public worship – other hooks for these intimate links that unite us: silence, the contemplative dimension, etc. We cannot even enumerate them all.

---

[31] Pius XII, *Mediator Dei,* nos. 14, 15, 37.

[32] *Sacrosanctum Concilium,* no. 23.

[33] In my paper 'Les conditions humaines du développement liturgique: Contribution pour expliquer une crise et en éviter d'autres', given at the 10th Colloquium Symposium of the Centre International d'Études Liturgiques (CIEL) in Rome, 3–6 November 2005.

[34] *Catechism of the Catholic Church,* no. 1207.

[35] Ferdinando Antonelli, 'Antecedenti, Importanza, Prospettive della Costituzione della Sacra Liturgia', *L'Osservatore Romano,* 8 December 1963, 6; cited in Nicola Giampietro, *The Development of the Liturgical Reform: As Seen by Cardinal Ferdinando Antonelli from 1948 to 1970* (Fort Collins, CO: Roman Catholic Books, 2009), 150.

3.2 Body, Sacramentality and Identity

In a certain way, we are engaged, in the West at least, not in a 'spiritualization' but rather in a 'rationalization' of the liturgy, notably through an inflation of verbal expression. This leads us to think that if we have trouble today with the understanding of the Church as a Mystical Body, the fact might be that we have trouble with the body in general, this body at once so adored and so scorned. It is no longer seen as a coherent whole, but only as a receptacle of more or less organized matter that one can reorganize at will. How then to understand all the expressions of St Paul about the Church as a Body? Finally, it might be difficult to admit that base matter could have its part in the identity of the very spiritual beings we believe ourselves to be![36] Spirit-bearing matter is what the fallen angels could never bear. The sexual revolution intended to break the objectivity of the physical link between two people, that astounding physical link which – following the theology of the body of St John Paul II – bases all of society under the model of the Trinity.

Perhaps you think we have digressed too far from the subject, but, to the contrary, we are at its heart. Jesus gives us his Body in order that we might be his Body, according to the famous formulation of St Augustine, who said that in communion we say 'Amen' to that which we are.[37] Heaven and earth join together in this God made man, God made body within the body of the Virgin Mary. 'Christianity does not reject matter,' said John Paul II, 'rather, corporeity is considered in all its value in the liturgical act, whereby the human body is disclosed in its inner nature as a temple of the Spirit and is united with the Lord Jesus, who himself took a body for the world's salvation.'[38] As a result, within the Church 'the life of the spirit is not dissociated from the body or from nature or from worldly realities, but lived in and with them,'[39] adds Pope Francis. The entire sacramental order depends upon this: 'a privileged way in which nature is taken up by God to become a means of mediating supernatural life. Through our worship of God, we are invited to embrace the world on a different plane. ... Encountering God does not mean fleeing from this world or turning our back on nature.'[40]

How are we to accept the full reality and demands of the Eucharist, summit of all liturgy, without fully consenting to this mediation of body and matter? And without admitting that this physical body is the very template of any social body? Pope Francis forcefully emphasizes this link:

> The Eucharist demands that we be members of the one body of the Church. Those who approach the Body and Blood of Christ may not wound that same Body by creating scandalous distinctions and divisions among its members. This is what it means to 'discern' the body of the Lord, to acknowledge it with faith and charity

---

[36] See Benedict XVI, Encyclical Letter on Christian Love *Deus Caritas Est* (25 December 2005), no. 5: 'Should he aspire to be pure spirit and to reject the flesh as pertaining to his animal nature alone, then spirit and body would both lose their dignity.'

[37] St Augustine of Hippo, *Sermo* 272 (*PL* 38,1247).

[38] St John Paul II, Apostolic Letter to Mark the Centenary of *Orientalium Dignitas* of Pope Leo XIII *Orientale Lumen* (2 May 1995), no. 11.

[39] Pope Francis, *Laudato Si'*, no. 216.

[40] Ibid., no. 235.

both in the sacramental signs and in the community; those who fail to do so eat and drink judgement against themselves.[41]

Thus, besides being the primordial place of mediation between matter and spirit, the body is also the least debatable and least manipulable model of unity we have. This is why, precisely because it is public worship, the liturgy cannot surpass this bodily dimension. The weakening or denial of this dimension is ultimately, in reality, a series of degradations, which we shall discuss later on.

But before getting to that, what we have discussed leads us to question: identity. It is certainly true that we are all together the Mystical Body of Jesus Christ, which worships the Father; but it is not enough to believe or to know this. It must also be perceived. And this is done through concrete familiar rituals: they ensure we can feel ourselves within us in a liturgy, that we can speak of 'us' when speaking about a rite, and that we seek to preserve and cultivate a common heritage, another type of link. Now, all things presuppose identification: 'I belong to the Roman rite, I belong to the Byzantine rite, etc.' In 1992, the Congregation for Divine Worship wrote: 'Liturgical reform, like all reforms, but especially those that relate to issues strongly associated with identity, ... require clarity in decisions and homogeneity in application, such that they might allow for a new education, for they offer a new identification.'[42]

There exist sociological human conditions that for a given rite might offer the framework needed for this necessary identification, but we cannot go into further detail here. Let us sketch just four principal characteristics, both hooks and links, that unite us: first, to feel at home, it is necessary that the house, the family and the people be recognizable in time and in space. For instance, with regard to the Latin rite, Cardinal Ratzinger wrote, 'Many of the faithful could not see the inner continuity with what had gone before. ... Certainly there is no awareness of [a Latin rite].'[43] The second characteristic is stability, which we have already briefly referred to with regard to time: changes that are too quickly implemented, even if justified, can render a rite unrecognizable and produce a loss of identity. The third characteristic is admiration: one is led to know and cultivate a liturgical identity if it produces admiration. Finally, these three characteristics can only exist in the context of a rooted culture. This is why it seems to me that although the Roman Liturgy now exists worldwide, it must emphatically not renounce the roots of its cultural origin. In my understanding, this is but a form of humility and is not due to some supposed 'liturgical colonialism', but it is especially necessary in order that the liturgy be perceived as a public act of an entire body, that of Jesus Christ.

---

[41] Pope Francis, *Amoris Laetitia*, no 186.
[42] Congregation for Divine Worship and the Discipline of the Sacraments, 'Credibilità della riforma liturgica', *Notítiae* 28 (1992): 625–8, at 626–7 (my translation).
[43] Joseph Cardinal Ratzinger, *The Feast of Faith: Approaches to a Theology of the Liturgy*, trans. Graham Harrison (San Francisco: Ignatius Press, 1986), 84. See also, from a different perspective, Joseph Gélineau, *Demain la liturgie: Essai* (Paris: Cerf, 1979), 13: 'In truth, it is another liturgy of the Mass. We must say without taboo: the Roman rite as we knew it no longer exists, it has been destroyed' (my translation).

3.3 Filiation, Society, Institution and Law

As soon as one discards the firm foundation of creation and of nature, inscribed within a body and an identity, the consequences multiply across all fields. The first of them in importance is filiation: being children of parents. Today there is a range of practices (test-tube babies, artificial uteri, etc.) through which our contemporaries seek to break the first non-chosen link, the first dependence imposed upon us: being children. By attacking this first fundamental link, man attacks the very image of God, for, as Pope Francis explains, 'The divine Persons are subsistent relations, and the world, created according to the divine model, is a web of relationships. Creatures tend towards God, and in turn it is proper to every living being to tend towards other things, so that throughout the universe we can find any number of constant and secretly interwoven relationships.'[44]

How could it be possible that this should not have practical consequences for the liturgical as a public act? For if filiation is effaced, leaving only isolated individuals who have no relationships other than those they have chosen and which they can always break, how can we then speak of family and of society? When one speaks of society today, it is generally understood as an agglomeration of people united only as a result of personal interest, and hence for reasons chosen by them and that can change: in other words, a social contract. Our world no longer perceives society as a social body prior and superior to individuals, to which they are attached in ways and for reasons independent of their will and that do not easily change. Our fundamental problem is therefore the current claim to individually determine all sorts of relationships, which sooner or later ends up transforming more or less all relationships into competitiveness, as C. S. Lewis so humorously explains in *The Screwtape Letters*.[45] On the other hand, relationships that are innate, intrinsic, arising from the Trinitarian model, orient us towards relationships of love. And upon this fact is founded the very definition of the liturgy that we have seen, the work of the entire Mystical Body of Jesus Christ.

We have already alluded to the concrete result: instead of voluntarily entering into a reality that surpasses and elevates us, our celebrations – I dare not speak of liturgy in these cases – are degraded into all manner of subjectivism. In liturgy, this produces the self-celebration of a particular group, a loss of the transcendent dimension and a terrible forgetfulness of the communion of saints. Cardinal Ratzinger observed:

> The liturgy is never a mere meeting of a group of people, who make up their own form of celebration and then, so far as possible, celebrate it themselves. Instead of that, through our sharing in Jesus' appearing before the Father, we stand both as members of the worldwide community of the whole Church and also of the *communio sanctorum*, the communion of all saints. ... And we know that we are

---

[44] Pope Francis, *Laudato Si'*, no. 240.
[45] C. S. Lewis, *The Screwtape Letters: Letters from a Senior to a Junior Devil* (London: Collins, 1960), Letter XVIII, 92: 'The whole philosophy of Hell rests on recognition of [this] axiom. ... What one gains another loses. ... "To be" means "to be in competition".'

not alone, that we are joining in, that the barrier between earth and heaven has truly been torn open.[46]

Akin to this 'dissociety' – a neologism by Marcel de Corte – from the moment when human links are no longer considered anything but the fruit of our personal choices, the Church is no longer accepted as an institution properly speaking, historically founded by Jesus Christ. She is no longer recognized as a constituted visible reality, the beginning of the Kingdom of God. The forcefulness of the prayers of the missal is no longer understood: 'Populi tui, Deus, institutor et rector ...'[47] One very often gets the impression that even entirely reputable Catholics have often adopted the Protestant theory of an invisible Church,[48] at least the temporal structure of which arises purely functionally from grassroots groups. I have even heard the marvellous Catholic philosopher Gustave Thibon use the expression 'the great thing' when speaking about the Church as an institution. How can we imagine in this case that a Christian could be officially designated and sent by this 'machine' to pray and to celebrate in its name, as we read in the General Instruction on the *Liturgy of the Hours?*[49] How could one grasp that one must be designated to distribute Holy Communion?[50] And so on.

Soon after the promulgation of *Sacrosanctum Concilium*, Bishop Henry Jenny suggested that the juridical conception of the Church's hierarchy should be adapted to the community of faith and prayer assembled for the Eucharist.[51] In this conception, several of the difficulties we have just mentioned implicitly arise. If the juridical aspect of the Church is set aside, we cannot expect adequate attention to liturgical law and rubrics, and this leads to all the consequences we are aware of.

Among the most unfortunate spiritual consequences of all these degradations of the public understanding of the liturgy is that the idea of a covenant between God and humanity becomes mitigated. As a result, the celebration of the New Covenant that is the Eucharist loses its true sense. The very thing that constitutes the summit, the final gift of Him who died and resurrected that we all 'may be one' (see Jn 17.11, 21-2), becomes undervalued, passing from the ontological depth of shared divine Life

---

[46] Joseph Cardinal Ratzinger, *God and the World: Believing and Living in Our Time*, A Conversation with Peter Seewald, trans. Henry Taylor (San Francisco: Ignatius Press, 2002), 412.

[47] *Missale Romanum ex decreto SS. Concilii Tridentini restitutum Summorum Pontificum cura recognitum*. Editio typica (Vatican City: Typis Polyglottis Vaticanis, 1962), Feria quinta post dominicam IV in Quadragesima, Oratio super populum.

[48] See Scott & Kimberly Hahn, *Rome Sweet Home: Our Journey to Catholicism* (San Francisco: Ignatius Press, 1993), 181–2.

[49] *Code of Canon Law* (1983), can. 834 § 2: 'Such worship takes place when it is carried out *in the name of the Church* by persons legitimately *designated* and through acts approved by the authority of the Church' (emphasis mine). See *The Divine Office: The Liturgy of the Hours according to the Roman Rite, As Renewed by the Decree of the Second Vatican Council and Promulgated by the Authority of Pope Paul VI*, approved for use in Australia, England & Wales, Ireland, New Zealand, Scotland, 3 vols. (London: Collins, 1974), General Instruction on the *Liturgy of the Hours*, no. 27: 'Wherever groups of the laity are gathered and whatever the reason which has brought them together, such as prayer or the apostolate, they are encouraged to recite the Church's Office, by celebrating part of the *Liturgy of the Hours*. For they should learn to adore God the Father in spirit and in truth especially through liturgical worship; they must remember that by public worship and prayer they can have an impact on all men and contribute to the salvation of the whole world.'

[50] *General Instruction of the Roman Missal* (Washington, DC: USCCB, 2011), no.162.

[51] See Henri Jenny, 'Introduction', in *Constitution de la Sainte Liturgie (de Sacra Liturgia)* (Paris: Éditions du Centurion, 1964), 2–30.

to the psycho-affective superficiality of 'living together'. The results are incalculable for the knowledge of our great and beautiful God and for entering into the fullness of his loving plan; in a word, for all spiritual life.

In the first section we have seen that the public nature of the liturgy is ultimately a consequence of the intimate links by which our Creator and Redeemer wished that 'they may be one, even as we are one ... perfectly one' (Jn 17.22-3). In this second section we have tried to see, with some examples, what is in play when these links become distended, because their foundations are weakened. Many other such enfeebled foundations might be examined, such as mission, authority, dependence and offering, but that would exceed the scope of this presentation.

To conclude this section, it seems nevertheless possible to detect already a common denominator of all these weaknesses in the full understanding of the liturgy: a certain rejection of mediation. For earthly affairs we accept the most compulsory sort of slavery with regard to material mediations: the media. But in our relationship with God, there is a temptation to seek to skip any mediation: sometimes even that of Christ, but more often that of his Body, of the Church, of institutions, of people and even of the things he has chosen. This ultimately goes back to the temptation of trying to become equal to God. The liturgy in its full public dimension is the place where all mediations, from the angels to the humblest material things, find their harmony in a unity that already anticipated glory, as is marvellously explained in the blessing of cement during the Rite of Dedication of a Church: '*Summe Deus, qui summa, et media, imaque custodis, et omnem creaturam intrinsecus ambiendo concludis, benedic hanc creaturam caementi*' – 'Most High God, who guard the heights, and the middle, and the depths, and encompass internally every creature, bless this creature of cement.'[52]

4 How to Foment a Fruitful Understanding of the Public Nature of the Liturgy

In a beautiful book describing his conversion to Catholicism, the one-time Protestant pastor Scott Hahn has a chapter entitled 'Teaching and Living the Covenant as Family'. This exactly what it is all about: the covenant between God and men as a family – in other words, the public aspect. Hence it is not a coincidence that in this chapter he discusses the importance of the liturgy in his conversion:

> As I shared these 'novel finds' about God's covenant family and the worship of his children, my parishioners grew excited. ... The elders even asked me to revise our liturgy ... so I began to study it. I came up with some questions: Why is our church so pastor-centered? Why is our worship so sermon-centered? Why aren't my sermons really designed to prepare God's people to receive communion? ... Going through the Letter to the Hebrews and the Gospel of John made me see that the liturgy and sacraments were an essential part of God's family life.[53]

---

[52] *Pontificale Romanum: Pars Secunda*, Editio Typica Emendata (Vatican City: Typis Polyglottis Vaticanis, 1961–2), Ordo ad ecclesiam dedicandam et consecrandam, no. 33 (p. 31).
[53] Hahn, *Rome Sweet Home*, 44–5.

Hahn still does not speak of the Church as the Mystical Body of Christ, but his research into the covenant leads him to the liturgy, and finally the liturgy leads him to Tradition and to the Church. And so a fruitful understanding of the public nature of the liturgy can be of utmost value in someone's life, and thus it behoves us to promote it.

4.1 The Celebration

The first place where this understanding must be developed is the Church, in the context of liturgical celebrations. Certainly one might find refuge behind the rubrics, saying that it is enough to apply them in order that the public sense of the liturgy be assured. Indeed, applying the rubrics in good faith is already an admirable step: each one sees himself humbly as the member of an institution from which he receives a mission. An ensemble of things would tighten the links of the one Body within which and in the name of which 'we dare to say Our Father'. But this does not suffice, especially when the rubrics allow considerable latitude and require choices to be made. It is troubling that many members of the Eastern churches, although they generally have fewer written rubrics than the Latin rite, often show better judgement about what is befitting and what is not, probably because their sense of the presence of God, of the communion of saints, and of sacramentality have not been dried up by Western scientific pretensions.

Where to begin then? Before anything, with a certain sense of the sacred. We will not enter into a debate about it when entire libraries have been written about the subject. But even if we cannot justify them here, we must, nevertheless, propose certain aspects in order to move forward.[54] If we take the enormous risk of trying to define 'the sacred', we should say that it is the proper character of persons, things and actions that transmit life, natural or supernatural. The more a person, a thing, or an action is a source of life, or close to the source, the more it shall be considered sacred. From this fact they will arouse an attitude where dependence, acknowledgement and attention are combined in a very strong link. This attitude is called piety, in its full Roman sense. By various analogical degrees, we also speak of piety towards God, the Church, one's parents, spouses or homeland, precisely because and insofar as they are sources of supernatural and natural life.

---

[54] I apologize for summarizing here, once again, the fruit of personal studies not yet formalized, with the consciousness that it would require enormous work to confirm or to correct these points of view. If it is useful, divine Providence certainly will find the right person to do that. The cross-shaped parallelism of Lev. 10.10 establishes equivalence between pure and sacred, impure and profane; and we know also the biblical bond between life and purity, between the partial or total loss of life (blood, semen, etc.) and impurity (dead, maximal impurity). It seems to give us a certain spiritual light, that I hope not totally unfounded. The point of view here briefly presented is not opposed to the notion of 'separated', 'reserved apart' that many authors justifiably attribute to the sacred. However it seems to me that this separation is only the most immediate and visible consequence of the bond with a source of life: because we protect this source as necessary, and also because we protect ourselves from it, as we confusingly know that a bad personal disposition can change this source of life into a source of death (see 1 Cor. 11.29), which in both the cases implies a distance. This distance is also owing to the mystery and the fear when facing life and death, because we do not act upon them at will.

Applied to the liturgy, this means that persons, things and actions must be brought into harmony with the source of life par excellence that is the Eucharist, as a sacrificial action and as presence. From there, by successive mediations, everything will fall into harmony, which extends to the bishop who acts as Jesus Christ, high priest and teacher, to the altar where Jesus Christ offers and is offered, then to the priest, to the deacon or the holy oils, etc. This is the principle that gives intimate value even with minimal rubrics: why does the priest perform certain actions at the altar, placing his hand over it, whereas the bishop performs them at his throne? It is because the priest does not have the fullness of the priesthood and his living-giving power is linked to the bishop. Why does one remove the Blessed Sacrament from the altar during a consecration of virgins? Because in this specific case the bishop must be perceived as Jesus the Bridegroom who calls upon the Church as Bride in the person of the consecrated virgin. Why does one turn towards the altar during the most important moments of the Divine Office? To link the public prayer of the Bride to the sacrifice of Jesus Christ who offers himself to the Father for our salvation. We could go on giving examples down to the details that, each on its own level, contribute to expressing and carrying out the union of the entire praying Body of Jesus Christ, the source of life.

Thus all efforts, all liturgical signs must tend, not only to the perception of the presence of God who comes from on high, but also to the fact that within the Mass this presence is active, that there is something going on in which all participants are involved. The Mass is not a simple 'machine to bring about the presence'. If one had on the altar a heap of enriched uranium, there would automatically be a whole series of clothing, gestures, signs and procedures that would regulate the behaviour of the people around it, since it would not be a matter of an inert treasure, such as the royal crown, but of an active reality. For someone seeing this spectacle, this choreography of precautions around a 'nuclear altar' would demonstrate that it is a very important matter, a matter of life and death, in which they are all involved. This is only a very limited metaphor, but the Mass is effectively about a real presence infinitely more active than uranium, and not because of death, but because of an unimaginable plenitude of life, which makes us all together 'another humanity for Jesus Christ', according to the expression of St Elizabeth of the Trinity.

Having proposed a principle that organizes and gives life to actions, it seems to me that the second thing that must be done is to bring order and hierarchy. This makes it immediately clear that there is an institution that is greater than ourselves and within which each one has his place. When there is no order, there is no proper place; if there is no proper place, no one feels in place and there is no personal identification with this Body. Concretely, this means that there must be careful attention during the ceremonies not only for practical reasons – to avoid disorder, which is certainly good – but in order that everyone might manifest their hierarchy and roles. This is done not only by the different positions of the assembly, but by the choice of vestments, of proper insignias, of signs of deference and many other things of this sort.

This is especially important during concelebration, in order to keep it on the level of meaning desired by the Church – the unity of the priesthood of Jesus Christ, at the heart of the public nature of the liturgy – and so that it does not break down into the sociological level of fraternal sharing. Fraternal sharing is very nice, of course, but is better suited for lunchtime. To continue on the subject, a bishop must never be seen as simply one more concelebrant among others during a Mass celebrated by a simple priest. This makes it impossible to perceive the very nature of the connections of the praying Body of Christ. It would be like putting the head where the arms should be, and it is worth noting that the Eastern Church is generally very sensitive to this incoherence.

But for a proper understanding, a beautiful hierarchy is not enough. It would be a mere skeleton if it found itself without any link to the liturgical assembly that is present. A fruitful understanding of the public nature of the liturgy can be promoted by anything that leads to common action in one Body, such as processions and common movements. For example, the fact that the president of the Bishops' Conference of the Philippines recently reminded the faithful that they must kneel after the *Sanctus* promotes in the hearts of the faithful not only piety, but also the perception of the public dimension of the liturgy. Liturgical orientation also contributes to making manifest this common action of one praying Body, of the priest and of the faithful walking towards the Lord who is coming.

To foment this, a properly understood architecture is a tremendous assistance. In the building of a church, it is not a valid principle that the assembly needs to be able to see everything during the liturgy. Besides the fact that this would underscore a rather individualistic outlook, it imposes reductionist choices (limited places, seating tiers, semicircles) that the Romans knew about perfectly well, but which they preferred not to adopt for the liturgy (basilicas, screens, iconostases) because they did not correspond to its public nature that demands a certain 'processionality' of the assembly.

In third place, everything that contributes to the sense of the universal during the celebrations allows each one to perceive the local community within the great reality of the Catholic Church. Certainly, rubrics also play their role here. But in the first place there must be a degree of stability, perhaps fewer optional formulas besides those that are truly necessary, in order that all may be found there more easily wherever they may go. Likewise, a certain dose of Latin, not understood as an absolute in itself but as an efficacious sign of universality, would also contribute to render the Latin rite recognizable everywhere. This would create an opportunity to identify with it – and this is part of the public dimension of the liturgy. Similar remarks would also be valid with regard to sacred music, especially the Gregorian chant.

The sacred, the order, the universal: three major lines of work to foment a proper liturgical understanding. But a proper understanding is not to have many ideas or to entertain many concepts. Liturgy certainly requires comprehension, but a specific type of understanding that is not so much the condition as the result of acts of worship of God, acts by which we enter into contact with the Father in the name of and in the Mystical Body of Jesus Christ. One does not understand anything except by knowing Someone, Christ. Before giving us ideas about God, the liturgy builds an image of God in our heart, an image of the Church – the Bride of Christ. It is this image that will condition our reflexes and then our understanding of and our love for God.

4.2 Formation

Formation begins at home, in the family. A sound education on the subjects we have mentioned will help give children a proper intellectual and affective background for strengthening the links that they have and that they are, inasmuch as they are men, and inasmuch as they are Christians. For instance, an education that inculcates a broad and beautiful view of creation where each being has its place, the awesome discovery of the laws inscribed in nature, respect for one's own body and for material things, a clear personal and familial identity, respect for family roles, a certain ritualism in family prayers, the communion of saints with its departed members, without mentioning participation in liturgies worthy of their name: these are the elements that would build a natural perception of this praying Body of Christ.

Much was said about formation during the Second Vatican Council and in its aftermath, and rightly so, but the present reality of seminaries seems globally, at least in the West, very far from addressing real needs. Many seminarians lack practical formation in the Mass and the sacraments. In all ages there would be enough material to write an entire thesis on 'sloth and liturgy', but in our days a certain minimalist mindset has generally settled in. It has had paradoxical contradictions, leading to sophisticated para-liturgies and a neglected liturgy, which is also due to the lack of an understanding of its public character and of responsibility towards the entire Body. It would be necessary at least to try to make use of this tendency to facilitate proposing in an authorized, accessible and structured manner a wealth of instruments useful for practical formation – for example, developing an official Roman ceremonial for parishes set up to be as accessible, practical and effective as possible. In the same spirit, proposing a more practical variant of the current ceremonial of bishops. And why not create a sort of school for masters of ceremonies, with different levels, etc. where dioceses could send those who will then serve in the seminary or with the bishop?

This pragmatic formation is a priority, not in itself, but, as we have said, in order to improve successfully the image people have of the liturgy and, consequently, of the Church and of God. But this must not lead to a neglect of the strengthening of the formation of seminarians in the philosophical, theological and spiritual principles that will prepare a soul for these efforts. In these fields, it seems to me that the most fundamental principle is a return to realist metaphysics, without which a common evaluation of the fundamental links that exist among men, from the facts of creation, of nature, of filiation, etc. becomes mere figure skating. A better anthropological formation would also produce similar benefits. Once these two bases have been mastered, the theology of the body and theology of the covenant could help deepen understanding of the link between ecclesiology and liturgy. Finally, a theological and spiritual understanding of law would give liturgical law its necessary place in a unitary and mystical order.

Properly understood, the same courses of formation would be beneficial for all the faithful, with perhaps a greater emphasis on their specific role as offerers during the course of the Holy Sacrifice. When the priest elevates the host, it is not only the offering of bread that will be transubstantiated, but also the offerings of all the faithful which this host represents and which they themselves must offer: 'In order that the oblation by which the faithful offer the divine Victim in this sacrifice to the heavenly Father may have its full effect, it is necessary that the people add something else, namely, the offering of themselves as a victim,' thus wrote Pius XII, then citing St Paul: 'I appeal to you therefore, brethren, by the mercies of God, to present your bodies as a living sacrifice, holy and acceptable to God, which is your spiritual worship' (Rom. 12.1).[55] The pope's words are forceful: 'in order that the oblation may have its full effect'. And this emphasizes precisely to what point this is about the oblation of the whole Body, social and mystical, in its entirety.

5 Conclusion: St Benedict, Master of Liturgy

To conclude, allow me to explain briefly why Benedictines are sensitive to this public nature of the liturgy. St Benedict never produced any theories about the liturgy. He was only a great Roman and especially a master of prayer. His Roman, perhaps patrician, culture instilled in him a structured, large and deep understanding of the family, of society and of law. It prepared this master of prayer, whose only goal was to put all means into effect for seeking the Lord, to detect in the liturgy he received from the Roman Church the means of the greatest perfection and effectiveness. And this is why he was able to write a monastic rule where remarks abound about this innate understanding of the public character of the liturgy and its unique value: the particular presence of God and the communion of saints in the Divine Office,[56] its marked distinction from private prayer,[57] the sense of a monastery's oratory,[58] rank within the community,[59] the minute prescription of the Office and its rubrics,[60] the importance of not losing the entire Office when one is late[61] and to say it outside of the choir kneeling,[62] public reparations for mistakes caused by their disorderliness,[63] etc. One might doubtlessly add even more examples of this confident liturgical sense, which is before anything else the result of a great theological and spiritual sense.

Giving one's life to seeking God by means of the great liturgy of the Church, in a community formed by the Benedictine rule: this conforms us every day to the thought of the patriarch of Western monks.

May this contribution be at once a filial offering to Mother Church, whose heart we have dared to lay open, and a homage to the liturgical spirit of St Benedict, which Dom Gérard Calvet – founder of my abbey – taught us to live so well.

---

[55] Pius XII, *Mediator Dei*, no 40.
[56] *The Rule of Saint Benedict*, trans. David Parry OSB (London: Darton, Longman & Todd,1984), Chapter XIX.
[57] Ibid., Chapter XX.
[58] Ibid., Chapter LII.
[59] Ibid., Chapters XLVII and LXIII.
[60] Ibid., Chapters VIII–XVIII.
[61] Ibid., Chapter XLIII.
[62] Ibid., Chapter L.
[63] Ibid., Chapters XLIII–XLIV.

5

The Ethical Character of the Mysteries: Observations from a Moral Theologian

Michael P. Cullinan

1 Introduction

I was asked to speak as a moral theologian, rather than as a liturgist or a sacramental theologian. In fact my area of expertise is in the ethics of St Paul, which you may well think is a long way from the particulars of liturgy. I am only too aware, therefore, of the danger of claiming knowledge which I do not possess, and all the more because I have always had a deep interest in liturgy. If professional liturgists can sometimes be regarded as somewhat dangerous people, at least in the eyes of those who do not agree with them, how much more dangerous may an amateur liturgist be! So I feel the need to begin rather defensively, with a few disclaimers. I do not claim to be a liturgist and I do not claim that the subject of this talk has been exhaustively researched. I intend only to offer a few observations rather than a closely connected analysis. But I hope that these observations may aid your thinking in the continuing implementation of the general restoration (*instauratio*) of the liturgy envisaged by Vatican II's Constitution on the Sacred Liturgy *Sacrosanctum Concilium*, no. 21, and the need to 'adapt more suitably to the needs of our own times those institutions which are subject to change'.[1]

What should a moral theologian say to liturgists? Once it would have been obvious. Like a great imperial power, moral theology (and its even greater neighbouring colonial power Canon Law) devoted much time to sacraments and liturgy – for example, half the manual of moral theology produced by Fr Henry Davis in 1935 is devoted to sacraments.[2] But we now live in a postcolonial theological world where Canon Law and moral theology have been pushed back to their home territories. It would still be possible, and maybe useful, to attempt to re-enter your territory by applying some moral principles to contemporary liturgical and sacramental practice, in the interests of validity, good order and the avoidance of anarchy and confusion. But this would be thinnish fare for an assembly of this kind, to say nothing of the risk of provocation – post-imperial powers have to be careful how they revisit their former territories,

---

[1] '... ad nostrae aetatis necessitates melius accommodare'. Second Vatican Council, Constitution on the Sacred Liturgy *Sacrosanctum Concilium* (4 December 1963), no. 21.

[2] Henry Davis SJ, *Moral and Pastoral Theology*, 4 vols. (London: Sheed and Ward, 1935).

particularly when they are in uniform. It seemed better to do the opposite: instead of applying moral principles *to* liturgy, consider how we can derive moral principles *from* liturgy. This immediately suggested the title 'The Ethical Character of the Mysteries', which is the title of a chapter in a book by a contemporary Orthodox lay theologian Christos Yannaras.

But why choose an Orthodox? First because for Yannaras, as for other Orthodox scholars such as Zizioulas and Guroian, there is a very close link between liturgy and ethics. But there are also more fundamental reasons for looking Eastwards, not only, of course, to Orthodox, but to our Catholic brethren too. The East tends, as Archbishop Kallistos Ware pointed out many years ago, to transcend our Western antitheses, particularly those developed after the Reformation. What a source from the East says always needs to be evaluated with a cool head before being assimilated, but its freshness often leads us to look at our own tradition anew.

There is another good liturgical reason for looking East. In contrast to our situation, their liturgy is unreformed, and so, in a sense, unremarkable and above discussion, as ours no longer is nor, perhaps, ever can be again, and their ecclesial tradition is very conservative and so can lead us back to our own Western tradition, even when it is not also actually part of our common Catholic tradition from the united churches of the first millennium. We too easily forget the Eastern half of this common tradition and, despite such documents as *Orientale Lumen*,[3] we are still not spending enough time studying it.

So the question arises of whether we can learn from the East, or at least from a few Eastern sources, in deriving ethical considerations from liturgy and in particular whether we can do the same with our own Latin-rite liturgy, either in its Ordinary or in its Extraordinary Form. This article does not claim to be comprehensive or completely up to date, so the approach will be merely through illustrative examples chosen from authors encountered in moral theology, to avoid the risk of an outsider venturing too cavalierly into the whole field of Eastern liturgy. Testimony from Zizioulas and Guroian is included, and there will also be two witnesses from the Reformation tradition: Paul Ramsey and Oliver O'Donovan.

Finally, it would perhaps be slightly too self-interested for a moral theologian to discuss only possible developments for his own subject in an assembly of liturgists. The only alternative is to venture briefly into your liturgical territory with some opinions of a moral theologian on some current questions in liturgy and in particular on the response of our age to the enormous changes that took place in the Roman rite from 1955 to 1970, prescinding as much as possible from personal liturgical opinions and speaking as a moral theologian.

In fact this article will argue a case, based on the evidence of the witnesses, for the grave moral importance of what people see and hear in our churches, for a re-examination of the individualization of penance, for the importance of our attitudes to material creation and, as an example, for the need for some reflection on the celebration of Christian marriage.

---

[3] Pope John Paul II, Apostolic Letter to Mark the Centenary of *Orientalium Dignitas* of Pope Leo XIII *Orientale Lumen* (2 May 1995).

2 Yannaras

Given the chosen title, Yannaras had to come first, but Yannaras is an especially difficult witness, because he is, even by Orthodox standards, militantly anti-Western. Neither does he seem to be a typical representative of mainstream Orthodox theology, if indeed there is such a thing. As a philosopher as well as a theologian he seeks to baptize existentialism. He passionately opposes individualism, legalist and conventional morality, and pietism, and he sees all these evils not only in the Protestant traditions but also very much in the Catholic Communion. The fruits of his ideas need to be selected carefully and picked over attentively before they can be served safely and this has as far as possible been done, even at the risk of failing to represent his ideas completely or with overall accuracy. On the other hand, his ideas, like those from other Eastern sources, do evince a degree of Paulinity, which has been a refreshing surprise. This article will attempt to show that Yannaras's ethical ideas on such matters as community, moral transformation by grace, law and the use of material things are important not only to moral theology but to liturgy too.

Yannaras's book *The Freedom of Morality* was published in Greek in 1970 during the dictatorship of the Greek colonels and after the heady years of the rebellious and Marxist 60s.[4] It emphasizes the freedom and personhood of God and attacks legalism and the reduction of ethics to convention and conformity with nature. In fact the title of his book is really the freedom of *ithos*, and it is ethos rather than simply ethics that Yannaras associates with the liturgy.

2.1 Introduction

Presenting Yannaras's views on morality and liturgy in a logical way requires a preliminary passage through his fundamental ideas on creation, sin, fall and redemption through Christ and the Church. These ideas reflect Yannaras's personalism and existentialism, and his utter rejection of legalism.

For Yannaras, the way God gives substance to being is personal. Personal distinctiveness forms the image of God in man and this image is not limited to parts of human nature, such as memory, understanding and will, or to the soul. Love is the supreme road to knowledge of the person. Man's ethical problem is 'how to be saved from natural necessity – from space, time, passions, corruption, and death' (p. 27). Man originally falls by 'the decision to reject personal communion with God for the autonomy and self-sufficiency of his own nature' (p. 30). This decision is sin because sin is defined by the fathers as 'missing the mark' (p. 33) – 'failure to realize their existential end, to confirm and conserve the uniqueness of their hypostasis through love' (p. 34).[5]

---

[4]   Christos Yannaras, *The Freedom of Morality*, trans. Elizabeth Brière (Crestwood, NY: St Vladimir's Seminary Press, 1984). Throughout this section page numbers in the text refer to this book. For some of the background information about this book and the author's biography, see Basilio Petrà, 'Christo Yannaras and the Idea "Dysis"', in *Orthodox Constructions of the West*, ed. George E. Demacopoulos and Aristotle Papanikolao (New York: Fordham University Press, 2013), 161–80. For this and more generally I am also indebted to some lectures by Professor Petrà given in Rome in 2001/2 based on his book *Tra cielo e terra* (Bologna: Edizioni Dehoniane, 1991).

[5]   Yannaras cites Maximus the Confessor, *Scholia on the Divine Names* (PG 4, 348C and 305B).

It is not a legal but an existential fact – an active refusal to be what we truly are, the image and glory of God (p. 46). The first sin fragments human nature into individual wills each expressing the individual's need to survive in self-sufficiency. Natural needs dominate and become an end in themselves, ending up as passions: 'causes of anguish and the utmost pain, and ultimately death' (p. 31). The first sin condemns the will of every other human person to be merely an individual will expressing and enforcing the necessities of the fragmented nature. Each new human being and his will are subject to the need to survive, thus perpetuating the fall (p. 31).

Man can be regenerated in Christ because Christ brings the divine and human natures together and harmonizes the human and divine wills (p. 52). For Yannaras, sin is also the measure of our awareness of separation from God and life and so the start of *metanoia* or repentance (p. 40). Man must entrust his whole life to Christ, sinful though it is. He does this through the Church (p. 41) because Christ 'constitutes her body' (p. 51) and because the fact of the Church manifests the Gospel and comes before even Scripture (pp. 49–50). This also requires *ascesis* (p. 53). God became man to transform man's nature but this cannot happen by individual effort but only by grafting man into Christ's body by total participation in it: 'The eating and drinking of Christ's flesh and blood changes individuals into members of a unified body and individual survival into communion of life and unity of life' (p. 81), that is, the Church. Elsewhere (p. 139), Yannaras describes the Eucharist as the fundamental mystery, before he discusses baptism, describing it as 'a realization of the new nature of the Church', as a regeneration and as giving a new hypostasis not based on natural necessity (p. 141).

Thus we have come inevitably and by a fairly short road from creation, fall and our need for salvation to the liturgy, to Sunday Mass in fact. Perhaps this already illustrates how an Eastern perspective can transcend Western antitheses. The idea of sin being the start of repentance would sit happily in the mouth of an evangelical Protestant, but the immediate emphasis on the Church would probably not. Yet both these ideas can be found in the Epistles of St Paul.

2.2 Specificity

Yannaras's idea of ethics raises the fundamental question of whether moral theology depends on revelation or is it an autonomous academic discipline. In his chapter on the ethical character of the mysteries (which is, of course, the normal Eastern word for the sacraments), Yannaras argues that the moral life of restoration to incorruptibility is itself a mystery, 'more of a mystery than natural life'. He goes on, 'If we draw the bounds of Christian ethics outside the realm of the mysteries of the Church, we shall inevitably end up with the shadows of conventional social requirements, with the fleshless, spineless ethic of legalistic "improvements" with no taste of real life and no correspondence in a real transfiguration of man' (p. 139). Earlier he says, 'The ethos or morality of Christians is the fact of the Eucharist, an existential fact of unity and communion' (p. 82). Indeed, repentance ('awareness of our failure and our fall') and Eucharist are the two poles of Christian ethics (p. 89). The Church's ethic is 'opposite to any philosophical, social, or religious ethic' (p. 82). Indeed, the mysteries are the 'sum and perfection' of the Church's ethics because in them ethos or morality identifies with being (p. 138). He also points out (p. 91) that both ethics and religion are the result of the fall of man.

This close identification of ethics and liturgy may surprise many of us. It certainly awakes a debate in moral theology about the specificity of Christian ethics, but it also provokes uncomfortable questions about liturgy.

There was a debate among moral theologians some decades ago about whether there are any specific moral precepts for Christians.[6] Apart from such matters as fasting on Good Friday and going to Mass on Sunday, is every moral precept derivable in principle from the natural law without recourse to revelation or magisterium? Moral theology as done before Vatican II often made little direct and explicit use of Scripture. Those who wanted to put the theology back into moral theology, sometimes known as favouring *Glaubensethik*, did not always find it easy to come down to specifics and were accused by the autonomist side of removing Christian ethical discussion and contribution from public debate in modern pluralistic societies. And it is true that St Thomas Aquinas said (or seemed to) that there no need for specific moral precepts in the new law beyond the moral precepts of the old law, which proceed from the dictate of reason.[7]

It seems clear which side Yannaras is on. The author would agree with the Anglican moral theologian Oliver O'Donovan's description of this as 'a rather unhelpful disagreement' because one cannot rule out *a priori* the possibility of revelation about 'the *humanum* that all men share'.[8] It follows that not only the reality of the *humanum*, but our fundamental essence and final destiny have to enter into fundamental moral theology. Neither can moral reflection ignore grace, indeed Servais Pinckaers is right to argue that the theology of grace is best taught as part of moral theology, as it once was generally and still is by the Dominicans in Rome, rather than being relegated in a somewhat desiccated form to the realm of dogmatic theology. Of course, once you bring grace in you then come to sacraments and so to liturgy.

Much of what Yannaras says here can, therefore, be taken very seriously. But it cuts both ways. If liturgy is so important to moral life, what of the liturgy most of our people actually encounter every Sunday – or maybe the one Sunday a month they bother to go – or when they go to weddings and funerals?

Yannaras has his own criticisms of Greek Orthodoxy here. For example, he criticizes the atomization of modern urban religion. 'Today', he says (and, remember, this was in 1970), consumer culture is 'incomparably stronger' than 'the culture and ethos of Eucharistic communion' (p. 224). People come to church 'to satisfy their individual religious needs' and to pray as individuals in parallel with the other members of the congregation, remaining 'more alone perhaps than on the sportsground or in the cinema'. They hear moralistic sermons. Their sense of mystical unity is atrophied, so atrophied that 'one wonders how far the Eucharistic synaxis today still preserves

6　For an excellent account of this debate, see J. Vincent MacNamara, *Faith and Ethics* (Dublin: Gill and Macmillan, 1985).

7　St Thomas Aquinas, *Summa Theologiae*, I-II, q. 100, a. 1, on the commandments belonging to the law of nature. See also q. 108, a. 2, especially ad 1 ('Et ideo in his non oportuit aliqua praecepta dari ultra moralia legis praecepta, quae sunt de dictamine rationis').

8　Oliver O'Donovan, *Resurrection and Moral Order: An Outline of Evangelical Ethics* (Leicester: Apollos, 1986, 1994²), 20.

the truth of the universal church' (p. 224). For Yannaras, the existence of Eucharistic community is not only important for Christians but for the whole modern world – indeed it is the world of today's last hope (p. 262). Yannaras's ideal is far different from the modern city. It is the Greek village of the past, of the time of Turkish domination: the 'free ethos of enslaved *Romiosyne* [Romanity]', with festivals, personal relationships, a liturgical structure to the community and communal virtue (pp. 222–3).

We, of course, have our own criticisms of ordinary parish church life. They would not, perhaps, be entirely different from Yannaras's, at least in big cities. Even after the liturgical changes people can come to church and personally ignore everyone else or, worse, be personally ignored by everyone else from priest to collector. Some of us also have our idealized models from the past, whether, for example, the English medieval village with its festivals or the Irish village of a century ago with its all-pervading faith.

Yannaras is surely right to highlight the importance of community for the proper realization of the Eucharist, and the author would agree with the late Jerome Murphy-O'Connor that St Paul's reference to the Corinthians 'eating and drinking judgement' (1 Cor. 11.29) has in part to do with the divisions in their community.[9] This does not mean, however, that we can or should long for a return to the tutelage of the village. Villages can have their own tyrannies of conformity and always limit freedom to be oneself, as, indeed, any community does to some extent. We would not want to replace the sports ground or the cinema with the tyranny of the parish. And Christianity began in large cities, not in villages, whereas the parish began in the countryside. But Yannaras's village may not after all be so far removed from the *urbs sacra* of *Ordo Romanus Primus*.[10]

Perhaps what Yannaras does force us to recognize is the importance to the Church's life and, indeed, survival of recreating community and personal relationships in cities. No doubt we already knew the problem existed but perhaps we did not realize how crucial it is. Both mass media and the weekday workaday world have corralled Christian culture into a short period of time on Sunday. Our feasts and our holidays have gone and almost everything about getting to heaven now has to depend on that homily and that short simple liturgy. If this does not frighten us and make us think, perhaps it should.

2.3 Asceticism

Yannaras does not only talk of feasts and holidays. He has a lot to say about fasts too: about Christian asceticism as a communal practice. Regeneration requires asceticism as well as repentance, where a person rejects the rebellion of his individual will and imitates the obedience of the second Adam (p. 53). Indeed repentance presupposes the dynamism of asceticism (p. 154). Only the knowledge gained by asceticism provides a real answer to the problem of death, in the effort to resist death in our own bodies (p. 115). But 'Christian asceticism is above all an ecclesial and not an individual matter'

---

[9] See Jerome Murphy-O'Connor, 'Eucharist and Community in First Corinthians', in *Keys to First Corinthians* (Oxford: Oxford University Press, 2009), 194–229.

[10] I am indebted to Revd Dr Stephen Morgan for this idea, as, indeed, for his comments on the draft of this article before it was presented.

(p. 109). Asceticism finds the completion of its purpose only in the mysteries of the church (p. 137). It is not an individual exercise of the will, nor is it a masochistic attitude to human needs and desires, but 'an opportunity for communion and an act of communion'. It represents a radical social and ultimately political action (p. 218). It involves abstinence from food so that autonomous individual desire for food becomes, by submission to the practice of the Church, 'an act of relationship and communion' (p. 110). It also includes sexual continence; physical prayer (prostrations); acts of service, altruism and charity; and submission to the liturgy.

The Orthodox canons on abstinence from food are very stringent. More than half the days of the year require some kind of abstinence and Lent requires going vegan for the whole period and, ideally, having only one meal a day. Of course few do all this in practice, but most know what the ideal is. It is also an important part of Eastern spiritual life to have a spiritual father and to ask his permission before doing penances.

We in the West have followed a very different path in the last few centuries. It is a long time since milk and butter were banned in Lent, although the tradition of Pancake Tuesday reminds us that once it was not only meat that was forbidden. The author's mother remembered meatless Lents a century ago in Ireland but it is many years since each weekday of Lent required us all to fast. Since Vatican II the emphasis has been on individually chosen works.

Once again, while we may not want to follow Yannaras all the way, what he says should make us think. The first question might be what ascetical practice has to do with liturgy rather than with moral and spiritual theology. It certainly is a moral and spiritual question, and yet it is in *Sacrosanctum Concilium*, no. 110 that current adaptations of fasting and abstinence begin. Liturgy does not only deal with services of worship but also with the sanctification of time and this includes both days of feasting and days of fast.

Then we might wonder whether all this emphasis on abstinence is of much value today. The original reason for the prohibition on marrying in Lent (now repealed anyway) has been almost entirely forgotten. And what, we might ask, has abstinence from meat to do with sanctification? Yannaras is clear that it has nothing to do with earning individual merit or subjugating matter to spirit or to any foods being unclean. Rather it is subjection to the common will and practice of the church (p. 110). We in the West might immediately retort that the Church can and has changed its will and practice on this issue, even if too readily. And yet we cannot abandon fasting entirely without endangering part of sacred tradition going back to the gospels.

Perhaps the most obvious link between fasting and the Eucharist is simply that both have to do with eating and drinking, and both have to do with communion. Do we really have to apologize for fasting and abstinence in a well-fed Europe that has never before had so much obesity, so much obsession with healthy diet, so much vegetarianism and veganism? Surely we must revisit the individualization of Lent and other days of penance. To some extent we moral theologians were to blame here. We erected every small infraction of the fasting rules into a mortal sin, leading to a very brittle discipline of fasting. Gradually, in response to such things as wars and secularization, the 'rules' (as we thought of them) were reduced until now there is no ideal left for us. We each have to plan our own Lents and it is an exceptionally pious and disciplined person who can do this well.

Here in England and Wales our hierarchy has already tried to restore Friday abstinence, still the universal norm, partly as a badge of identity. May we hope that the universal Church will explore ways to restore some simple rules for Lent that will allow of sensible exception and will restore to our people a sense of their identity, a focus for their religion outside Sundays, and, indeed, a greater sense of sin. In a world where Ramadan is increasingly noticed and accommodated outside the Muslim community, would some simple solution such as the alternative of either fasting or abstaining each day be worth some consideration? The Eastern way seems to be to contrast a festal liturgy with a great deal of penance. One wonders whether we in the West have perhaps emulsified and pasteurized the vivid tastes of fast and feast into an insipid gruel.

2.4 Marriage

Marriage is, as many will know far better than the author, often very difficult and challenging. This is also true of the moral and sacramental study of it. Venturing into this area was not done without hesitation, but it is, perhaps, the main intersection between the moral and liturgical, at least in terms of academic subjects if not also in practice. It also comes up in the evidence of many of the chosen witnesses. So what Yannaras has to say about it will be presented briefly.

Yannaras insists on the distinctiveness of Christian marriage as a mystery (or sacrament). The mystery of marriage transforms natural necessity into personal communion and makes the couple's ultimate and real relationship not their family, but the Church – linked to the Eucharistic *synaxis* (p. 161).[11] Freedom from the exclusiveness of the biological bond requires asceticism – indeed, he says, 'The mystery of marriage ... has more in common with the asceticism of the monks than social institutionalization of the reproductive process.' It transfigures natural relationship into a possibility for personal relationship with the whole body of the Church who 'crowns the newly-wed couple as "martyrs", *witnesses* to her truth' (p. 167).

Yannaras then argues that the culture of today undermines true marriage – relationship becomes only subjection (p. 169). Extremes of subjectivity and objectivity make Western man 'an idea devoid of content, a unit of autoerotic satisfaction' in 'a culture of autoeroticism' (p. 170). Yannaras then blames the church authorities for being involved in this 'alienation' of marriage. Marriage celebrations are now 'dissociated' from the Eucharistic community of the Church, with many individual weddings being celebrated on the same day. The mystery must not be a precondition of civil marriage but only for those who want to experience the transfiguration and asceticism (p. 172).[12] Its challenge to both moralists and liturgists is to reflect on the Christian attitude to *eros* and to avoid reducing the understanding and celebration of Christian marriage to the underlying natural institution that marriage is.

---

[11] Quoting John Zizioulas, 'From Prosopeion to Prosopon: The Contribution of Patristic Theology to the Concept of the Person', in *Charesteria: Tributes in Honour of Metropolitan Meliton of Chalcedon* (Thessaloniki: Patriarchal Institute for Patristic Studies, 1977), 287–323 [in Greek], at 319, fn. 52.

[12] This was, of course, written before 1970 when there was no civil marriage in Greece.

2.5 Matter

Thus far this article might be accused of saying something about sacraments but little about liturgy. We in the West like to divide subjects up – not always for the best – just as we divide moral and spiritual theology, for example. When reading Yannaras the question arose of whether much of what he was saying might fail to be specifically applicable to questions of liturgy rather than sacraments. But in fact there is a possible bridge into liturgy, through his ideas on art and, more fundamentally, on the Christian relationship with matter.

We have already seen that Yannaras rejects any depreciation of matter, whether in the importance of a person's body or in ascetical practice. On the contrary, he argues that because 'the liturgy of the Church is not simply an expression of religious worship, but the core and sum of her life and truth, of her faith and ethics' (p. 85) and because the liturgy is also cosmic, we cannot then despise material reality. But neither can we make the material into an autonomous absolute as capitalism and Marxism do (pp. 86–7). For Yannaras, 'the ethos of the Church creates a mode of social coexistence, a way of using the world, and consequently a culture' (p. 88). The objects of the material world have to be seen as acts of God's love and transfigured together with one's life (p. 87), transfigured through living the ethos of the Eucharist and not simply improved (p. 217). Yannaras argues that the ontological content of the Eucharist as communion presupposes matter and the use of matter (p. 231). The word used for this in the English translation is 'art' but the Greek, we are told, is *techne*, including not only painting but music, vesture, architecture and everything else associated with the celebration of the liturgy. So worship is art and the Church's art is worship. This seems to be the bridge between Eastern and Western categories in this area. What the East says about sacred art or *techne* is of potential relevance in the West specifically to liturgy.

Yet again, however, we first have to answer some fundamental questions. Historically, certainly since the late Middle Ages, we in the West minimized sacraments to their essential requirements for validity, we simplified and individualized liturgy to allow Low Masses, and then all too often we regarded the whole world of art, music and architecture as mere icing on the cake – delicious and sweet but not particularly nourishing or essential. So we have to convince ourselves that what people see and hear at Mass is important to their moral lives. Any advertiser will very quickly assure us that these things are indeed very important, at least sociologically speaking. It is, of course, true that 'it's the Mass that matters' and that its valid celebration is far more important than the quality of the materials that accompany it. But knowing this requires faith, often deep faith, and such faith is not always easily found today.

The depreciation of matter has also been exacerbated in recent times by a kind of cult of simplicity. Noble simplicity[13] is one thing, but in order to understand what it means we perhaps need to contrast it with simple nobility, with ignoble simplicity and with noble complexity. But very often the next question we encounter in an argument in favour of the best liturgical *techne* is, 'But what would you do in a concentration camp?' The implication is that a liturgy celebrated with the simple materials available can mean more than High Mass in St Peter's. This is surely true, but using the simple

---

[13] Enjoined by *Sacrosanctum Concilium*, no. 34, at least for the Roman rite.

materials available is not the same thing as using the *simplest* materials available. To do the very best with what you can is not at all the same as doing the least you can. In fact we have evidence that priests both in Dachau and the Gulag did the very best they could. A priest in Siberia fasted from midnight until the afternoon – despite doing hard labour – in order to celebrate Mass according to the Church's law of fasting. Pontifical regalia required by the rubrics were brought into Dachau for the ordination to the priesthood of a dying deacon and a mitre and pontifical sandals were actually made in the camp.[14]

What seems to have happened recently is an exaltation of simplicity, not as one artistic principle among many but as a kind of overarching axiom or super-rubric. For the first time in religious history, people do not seem to want to offer to God the best they have and they do not see anything wrong in this. Often it is the people who have most, perhaps far more than their parents and grandparents, who want the barest worship spaces, whereas it is often the poorest who want to subscribe to statues and richly ornamented vestments. The moral theologian should suspect that something may be going on here, to do with both psychology and sociology.

It is, therefore, worth hearing what Yannaras has to say about Western attitudes to matter, even though he may be very prejudiced. He claims that modern man is cut off from the study and the respect for natural reality that comes through *ascesis* and is instead 'isolated in the autonomous self-sufficiency of technology' (p. 234). Western civilization has tried to subjugate matter in a totalitarian way and Yannaras sees this in everything from scholasticism through capitalism and technocracy to the Gulag Archipelago, which he describes, rather astonishingly, as 'the cutting edge of the West' (p. 206, fn. 11). More concretely, Yannaras also sees this in the Gothic architecture of the huge German cathedrals: both the huge Gothic cathedrals and scholasticism each subjugate human beings and this leads to 'the rebellion of the Reformation' (fn. 19) and to later Western attitudes to matter (pp. 239–43).

For Yannaras, art reveals an underlying ethos and maybe theology. While he exaggerates, if he does not actually caricature, the problems with medieval art and theology, once again he deserves a hearing. We ourselves might well ask what ethos and theology modern Catholic art and architecture reveal. This is, of course, a very hard question, and one the author is not qualified to answer. But we are wise, perhaps, as part of this process, to ask for light to examine our own individual aesthetic preferences conscientiously with a degree of humble insight and, maybe, of repentance. A sacramental religion cannot ignore the effect on people of what they see and do as well as hear.

3 Other Contributors

By now the reader may be feeling a little unsettled. If Yannaras were a lone voice in this area, a certain degree of puzzlement or even resentment would certainly be

---

[14] See, respectively, Walter Ciszek SJ, *He Leadeth Me* (London: Hodder and Stoughton, 1973), 134 and John Lenz, *Christ in Dachau* (Fort Collins, CO: Roman Catholic Books, 1960), 200.

understandable. Why, it might very reasonably be asked, has this moral theologian chosen to examine such a maverick and someone so far away in mentality from where most of us are? Yannaras is not the only ethicist to venture into the territory of liturgy. There are other Orthodox voices such as Zizioulas and Guroian but, as far as I know, few Catholic ones. It might also be as well to give a brief summary of some other contributions. The other Orthodox voices will be taken first because their view of liturgy and liturgical change is much closer to ours than that of many Protestants.

3.1 Zizioulas

John Zizioulas is a Greek Orthodox theologian who has spent many years in Scotland.[15] He contrasts the two traditions of East and West as equally ancient and each needing the other, commenting that 'both traditions know of ethics and both know sacrament. But one of them uses the sacrament in order to qualify the ethics whereas the other one uses ethics in order to qualify the sacrament. The difference is enormous in terms of spirituality and ethos.'[16]

The Western tradition, Zizioulas argues, approaches ethics through action and imitation of Christ. It is based on a historical approach and emphasizes the cross and passion. The Eastern tradition, on the other hand, is based on the eschatological and emphasizes the resurrection. The incarnation introduces eschatology into history but the eschatological God is not enclosed by history. The fundamental image is the holy city coming down from heaven in glory. The kingdom in glory is visible but through iconic, liturgical language and through the relationships of the dispersed people of God. Iconic language is not dependent on history, so, for example, the icon of Pentecost shows St Paul receiving the Spirit along with the Twelve. Ethical actions can only come out of the community and not be prior to or independent of it. Personal identity is derived from community and is destroyed by individualism. Zizioulas admits that the Eastern approach often leads in practice to indifference to ethics and history but argues it need not do so. Orthodoxy needs 'to draw the ethical implications of the Eucharist' while Catholics need 'to continue to liberate sacramental theology from notions of historical causality imposed by scholastic medieval theology so that the pneumatological and eschatological aspects become more evident.'[17]

Some of this is similar to the views of Yannaras. Two points can, perhaps, be made. We do not need to follow Zizioulas's criticism of medieval theology to accept the importance of the pneumatological and eschatological for our worship. The presence of God in our churches and on our altars is an eschatological presence, not merely a historical one. We have tended to fight shy of depicting the glory of the kingdom of heaven in case it is mistaken for clerical or ecclesiastical triumphalism, but in doing so we have all too often reduced the mysteries to the mundane and parochial, if one

---

[15] He became Metropolitan John of Pergamon in 1986 and spoke on liturgy and ethics in a symposium at the World Council of Churches the same year, published as John Zizioulas, 'Action and Icon/ Messianic Sacramentality and Sacramental Ethics', in *Whither Ecumenism? A Dialogue in the Transit Lounge of the Ecumenical Movement*, ed. Thomas Wieser (Geneva: World Council of Churches, 1986), 62–73.

[16] Ibid., 65.

[17] Ibid., 71.

may use the word. Our Western glory may be less exuberant than that of the East but it should be there, and not only in cathedrals and Oratories but in every parish church. Perhaps one reason for our problems is that even though we may pay lip service to aphorisms such as 'The Eucharist makes the Church', in practice we tend to see the Church primarily in institutional and hierarchical terms rather than, as the East seems to, primarily as the Eucharist.

A second conclusion is more tentative, because it raises aesthetic issues. Icons deliberately do not try to be historical. They are in many ways symbolic and otherworldly. Yannaras severely criticizes Western naturalism in art since the thirteenth century. Can we at least think about the need for our art, including music, vestments and architecture to be eschatological as well as historical?

3.2 Guroian

Vigen Guroian is an Armenian Orthodox lay theologian in the United States. For Guroian, Christian ethics is necessarily baptismal and Eucharistic. Baptism rather than natural generation, social reform or revolution produces a new people and the kingdom. The new people is corporate and relational and a baptismal ethic is incomplete apart from 'the Eucharistic action by which persons gather and constitute themselves as Church'. Christian ethics begins by affirming the good of creation 'as that creation comes from the hand of God and returns to his bosom through the eucharistic action of the Church', but it must also pay attention to the 'surd of evil in the Christian story'. Liturgy is not merely didactic but seeks to recreate the world by forming a 'eucharistic public' and sending it into the world.[18]

Freedom for Christians is different from the false 'gnomic' freedom of the world. Interestingly, Guroian then comments: 'This will be offensive ultimately to a secular and pluralistic society such as ours, because it defies the "privatization" of religion which that society promotes and escapes the place it provides for religion among a panoply of alternative ideologies good for private consumption but discouraged in the name of tolerance from public enactment.'[19] Guroian argues that many American Orthodox churches have failed to do this by assuming they were still a 'sacramental organism of the political society' and by turning the Eucharist into the privilege of an ethnic, social, economic or racial cult. The most powerful liturgies in our society are now those of civil religion or media: 'The liturgists of our age are the writers of advertising jingles and television "sitcoms" and the choreographers of football half-times. ... But these are liturgies and liturgists without a church.'[20] He then points to Poland as an example of how liturgy can judge political institutions. All this should challenge us.

Guroian also makes an interesting point about the Eastern attitude to creation and the eschatological aspect of the kingdom, by pointing to the exorcism of things as well as people in the baptismal rite. We have recently tended to move away from exorcizing

---

[18] Vigen Guroian, 'Seeing Worship as Ethics: An Orthodox Perspective', *Journal of Religious Ethics* 13 (1985): 332–59, with the quotations at 343 and 337.

[19] Ibid., 346.

[20] Ibid., 349, citing William J. Everett, 'Liturgy and Ethics: A Response to Saliers and Ramsey', *Journal of Religious Ethic* 7 (1979): 203–14, at 208.

or blessing things as well as people. Perhaps we should ask ourselves what this reveals about our attitude to matter, and to the genuinely Pauline ideas of creation in travail and of new creation.

3.3 Ramsey

An important earlier source was a paper by the American Methodist ethicist Paul Ramsey in a special issue of the *Journal of Religious Ethics* devoted to liturgy and ethics.[21] His contribution later inspired his one-time student Oliver O'Donovan to write a booklet also entitled *Liturgy and Ethics*.

Following Barth,[22] Ramsey sees liturgy, faith and life as three mirrors that can either reflect the divine event or be clouded by what he describes as 'pollutants in the atmosphere'. He wrote at a time of great liturgical revision and has very severe words for those he refers to as 'tinkerers': 'Those who elect themselves to draw up modern creeds, devise new liturgies and experiments or proposals for Christian living when there is no crisis of the church's struggle for its authentic witness in the world against invasion from the world turn out to be at best plunderers and looters or at worst petty pilferers of the Christian tradition'. There are 'well-meaning people in the churches who tamper with Christian liturgy and remove the ancient landmarks in the Christian moral life as well from proposing bland and novel rituals'. Later there will need to be 'some returning renewal, correction and nourishment of liturgy from the vitalities of faith and life'. He mentions in particular rituals of divorce and the revision of creeds. Interestingly for a Methodist he also argues that 'where the "Christian year" shapes the devotion of churches, or within this when every Sunday is an Easter and every Friday 'good', observed by fasting from meat other than the symbolic fish, that is liturgy'.[23]

Ramsey also highlights the importance of language: 'Even the impoverishment of the English language, the loss of elevating cadences, in much contemporary worship has paramount importance when at issue is the liturgy of the church, and as well Christian faith and moral life.'[24]

He concludes that 'an impoverished or distorted, shapeless liturgy influences the morality we credit' and argues that liturgists and ethicists need to criticize each other's work: the former when theological or ethical developments are incompatible with 'a living and authentic liturgy'; the latter on 'developments in liturgy that run against Christian believing and doing well'.[25]

This time we have a Methodist viewpoint, but once more there is an insistence on the relationship between liturgy and ethics, indeed of the duty of ethicists and liturgists to criticize each other, and on the importance of asceticism and good liturgical language. Interestingly for those favouring a 'reform of the reform', there is the prediction of the need for revisions of the liturgy made in the 1960s and 1970s to be revisited.

[21] Paul Ramsey, 'Liturgy and Ethics', *Journal of Religious Ethics* 7 (1979): 139–71. The Society of Christian Ethics currently has a group devoted to liturgy and ethics.
[22] Ibid., 143, citing Karl Barth, *Church Dogmatics* III/4, 17 and 18.
[23] Ibid., with the quoted sentences at 140, 152, 148 and 143.
[24] Ibid., 164.
[25] Ibid., 139 and 162. There are clear echoes here of *lex credendi legem statuat supplicandi.*

3.4 O'Donovan

Oliver O'Donovan's contribution came from a lecture at St John's College, Nottingham, in 1992.[26] The context is, therefore, evangelical Anglican and at a time when Anglican liturgy had recently changed greatly. O'Donovan makes two interesting and very questionable assumptions. The first is that the church constantly adapts its liturgy; the second is that liturgy is essentially speech, which leads him also to discuss preaching and revisions of the lectionary.

O'Donovan argues that moralists need liturgy to remind them that moral life 'must express what God has done in Jesus Christ'; and that liturgists need morals lest they overlook 'the enormous challenges which confront the witness of the people of God'. If people do not learn about morality from liturgy the moral categories in their minds will resemble 'a rubbish dump of contemporary cliché' from 'tired journalistic turns of phrase'. He points out that moralists failed to teach the liturgists who revised the Anglican marriage rite that the rite should explicitly link marriage to promoting the individual holiness of the spouses. He warns against lectionaries that 'cut' the text 'about with pen-knives', overprotecting people from the words of the ancient people of God and so 'locking us into our own cultural prejudices'. But when asked about non-verbal aspects of liturgy, O'Donovan has nothing to suggest.[27]

Once again the link between moral theology and liturgy is made, however uncomfortable we may be about mutual criticism. Once again there is a reference to the marriage liturgy and also to the importance of language. There is also the question of lectionaries. A scholar of Paul and of morals must remain somewhat astonished and dismayed that the text of 1 Cor. 11.27-32 on fitness to receive Holy Communion has been cut out not just from the Mass readings on Maundy Thursday but also from the serial reading of this epistle in the weekdays of Ordinary Time. Sharp penknives here, it seems.

4 Conclusion

You have listened with patience to a moral theologian's examination of other moral theologians on the question of the relationship between liturgy and morals. We have now come to the closing speech of the case. But, as promised in the title, the objective is not to convict anyone or to tell liturgists how to do their job, but merely to make some observations on what liturgy can teach morals and – necessarily more tentatively – on what morals can teach liturgy.

The clearest conclusion this study has suggested is the fundamental link between liturgical, sacramental life and Christian moral life. A Catholic ethic that has nothing to say about the ethos of the Eucharist, whether as sacrament, sacrifice or popular *synaxis* is not an adequate moral theology. Neither can a liturgy that ignores the moral life of grace be adequate for the needs of the People of God.

---

[26] Later published in Oliver O'Donovan, *Liturgy and Ethics*, Grove Ethical Studies, 38 (Nottingham: Grove Books Limited, 1993).
[27] Ibid., 5, 4, 9 and 13.

It is a short road from creation, fall, redemption and grace to Sunday Mass. What people see and hear in our churches is often not only their only moral instruction but also their only experience of the Body of Christ, not only as it exists struggling in this world but also as it exists glorified in heaven. What happens at Sunday Mass and also at baptisms, weddings and funerals matters crucially for our moral lives and, indeed, our salvation.

Part of our experience together should involve a foretaste of heaven, and part should make really present the whole communion of saints, the ecclesial community of persons in which and by which we are saved. This life together should involve not only the liturgy in church but the sanctification of the rest of our lives through feast and also through fast, which involves a rediscovery of the communal nature of Christian asceticism. This asceticism involves right attitudes to material creation, avoiding aversion and flight on the one hand and prideful subjugation on the other. Liturgical preferences can reveal the integrity or otherwise of these attitudes and are worth examining.

So far the moralist has spoken. But now he ventures into your liturgical territory. As already said, marriage can be dangerous. Perhaps two points about it can be suggested here by a non-liturgist. Both relate not only to marriage but to wider questions of liturgical change. Unlike the Protestant traditions, this is a fairly recent and controversial matter for us Catholics. We have left behind the Orthodox innocence of an unchanging, unquestionable liturgy which is a source for our faith partly because of its antiquity. But neither have we embraced the Protestant idea that liturgy is ordinarily changed to reflect belief, which makes it at best only a very secondary source for faith. We have, officially at least, used the word *instauratio*, perhaps best rendered as 'restoration', which is somewhere in-between. This leads to the question of to what extent the *lex orandi* is or should be the *lex credendi*. This is really a question beyond the scope of this article, but it is pressed on our consideration by the question of changes to the Rite of Marriage.

The Catholic Bishops of England and Wales have recently adopted a new marriage rite, which is a translation of the latest version of the Roman rite restored after Vatican II. The medieval English rite was retained in this country until just after Vatican II. Apart from a few details, such as the gold and silver with which the groom wedded the bride, this rite was largely retained by Cranmer and so passed into the consciousness of the English-speaking world.

A moralist can easily see the need for change to reflect the developed understanding of marriage, which is the fruit of the last century and of *Gaudium et Spes* in particular, and also (with reluctance) that it is no longer strictly correct to say 'With this ring I thee wed' because you actually wed by the words of consent, and that 'I join you … in Holy Matrimony' (a phrase found in the former Roman rite also) is also wrong because the priest or deacon is a witness not the minister of the sacrament. But one is left wondering how, then, our ancient rite can be a source of faith and understanding from tradition on what is, after all, the only sacrament which originates from a rite natural throughout human history.

As somewhat of a romantic, I venture a second, and secondary, question. When I look at the five-shilling piece on which my parents were married in the ancient English rite, I have to confess to a twinge of sadness at its demise, prompting a concern that the loss of its beauty may, as Ramsey points out, have significant deleterious consequences for our people. Even the best attempts at beautiful English today seem to lack the heights of the past, and this perception, because subjective perception counts here too, is valid and of concern here even if it is largely the familiarity of the old that is the source of its beauty. The language of recent Anglican weddings I have attended was good English, but it struck me as more that of the Civil Service than either the colloquial or the sacred. Judgements on our current language must be left to others. But the celebration of marriage will reveal much about what our understanding is in practice about its distinctively Christian sacramental nature.

I dare to end with a bit of a peroration – this was a risk you took when you invited a moral theologian! What happens in our churches matters for the salvation of our people. Moralists need to reflect on this and so do liturgists. If what happens fails to present our people with the challenge and the glory of the Christian life, if it fails to teach them the fullness of the Gospel, if it fails either to lift them up towards heaven or to show them a glimpse of heaven on earth, if it bores them by its dullness or offends them by the brutal ugliness of its language, music and surroundings, if it leaves them isolated as individuals or couples, or even as closed self-selecting groups, if it gives them gruel rather than the bread of heaven, where will they go for grace and how shall they – and those who let them down – be saved?

6

Doing the World Liturgically: Stewardship of Creation and Care for the Poor

David W. Fagerberg

I do not have the intelligence to mimic Thomas Aquinas all the way to the end, but I would like to mimic him briefly here at the beginning. You all know the layout of the *Summa*: he presents a question asking whether such and such is the case; he responds with a series of objections that either say 'it seems so' or 'it seems not', followed by a contrary opinion before he reaches his own conclusion with 'I answer that'. And you all know that whatever is said in that first objection is the opposite of where Thomas intends to wind up. I briefly follow suit.

Question: 'Whether there is a connection between liturgy and social justice, especially concern for the poor and stewardship of creation?' Objection: 'It would seem not.' (You now know where I intend to wind up.) I borrowed the wording of that question from the first email contact inviting me to participate in this conference, and I have been thinking about the connection ever since. But I am momentarily sidetracked by this Thomistic exercise to consider whether anyone would have objections to the proposition. I am sidetracked to ask why we would *want* there to be a connection, anyway? Why regret the divide between liturgy and social justice? Why not leave concern for the poor and stewardship of creation to the moral theologians, and leave liturgy comfortably at home with its candles and choirs, its vestments and versicles? Why would the liturgical theologian want to butt his sacred nose into the profane world's business? Never mind *how* we are going to do it, first ask *why* we want to do it. After all, liturgy has to do with heaven, and social justice with the earth; liturgy with our soul, and social justice with our body; liturgy with our salvation, and social justice with our neighbour's good; liturgy is for the weekend, and social justice is for the week. Why even include this paper in our conference?

Under one definition of liturgy, that might be hard to justify. A thin definition reads only the surface of liturgy, like someone looking at the surface of a pond but not seeing the teeming life of the underwater ecosystem. Can we see the teeming supernatural ecosystem beneath liturgy? If not, then we are hard-pressed to explain how liturgy can get past the threshold of the narthex out into the world. The symbolism of temple topography has understood the sanctuary as heaven, the nave as the Church, and the narthex as the threshold between Church and world. My set of questions was intended to ask whether liturgy has any contact with the world across this threshold? The narthex is the membrane between sacred and profane: is it permeable? The Liturgical Movement persuaded us that liturgy overflows the boundary of the sanctuary to involve the nave, but has it persuaded us that liturgy overflows the boundary of the narthex to concern the world?

I will repeat the question: Is there a connection between liturgy and social justice, especially concern for the poor and stewardship of creation? And now 'I answer that' it seems so, because Christ comes to make his mercies flow far as the curse is found; because cult is the basis of culture; because of the relationship between cult and cosmos; because the tip of the liturgical iceberg that we can see is connected to a divine economy below; because the liturgy needs the world as material for sacrifice and matter for sacrament; because after liturgy, we crave mission; because Christ heads a parade from the empty tomb, through the dislocated gates of Hades, to the Heavenly Jerusalem, and this liturgical procession marches straight through the valley of the shadow of death; because liturgy makes the Church, and the Church's reason for being is as a herald of salvation; because the *sphragis* has inscribed the Paschal Mystery on our brow as a phylactery; because the Church-at-liturgy is not a new world, it is the world renewed; because liturgy is to world as form is to matter; because the coin of the realm in liturgy is grace, and grace perfects nature; because we must be able to see the supernatural end of our creation in order to do justice to nature at the moment; because without the rational tongue of liturgists, mute matter could not symphonize with the angels; because of incarnation in a body and resurrection of a body; because liturgy puts man and woman in their true cosmic location. Let us give Benedict XVI the final word:

> The true liturgical action is the deed of God, and for that very reason the liturgy of faith always reaches beyond the cultic act into everyday life, which must itself become 'liturgical', a service for the transformation of the world.[1]

> Cult, liturgy in the proper sense, is part of this worship, but so, too, is life according to the will of God. … Ultimately, it is the very life of man, man himself as living righteously, that is the true worship of God, but life only becomes real life when it receives its form from looking toward God. Cult exists in order to communicate this vision and to give life in such a way that glory is given to God.[2]

If the idea of a square triangle sounds more intelligible than liturgical action reaching beyond cult into the bedroom and the boardroom, the political circle and the market square, then perhaps our definition of liturgy is too thin – not high enough to kiss heaven, not deep enough to pressure Hades, not broad enough to touch the world and comfort the poor in it. Liturgy should overflow the sanctuary. Stewardship of creation and care for the poor is not just a moral duty, it is a liturgical responsibility. We look upon the poor not with human sympathy but with divine compassion; we look at our enemies with the same urgent desire for reconciliation that God has when he looks

---

[1]   Joseph Ratzinger, *Spirit of the Liturgy*, trans. John Saward (San Francisco: Ignatius Press, 2000), 175.
[2]   Ibid., 17–18.

upon us sinners; we look at suffering and feel the same willingness to embrace the cross that Christ felt. This is mundane liturgical theology.[3]

In order to think this through, I am going to use the hermeneutic of microcosm, applied on three fronts: first to say human beings are royal priests; second, that cultic liturgy is microcosmic; and third, to flip the idea and see the world as *macro*cosmic liturgy, though this is only accomplished at the cost of asceticism. I will consider these to be examples of *liturgical anthropology, liturgical cosmology* and *liturgical ecology.*

1 Liturgical Anthropology

Let us first consider a liturgical anthropology that sees the human being as microcosm. You recall that 'micro-cosm' means 'little house', which does not mean a fraction, it means a miniature. The kitchen is not a microcosm of a house, rather a dollhouse is, because everything in the big house can be found in the small house. The Church fathers describe man and woman as a hybrid, a mixture, because both matter and spirit can be found in the human being. Almost any card you are dealt from the patristic deck will include this idea, and I will play my hand with only three cards: two Gregories and a Maximus. Gregory of Nazianzus says:

> The great Architect of the universe conceived and produced a being endowed with both natures, the visible and invisible. … Thus in some way a new universe was born, small and great at one and the same time. God set this 'hybrid' worshiper on earth to contemplate the visible world, and to be initiated into the invisible; to reign over earth's creatures, and to obey orders from on high.[4]

His friend, Gregory of Nyssa, says man was created last because a good host does not bring his guest to the house before the preparation for the feast is finished. God first prepared the *kosmos* – which means 'well-disposed, prepared, ordered and arranged' – and then placed the human being in it to play his particular role.

> For this reason [God] gives him as foundations the instincts of a twofold organization, blending the Divine with the earthy [sic], that by means of both he may be naturally and properly disposed to each enjoyment, enjoying God by means of his more divine nature, and the good things of earth by the sense that is akin to them.[5]

And Maximus the Confessor thinks the human being is last because God intended to unite five extremes in him. Man is, he says, 'the laboratory in which everything is concentrated'. Andrew Louth explains why:

[3] David W. Fagerberg, *Consecrating the World: On Mundane Liturgical Theology* (Kettering, OH: Angelico Press, 2016).

[4] Gregory of Nazianzus, *Oration 45 (Second Oration on Easter)*, 7 (PG 36,850), cited by Olivier Clement, *The Roots of Christian Mysticism* (New York: New City Press, 1996), 77.

[5] Gregory of Nyssa, *On the Making of Man*, II.2, in *Nicene and Post-Nicene Fathers*, vol. 5 (Peabody, MA: Hendrickson Publishers, 2004), 390.

Human beings are found on both sides of each division: they belong in paradise but inhabit the uninhabited world; they are earthly and yet destined for heaven; they have both mind and senses; and though created, they are destined to share in the uncreated nature by deification. All the divisions of the cosmos are reflected in the human being, so the human being is a microcosm.[6]

All three of these passages see the reason for a person's unique, microcosmic make-up as serving the purpose of linking heaven and earth, spirit and matter. Human beings were constructed for the express purpose of serving God's glory by being the tongue of material creation's praise. Thomas Aquinas defined the good as something having the perfection proper to it. A pen is good when it writes, a knife is good when it cuts, a table is good when it holds the weight it is meant to bear. And what is a good person? I submit that the perfection proper to a human being is to join in the life of God. Between the Father, the Son and the Holy Spirit flows an exchange of love that tradition has called *perichoresis*, and I define liturgy as 'perichoresis kenotically extended to invite our synergistic ascent into deification'.[7] Liturgy is our perfection, for there we are being filled with the love of God by joining the choreography of his divine love, and performing the work of a cosmic priesthood.

We could reveal the microcosm by calling man and woman 'royal priests'. As befits their royal status, they were created as the climax of creation and given power and dominion and responsibility. As befits their priestly status, they were given stewardship in order to bring creation into the circulation of *agape* and Eucharist. To deny man and woman's royal vocation, or to separate that vocation from their priestly identity, equally flunks a full anthropology. On the one hand, man and woman are called to exercise dominion over the environment in which they are placed, which is why the *Catechism* has such a confident description of the human being: man occupies a unique place in creation as the image of God;[8] man is the only visible creature able to know and love his creator;[9] and he possesses the dignity of person with self-knowledge and self-possession.[10] On the other hand, man and woman's royal dominion exists for latreutic purposes. When it comes to humanity, a half-definition is a half-truth: lose either dimension – royalty without priesthood, or priesthood without royalty – and something goes awry. Some secular anthropologies are drawn to the former error and place no Godly limits on man's royalty; some spiritual anthropologies are drawn to the latter error and see man as so heavenly minded that he is of no earthly good. But the *Catechism* locates anthropology within the context of liturgical cult: 'God created everything for man, but man in turn was created to serve and love God and to offer all creation back to him'.[11] Just as a planet must balance both centrifugal force and

---

[6] Andrew Louth, *Maximus the Confessor*, The Early Church Fathers (New York: Routledge, 1996), 73.

[7] My operating definition of liturgy. See David Fagerberg, *On Liturgical Asceticism* (Washington, DC: The Catholic University of America Press, 2013), 9.

[8] *Catechism of the Catholic Church*, 2nd edn (Washington, DC: United States Catholic Conference, 2000), no. 355.

[9] Ibid., no. 356.

[10] Ibid., no. 357.

[11] Ibid., no. 358.

gravitational pull, so a human being must find the exact midpoint between heaven and earth so as neither to desert the world nor be marooned on it.

As microcosm, human beings are called to take the world into themselves in order to speak the worship that the universe wordlessly offers. Man and woman are cosmic priests for standing with one foot in the *kosmos noetos* (the intelligible world) and the other in the *kosmos aisthetos* (the sensible world).[12] Cities were founded where traffic crisscrossed along trade routes that connected extreme geographical points; liturgies are found where traffic criss-crosses from extreme ontological points: spirit and matter, heaven and earth, mind and senses, man and beast, man and angel, life and death, justice and mercy, time and eternity, history and *eschaton*, chaos and cosmos, truth and beauty and goodness. Liturgy balances atop these crossbeams because the human liturgist has a foot in each of them. The human being as microcosm is the anthropological possibility for liturgy.

2 Liturgical Cosmology

Aristotle claimed that for a story plot to be understood, it must be of a length the audience can grasp as it unfolds between beginning and end. He makes his point by comparing a literary grasp to a grasp of beauty. 'To be beautiful, a living creature ... must not only present a certain order in its arrangement of parts, but also be of a certain definite magnitude. Beauty is a matter of size and order...' and just as an extremely minute creature could not be discerned as beautiful, neither could 'a creature of vast size – one, say, 1,000 miles long – as in that case ... the unity and wholeness of it is lost to the beholder'.[13] His observation inspires the thought in me that we cannot judge history because it is a thousand centuries long and we cannot see the whole thing at once. We cannot understand history's plot because its end and its beginning are beyond the range of our natural eye, which has put some people in a quandary. They do not know if existence is beautiful or not, or if it is true or not, and, sadly, some even wonder whether life is good or not, because they are only seeing a piece of it – their piece, this particular moment. But there is a height from which to see the whole, the plot line of history from start to finish. Liturgy is a microcosmic celebration of the Alpha and the Omega, which provides us with a protological and eschatological vantage point from which we can see why God created, and what God created, and what God hopes for his creation.

'Let us make human beings in our image, after our likeness,' God decreed on the sixth day, and 'let them have dominion over the fish of the sea, the birds of the air, the tame animals, all the wild animals, and all the creatures that crawl on the earth'

---

[12] 'Alongside "*kosmos noetos*" (the intelligible world) Holy Tradition sets "*kosmos aisthetos*" (the sensible world). This latter encompasses the whole realm of what belongs to the senses in the sacraments, in the liturgy, in icons, and in the lived experience of God. ... The beautiful then is as a shining forth, an epiphany, of the mysterious depths of being, of that interiority that is a witness to the intimate relation between the body and the soul.' Paul Evdokimov, *The Art of the Icon: A Theology of Beauty* (Redondo Beach, CA: Oakwood Publications, 1990), 26.

[13] Aristotle, *Poetics*, 7 (1450b34–1451a1), in *The Basic Works of Aristotle* (New York: Random House, 1966), 1462–3.

(Gen. 1.26). We are stewards, then, of creation, a steward defined as someone who looks after another person's resources. That is the sole basis of our dominion, and we have every bit as much reason to be concerned about our job performance as did the man in Luke 16. 'A rich man had a steward who was reported to him for squandering his property. He summoned him and said, "What is this I hear about you? Prepare a full account of your stewardship..."' (Lk. 16.1-2). One day we will be asked to prepare a full account of our stewardship, and whether we have done the world righteously, prudently, justly. We best sense that obligation when we are kneeling before the true King, because we are otherwise tempted to slip ourselves onto the throne. We can only stand rightly before our neighbour if we are kneeling before God. Worship provides a sort of supernatural ballast to equalize every exercise of our stewardship. When Adam named each animal, he was blessing God for each one; remove that act of worship and we name things for selfish utility. How do we view God, identify our neighbour and call the world around us? What is our place in the world?

The Lutheran theologian Regin Prenter describes the effects of the Fall upon the ontological location of man and woman this way:

> Man is created by God in his image. That is, he stands before God and is addressed by him; he stands beside his fellow man in a dialogue of love; and he stands over his co-creation in terms of knowledge. The fall is man's unexplainable rebellion against his creatureliness through disobedience to God's word. ... Sin, understood as rebellious disobedience, is vastly more than an isolated act; it is, then, a destruction of man's very humanity, affecting his relation to the Creator, to his fellow man, and to his co-creation.[14]

That passage took up residence in my memory in this shorthanded version: we were created to stand *under God, beside our neighbour* and *over creation*. It led me to imagine the Fall in a way that, although upsetting to its natural gravitational symbolism, did justice to the inflationary power of pride: the Fall is the attempt to rise one step higher in the cosmic order than we are supposed to. *Superbia* is the sentiment that makes us want too much elevation. Adam and Eve evacuated the liturgical sweet spot at which they were to exercise their royal priesthood under God, beside their neighbour and over creation; and when they did, they upset the liturgical orbit of existence. Now pride bristles at being under God and seeks to stand on equal footing with him (thus we neither submit to God, nor render him worship ahead of ourselves); envy bristles at standing beside our neighbour and seeks to stand over him (thus we impose our will and make him our utility); and selfishness reneges at governing creation, and instead we exploit it (thus losing our sympathy for fellow-creatures and abandoning solicitous care for earth and air). By our arrogant self-promotion to deity, we lose our connaturality with both neighbour and world.

Pope Francis's Encyclical Letter *Laudato Si'* observes the same fact. '[The creation accounts in Genesis] suggest that human life is grounded in three fundamental and closely intertwined relationships: with God, with our neighbour and with the earth itself. According to the Bible, these three vital relationships have been broken, both

---

[14] Regin Prenter, *Creation and Redemption* (Philadelphia: Fortress Press, 1968), 251.

outwardly and within us. This rupture is sin'.[15] That is why the Holy Father concludes that 'a true ecological approach *always* becomes a social approach; it must integrate questions of justice in debates on the environment, so as to hear *both the cry of the earth and the cry of the poor*'.[16] Liturgy puts us in our place.

3 Liturgical Ecology

Third, we can now flip our perspective and instead of seeing the liturgy as microcosmic world, see the world as macrocosmic liturgy. I am led to think of this as a kind of *liturgical ecology*. Ecology means the 'study of a house' (*oikos-logos*), and the house we are studying is God's creation. If I had more nerve, I would title my paper 'Doing Liturgy in the Big House'. Instead, I have based my title on Aidan Kavanagh's oft-repeated line in class that 'liturgy is doing the world the way the world was meant to be done'. But doing the world the way it was meant to be done carries a cost, because it requires we first be ascetically freed from the passions.

God laid the foundations of this house by wisdom (Prov. 3.19), and he tends its good by divine economy (*oikonomia* being 'household management'). Towards what end? It behoves us to know this, so that when we tend creation we will align our dominion with God's tendencies. Towards what does God direct his creation? There are two ways to answer this question. The first is catabatic, meaning creation was constructed in such a way as to expect God's arrival. The second is anabatic, meaning creation was constructed with an upward-current-carrying man and woman at its apex. And human beings are commissioned to be involved in this economy. They are *oikonomoi*, managers in God's project: they are *liturgical economists* who steward creation towards its eschatological end. That is our job description, and we can do it justly or unjustly.

Justice means giving someone or something its due. When Thomas treated the virtue of religion in the *Summa*, he located it in the section dealing with the cardinal virtue of justice, because religion is giving God the honour he is due. Why would we not? Why would we even think of acting unjustly towards God? Because the honour due God is glory, and we have a preference for self-glory (even if that glory is vain). Giving thanks to the Lord our God is right and just, but we must be reminded of that fact at every Eucharistic dialogue. One way of defining 'liturgy' is to understand it as a restored participation in the original created order. Failing this, the signs of creation no longer point to the Creator, and nature quickly becomes opaque, then a substitute, and finally an idol. Injustice and idolatry are bound together. Failing this, our neighbour is no longer seen as a fellow image of God, and he quickly becomes a competitor, then an opponent and finally an enemy. Uncreated justice and created justice are bound together.

According to some Old Testament commentators, being *imago Dei* means more than possessing reason, it means being a representative of God. The Hebrew word used, *selem*, means a duplicate, like a statue that corresponds to the original. Thus, by

---

[15] Pope Francis, Encyclical Letter on Care for Our Common Home *Laudato Si'* (24 May 2015), no. 65.
[16] Ibid., no. 49.

erecting his image a king indicated that he ruled the territory in which his image stood.[17] The Second Council of Nicaea concluded that an icon and its prototype are connected in such a way that the honour paid to the icon is received by the prototype. It would seem, also then, that any injustice paid to a living icon would be received by his divine prototype. Consider: if someone gouged the statue of Caesar with a nail, disfiguring it, he would be guilty of treason against the emperor; and if someone defaces, disfigures or violates an *imago Dei* in some basic way, he is guilty of an act against God. The First Letter of John says 'if anyone says "I love God," but hates his brother, he is a liar; for whoever does not love a brother whom he has seen cannot love God whom he has not seen' (1 Jn 4.20). We can adapt it to say that if anyone thinks he can be just to God but unjust to his brother, he is a liar; for whoever does not give justice to his brother whom he has seen cannot be just towards God whom he has not seen. Justice towards the Uncreated is linked to justice towards the created. Uncreated justice is expressed by worship, adoration, sacrifice, devotion, piety, honour, subordination and latreutic cult. Created justice is expressed by charity, generosity, self-giving, kindness, magnanimity, benevolence, mercy and commitment to the common good. That is why the *Catechism* can say, in one breath, 'Justice consists in the firm and constant will to give God and neighbour their due'.[18] If the secularist unlinks them, ignoring God as he works for goodness on earth, his justice is deficient; if the spiritualist unlinks them, ignoring goodness on earth as he worships God, his justice is deficient.

The sacred liturgy and custody of the profane do not cancel each other out. The sacraments do not evacuate us from the world, they equip us to protect it. Sacraments are designed to stimulate the Holy Spirit within us, and what does the Spirit of God want to do? According to his sacrament (Confirmation), he wants to breathe wisdom, understanding, right judgement, courage, knowledge, reverence and the spirit of wonder and awe over the face of the earth. The life of Christ in us – ecclesiality, as Pavel Florensky calls it – consists in observing the movements of the Spirit of God in our soul, then fortifying these movements with prayer, sacrament and the practice of virtues. We become conspirators with God: we *con-spire*, breathe together. Liturgical cult stimulates the ministry of justice, mercy, care of the poor, care of the land. Sometimes a shabby reading of the Old Testament pits prophet against priest, profane against sacred, world against temple. But this is a false reading. The prophet does not mind someone going into the temple; the prophet is only bothered if that person does

---

[17] 'It is precisely in his function as ruler that [man] is God's image. In the ancient East the setting up of the king's statue was the equivalent to the proclamation of his domination over the sphere in which the statue was erected. When in the thirteenth century BC the Pharaoh Ramesses II had his image hewn out of rock at the mouth of the *nahr el-kelb*, on the Mediterranean north of Beirut, the image meant that he was the ruler of this area. Accordingly man is set in the midst of creation as God's statue. He is evidence that God is the Lord of creation; but as God's steward he also exerts his rule, fulfilling his task not in arbitrary despotism but as a responsible agent.' Hans Walter Wolff, *Anthropology of the Old Testament*, trans. Margaret Kohl (Philadelphia: Fortress Press, 1974), 160. 'Selem (image) means predominantly an actual plastic work, a duplicate, sometimes an idol. ... Just as powerful earthly kings, to indicate their claim to dominion, erect an image of themselves in the provinces of their empire where they do not personally appear, so man is placed upon earth in God's image as God's sovereign emblem. He is really only God's representative, summoned to maintain and enforce God's claim to dominion over the earth.' Gerhard von Rad, *Genesis: A Commentary*, trans. John H. Marks, The Old Testament Library (Philadelphia: Westminster Press, 1972), 60.

[18] *Catechism of the Catholic Church*, no. 1836.

not take the temple with him when he comes back out again! The prophet is criticizing the fact that what has been tilled in the sacred cult (*cult-ivated*) does not take root in the mundane and produce fruit. That is why, in order to cultivate creation and care for the poor, we must first deal with the corruption of sin within, which brings us to liturgical asceticism.

Satan was shrewd. He did not promise Eve something unthinkable to her. To draw her away from God he bent God's own plan for her deification and dominion. His temptation would only have worked if he were tickling an aspiration placed in Eve's heart by God himself, so he said to her 'you will be like gods'. Eve opened her eyes because deification was precisely her *telos*. And Eve opened her ears because dominion was precisely a responsibility she should have exercised as an adult and not as a child. But Satan bent the path to these God-given ends until the arrow missed the mark (sin is *hamartia*) by seizing the gifts prematurely and independently. As a result, and ever since, we have sought a deification that is actually nothing but our own exaltation, which is of no help to my neighbour at all and has serious consequences for the natural world. Now instead of exercising dominion, we sinners domineer. The latter means to rule arbitrarily or arrogantly, the former means to govern and control, directed by legitimate authority – in this case, an authority granted by God himself. The fall was the forfeiture of our liturgical career and we have lost our balance.

Sin is the cause of injustice, but can we be any more precise? The created environment is God's good gift, over which he exclaimed satisfaction on the sixth day of Genesis, and in which we should find happiness. So why don't we? The mystery of iniquity is that the world can cause worldliness in us; Satan has seduced us into inserting ourselves between the cause and its proper effect. Worldliness is using the world without reference to God. That makes for a contradiction that is reflected in Scripture's own vocabulary. The same gospel that says God so loved the world that he gave his only Son to die for it (Jn 3.16) also says that Jesus' disciples do not belong to the world (Jn 17.16), that the world hates them (Jn 15.19), that they must hate their life in this world (Jn 12.23) and that Jesus does not pray for the world (Jn 17.9). Scripture uses the word 'world' in both ways – as a good gift and as a source of temptation – and while we do not go into the temple to abandon the world (in the first sense), we do go there in order to escape the world (in the second sense). This is the liturgical paradox: that there is nothing wrong with the world, but we must leave the world and bless the kingdom of God. Alexander Schmemann wrote, 'This exodus from the world is accomplished in the name of the world, for the sake of its salvation. ... We separate ourselves from the world in order to bring it, in order to lift it up to the kingdom, to make it once again the way to God and participation in his eternal kingdom.'[19]

One chooses between two economies: one obedient and the other disobedient, one worshipful and the other idolatrous, one just and the other unjust, one natural and the other rebellious. Conversion is the act of opting out of the latter for the former. 'Do you reject Satan, and all his works and all his empty promises?' The New Testament uses the term *arche* to name the powers or principalities that hold this world captive, a concentrated roster of those malevolent forces being named in Eph. 6.12. 'For our

---

[19] Alexander Schmemann, *The Eucharist: Sacrament of the Kingdom*, trans. Paul Kachur (Crestwood, NY: St. Vladimir's Seminary Press, 1987), 53.

struggle is not with flesh and blood but with the principalities, with the powers, with the world rulers of this present darkness, with the evil spirits in the heavens.' But Christ's victory has unleashed a new *arche* into the world, a new power. Not rebellious, but obedient; not selfish, but sacramental; not diabolically dividing, but symbolically uniting. It is a priestly power, a *hiereus arche*. Satan upset creation with *anarchy*, but we join Christ in restoring all creation to liturgical *hierarchy*. And so the Collect for the Solemnity of our Lord Jesus Christ, King of the Universe prays: 'Almighty ever-living God, whose will is to restore all things in your beloved Son, the King of the universe, grant, we pray, that the whole creation, set free from slavery, may render your majesty service and ceaselessly proclaim your praise.'[20] Liturgy is the activity of Christ, and Christ is king of the world.

I pause only briefly to note that this means 'all creation', every creature that God has created, and this includes time. Time was created; it is a creature to be valued, but mastered. We must also approach time ascetically if we are to use it justly. Most of our abuse of the environment comes from wanting too much, too fast, too soon, too eagerly. The disruptive passion seems to be gluttony, which John Climacus defined as 'hypocrisy of the stomach',[21] whose antidote is temperance, which can be trained by fasting. Liturgical fasting has as much to do with patience as it has to do with food. Satan combined gluttony and disobedience by asking 'Can't you have that?' The proper response both in the Garden of Eden and on the fields of our farms today is, 'We can, but not yet. We must be patient.' The environment has an amazing power to renew itself, but our technologies must not push its rhythms beyond its limits. The virtue of prudence is required to read natural law, but the virtue of temperance is required to let that natural law take its course.

So how is it that the good gifts of God (both property and neighbour) cause in us such concupiscence that we abuse them in order to take our own advantage? The ascetical tradition has studied this riddle for a long time and has concluded that there is nothing wrong with the world, but something goes wrong when we put our hand upon it. The passions are our faculties misfiring. Evagrius provides an individuated list that includes gluttony, lust, avarice, sadness, anger, sloth, vainglory and pride, but Isaac the Syrian groups them under one name, saying 'When we wish to give a collective name to the passions, we call them *world*.'[22] Maximus adds, 'The one who has self-love has all the passions.'[23] The problem is not money, sex or beer; the problem is avarice, lust and gluttony. The objects of the world are the matter on which our passions feed. Nature is good, as given, but we do not do nature naturally any more, and if we wish to clean the oceans and the air, we must begin by cleansing our hearts, because the passions have gotten in the way of our peaceful relationship with matter.

---

[20] *The Roman Missal: Renewed by Decree of the Most Holy Second Ecumenical Council of the Vatican, Promulgated by Authority of Pope Paul VI and Revised at the Direction of Pope John Paul II* (Washington, DC: USCCB, 2011), 505.

[21] John Climacus, *The Ladder of Divine Ascent*, trans. Colm Luibheid and Norman Russell, The Classics of Western Spirituality (New York: Paulist Press, 1982), 165 (Step 14: On Gluttony).

[22] Isaac the Syrian, *Homily 2*, in *The Ascetical Homilies of Saint Isaac the Syrian*, trans. Dana Miller (Boston: Holy Transfiguration Monastery, 1984), 14–15.

[23] Maximus the Confessor, *Four Hundred Chapters on Love*, III.8, in *Maximus Confessor: Selected Writings*, trans. George Charles Berthold, The Classics of Western Spirituality (New York: Paulist Press, 1985), 62.

We are surrounded by a good creation (we have God's word on that), and it is filled with gifts that will bend submissively under our own hands as sub-creators. Our capacity as royal priests includes a power of creation (*poiesis*) that can make art, found societies, develop science and cities and technology, cooperate with God in civilizing chaos. What good is liturgy without a material on which to exercise it? And what good is chaos without a form that shapes it? But the question still remains whether man's sub-creativity will iconograph God or idolize himself. When the world functions properly, the created serves its sacred function to lift our eyes to heaven, and the created serves its profane function to be material for civilization. But when self-love corrupts our eyesight, then the world fails both functions, though it is not the world's fault.

Strange to say, then, but we cannot do the world rightly until we are indifferent to it. This sounds counterintuitive, but so long as the passions reign we are slaves to creatures. Indifference must defuse our selfishness. We must find liberty before we can rule. If we are enslaved to the objects of the world, then how can we do the world the way it was meant to be done, and treat our neighbour fairly, and make just distribution of common goods, and tend the environment with true dominion? This is behind Maximus's definition of perfect love: it is equal love towards all, loving all men equally. It is a deceptively simple definition. Think about it: do you love *all* human beings equally? Or do you give preference to some, have greater attachment to others? In the words of Lars Thunberg's study of Maximus, 'He who devotes his loving desire entirely to God, is not affected by any partial attachment to the world and is thus able to love all men equally in imitation of God's own love for all. Resentfulness, on the other hand, is a sign of worldliness and implies a worship of creatures instead of the Creator.'[24] The sort of love for our neighbour that is required to bring about justice can only stem from imitation of God's own love for all, freed from favouring parts of the world and parts of the human community.

Liturgical asceticism is required to make the heart supple and train it in divine charity so that we can steward creation and care for all the poor, not just some of them. A crucial practice, the desert monks discovered, was poverty expressed in lifestyle, but I am thinking now of poverty of spirit reigning over the heart in the simple sense of not being attached to any creature. I will not be able to stand aright and offer my holy oblation in peace so long as I am bent over some paltry pebbles of gold in the undignified posture of someone *incurvatus in se*. I will not be able to treat my neighbour with justice so long as I look at him enviously, or his wife lustfully or his property avariciously. As long as the passions stop up my ears I cannot hear either the cry of the poor or the needs of the earth. Until the cataracts of sin are removed by asceticism, I will see both my neighbour and the world falsely, distortedly, as if in a fun house mirror. Pope Francis says his namesake, St. Francis, taught this same integration of truths. 'He shows us just how inseparable the bond is between concern for nature, justice for the poor, commitment to society, and interior peace.'[25] Liturgical asceticism is the search for that interior peace, called *apatheia,* which is required in order to look upon all things rightly.

The liturgy within the temple is connected to the liturgy outside the temple. John Chrysostom says nothing is better suited to prolonging the effects of the Eucharist than

---

[24] Lars Thunberg, *Microcosm and Mediator* (Chicago: Open Court Publishing, 1995), 313–14.
[25] Pope Francis, *Laudato Si'*, no. 11.

a visit paid to Christ in his little ones. The poor standing in the public square remind the golden-mouthed saint of the majesty of an altar made ready for the sacrifice.

> This altar [of the poor] is composed of the very members of Christ, and the Lord's body becomes an altar for thee. Venerate it; for upon it, in the flesh, thou dost offer sacrifice to the Lord. This altar is greater than the altar in his church. … Do not protest! The *stone* altar is august because of the Victim that rests upon it; but the *altar of almsgiving* is more so because it is made of this very Victim.[26]

What generosity by God! He provides us an altar for sacrifice wherever we are. The poor await us anywhere.

> This altar you can see everywhere, in the streets and in the market place, and at any hour you may offer sacrifice thereon; for it too is a place of sacrifice. And, as the priest standing at the altar brings down the Spirit, so you too bring down the Spirit, like the oil which was poured out in abundance.[27]

Now the narthex becomes truly liminal: a threshold or entrance upon the world. We build up a static charge of *eucharistia* all week long by rubbing shoulders with the world, and discharge it in the glory we give God at the altar; we receive a charge of mercy and grace at that same mass, and we discharge it throughout the coming week.

Folly is the opposite of wisdom. Folly judges by some temporal good, while wisdom judges by first principle and last end. Liturgy teaches us wisdom, teaches us those first principles and last ends so that we can take the proper measure of all created things, and that is why we go to the temple on a scheduled basis. There, in the sacred space, we learn how the secular should be constructed. There, in the vestibule of heaven, we learn what the earth is for and how to use it prudently. There, in the midst of the community of saints, we learn the eternal value of a single soul and are flooded with love for every one of them, equally, no matter how poor or disreputable. There, before the cross, we find firm footing so that we are no longer swayed by passing honours and pleasures, natural reputation, praises, comfort and flattering self-love. Our failure to steward creation and care for the poor comes from placing ourselves at the centre, and the only way to solve this problem is to put someone else at the centre. This is called conversion. This is called love. And love is liturgy's heart.

4 A Brief Postscript

That was my conclusion, but I have a postscript in the form of a challenge to liturgical theology, because, after all, this is not a conference on ecology or social justice, it is a conference on the liturgy.

---

[26] John Chrysostom, *Homily 20 on II Corinthians*, quoted in Emile Mersch, *The Whole Christ: The Historical Development of the Doctrine of the Mystical Body in Scripture and Tradition*, trans. John R. Kelly (Milwaukee, WI: The Bruce Publishing Company, 1938), 335.

[27] Ibid.

I began with a propaedeutic Thomistic exercise that considered what objections there might be to even including this paper in our conference. I concluded that failure to connect the liturgy with the poor and with stewardship of creation might arise from too thin a definition of liturgy, one that reduced its range. It is my metaphor, but I think Benedict XVI is expressing something similar when he analyses the liturgical situation across his lifetime. He thinks it was an important step when the *Catechism* placed its treatment of the sacraments within the context of the celebration of divine worship because

> Medieval theology had already detached the theological study of the sacraments to a large extent from their administration in divine worship and treated it separately under the headings of *institution, sign, effect, minister,* and *recipient.* ... Thus divine worship and theology diverged more and more; dogmatic theology expounded, not on divine worship itself, but rather on its abstract theological contents ... and liturgy necessarily seemed almost like a collection of ceremonies that clothed the essentials...[28]

But when the pendulum swung, and liturgy edged its way back on stage, he says liturgics became nothing but 'the study of prevailing norms in divine worship and thus came close to a sort of juridical positivism'. He therefore approves of the Liturgical Movement at its origin when it sought to overcome this dangerous separation. It 'strove to understand the essence of a sacrament from the form in divine worship' and to think of liturgy 'as the organically developed and suitable expression of the sacrament in the worship celebration'. And, in his opinion, *Sacrosanctum Concilium* set forth this synthesis more adequately than had been done in the past, allowing us to understand the Church's divine worship and her sacraments in a new and more profound way. But alas, the professor warns,

> Unfortunately very little has been done so far to complete this assignment. Liturgical studies once again have tended to detach themselves from dogmatic theology and to set themselves up as a sort of technique for worship celebrations. Conversely, dogmatic theology has not yet convincingly taken up the subject of its liturgical dimension, either.[29]

In this remark, Benedict XVI is specifically thinking of reconnecting liturgical studies with the dogmatic theology of sacraments, but I would recommend 'completing the assignment' by expanding our syllabus a bit further. *Lex orandi* is not only the foundation (*statuat*) of sacramentology, but also the foundation for the dogmatic understanding of man and matter, time and eschatology, sin and salvation history. I have attempted a small-scale exercise here, in the form of liturgical anthropology, liturgical cosmology and liturgical ecology, but my next project will be to explore the idea further, and I think to call it 'liturgical dogmatics'. How can we know what to build with the bricks in our hands if we do not know about temples? How can we know how

---

[28] Joseph Ratzinger, *On the Way to Jesus Christ*, trans. Michael J. Miller (San Francisco: Ignatius Press, 2005), 153–4.

[29] Ibid., 154.

deep is our connection to the Lazarus on our doorstep if we do not know about the community of heaven? How can we do justice to mortal things without the eternal horizon against which to place them? Exercising stewardship of creation and care for the poor will require doing the world liturgically, whereby our dominion will become *diakonia*, as Jesus on the cross showed it to be. Liturgical dogmatics should teach us how to do the world as it was meant to be done.

7

Liturgy Beyond the Secular

Joris Geldhof

All too often there seems to be a diametrical opposition between the liturgical tradition of the Church and the sociocultural conditions of life in the Western world, which are commonly characterized as secular. Clearly, there is quite some animosity from both parts, sometimes even enmity. On the one hand, there are promoters of a harsh kind of secularism, who want to ban religion altogether from the public realm. Convinced as they are that monotheism is intrinsically connected to violence, they aim above all at classical shapes of Christianity; depending on how far they want to go in a discourse of political correctness, they also have severe difficulties in coming to terms with Islam and Judaism. In general, secularism here means the neutralizing of religion and its banishment to the private sphere, where it is held not to do too much harm. On the other hand, one observes religious leaders and opinion-makers who develop an entirely anti-modern and sometimes even aggressive anti-secular rhetoric – a rhetoric that supposes that, because of one's being religious, one has to combat anything secular. Religion, or at least a specific expression of it, is supposed to keep the values one cherishes or to be the safe warrant against attacks on holiness and one's identity. They assume that, because secularism threatens religious identities and expressions, one has no choice but to construct fortresses against it.

The picture I just sketched of the opposite poles of this continuum may be too extreme but I am convinced that many debates in contemporary politics and theology are representative of these positions, either explicitly or implicitly. If you are secular, you cannot be reasonably religious, and if you are religious, you ought to be against secularism. In the present paper, I want to challenge the very assumptions underlying this continuum. Not only is seeing things this way both unfruitful and unnecessary, none of these positions understands the true nature of Christian sacramentality, for Christian sacramentality does not allow itself to be caught in any binary opposition. Rather, it installs an asymmetry into every symmetry, also into the opposition between the sacred and the secular. In particular, however, I will argue that it is precisely the liturgy which keeps one, and should keep one, from getting bogged down in the aforementioned deadlock.

I will build up my case cumulatively through the synthetic combination of several elements.[1] First, I will venture a description of the concept of the secular. With the help of Charles Taylor's inevitable work,[2] I will propose an understanding of the term according to a spatiotemporal circumscription. Second, I will use this interpretation key to advance not a definition but a topography and chronography of liturgy. Third, this understanding of the liturgy will give rise to a renewed approach to the history and economy of salvation and to what 'sanctification' means in a Christian register. Fourth, the proposed interpretation of the universal liturgical dynamics of sanctification will help us see some allegedly contradictory realities like Church and world, heaven and earth, cult and culture, religion and politics, etc. in a different light. I will conclude with a summary of my major argument as well as with some practical suggestions to overcome the aporetic circumstances in which many faithful believers have found themselves when they reflected on the transmission of what is so dear to them in the present age.

1 Situating the Secular

To explain what secularism means is to look at the intellectual heritage of Western culture. According to widespread anthropological theories, every civilization knows about a difference between the sacred and the profane.[3] It seems impossible that sacredness determines the entirety of people's lives, just as it seems equally unthinkable that one operates from birth to death totally, and exclusively, in the atmosphere of the profane. In other words, there must be rupture and difference, if life is to be liveable. However, according to renowned scholars, in Western societies, the very conditions of this difference changed drastically with the rise of modernity. The traditional equilibrium between the metaphysical triad of the world, the soul and God was shaken when autonomous subjectivity took the lead both in the acquisition process of knowledge and in deciding about good and evil.[4]

This slow but thoroughgoing revolution in epistemology and ethics, and from there in many other areas of life, evidently occasioned fundamental reinterpretations of faith and religion. Louis Dupré observes: 'The anthropocentric position has installed itself solidly in the modern mind. The turn to the subject, once taken, cannot be unmade. Yet it need not result in the reductionist conclusions that secularism has drawn from it.'[5] It seems, therefore, that variations of a middle position are necessary to cope with

[1]   The inspiration for the method of a cumulative case is taken from Brian Hebblethwaite, *In Defence of Christianity* (Oxford: Oxford University Press, 2005).
[2]   Charles Taylor, *A Secular Age* (Cambridge, MA: Belknap Press of Harvard University Press, 2007).
[3]   Mircea Eliade, *The Sacred and the Profane: The Nature of Religion* (New York: Harper and Row, 1961).
[4]   See the trilogy of Louis Dupré, *Passage to Modernity: An Essay in the Hermeneutics of Nature and Culture* (New Haven, CT: Yale University Press, 1993); *The Enlightenment and the Intellectual Foundations of Modern Culture* (New Haven, CT and London: Yale University Press, 2004); *The Quest of the Absolute: Birth and Decline of European Romanticism* (Notre Dame, IN: University of Notre Dame Press, 2013).
[5]   Louis Dupré, *Symbols of the Sacred* (Grand Rapids, MI and Cambridge: William B. Eerdmans, 2000), 126.

the present crisis of Catholicism in secular environments. Before we go any further, however, it is preferable to continue to specify what secularism means.

Charles Taylor reminds one of the etymology of the term. It is 'a category that developed within Latin Christendom. First, it was one term of a dyad. The secular had to do with the "century" – that is, with profane time – and it was contrasted with what related to the eternal, or to sacred time'.[6] Later on, roughly from the seventeenth century onwards, Taylor holds, the meaning of the concept of *saeculum* was significantly extended: 'The contrast was no longer with another temporal dimension, in which "spiritual" institutions had their niche; rather, the secular was, in its new sense, opposed to any claim made in the name of something transcendent of this world and its interests'.[7]

This enlargement of the meaning of the word and the fact that it was no longer seen as one component of a dyad, had radical consequences: 'Secular and religious are opposed as true and false or necessary and superfluous. The goal of policy becomes, in many cases, to abolish one while conserving the other'.[8]

In a way similar to Dupré, Taylor sees the problem with secularism and its stance towards religion not as an intrinsic evil. The real problem is that secularism often goes along with a certain kind of reductionism or exclusivism: it focuses only on certain aspects of human conscience, intelligence, society, science, culture, etc. and refuses to see 'other dimensions'. Dupré explains:

> The modern age has transferred the primary source of meaning and value from nature, and thus ultimately, from the Creator of nature, to the human mind. Any reality other than that of the mind itself becomes thereby reduced to the status of an object. But once the constitution of 'objectivity' has become the principal function of the mind, the mind itself ends up possessing no content of its own. … The self has become a mere function of its own mental acts.[9]

Or, in other words, the self has become fundamentally lonely. Nevertheless, it remains possible to develop visions of humanity and divinity and the ways they interact within a context which is determined by modern secular conditions. The task is, Taylor suggests, 'taking our modern civilization for another of those great cultural forms that have come and gone in human history, to see what it means to be a Christian here, to find our authentic voice in the eventual Catholic chorus'.[10] My own additional suggestion would be that nothing but the liturgy, substantially understood, is primordial in this exercise of discernment.

From a meta point of view, it is interesting to observe that there has been a shift from the temporal to the spatial in the meaning of secularism. The secular now refers above

---

[6] Charles Taylor, 'What Does Secularism Mean?', in *Dilemmas and Connections: Selected Essays* (Cambridge, MA and London: The Belknap Press of Harvard University Press, 2011), 303–25, at 304.

[7] Ibid., 304.

[8] Ibid., 307.

[9] Louis Dupré, *Religion and the Rise of Modern Culture* (Notre Dame, IN: University of Notre Dame Press, 2008), 114–5.

[10] Charles Taylor, 'A Catholic Modernity?', in *Dilemmas and Connections: Selected Essays* (Cambridge, MA and London: The Belknap Press of Harvard University Press, 2011), 167–87, at 169.

all to the space or the room within which we live today. It has become the fundamental quality of the environment of life; it determines the very coordinates of where we are. We cannot situate ourselves unless we refer to the secular conditions of our *Lebenswelt*. Yet, it has become fashionable in some circles to use the concept of the 'post-secular'. This usage supposes that the secular is something which determines a certain period of time and that this time has come to an end. It is indeed the conviction of several scholars that the concept of the secular no longer adequately captures the nature of our time and that in the meantime a new era has emerged.

Whether or not this is true, largely depends of course on one's interpretation of the secular. Inasmuch as the secularization hypothesis, which predicted the disappearance of religion, as the impact of science, technology, economy and democracy would continue to increase, was enfeebled, there is definitely something to say in favour of a discourse about the post-secular.[11] But just as it is the case with the relationship between modernity and postmodernism, the post-secular does not entail something substantially different vis-à-vis secularism. In particular, post-secular conditions do not miraculously occasion the rebirth of religion and faith or a revival of a natural sense of sacredness. We will see that, whatever happens to such revivals, does not really matter. For Christian liturgy is not there to nourish one's sense of the sacred, but to sanctify the world.

2 A Topography of Liturgy

In line with these explorations of secularism we now shift our attention to the liturgy. We saw that secularism has to be understood as a bundle of factors impacting heavily on the very space and time in which we live. As a matter of fact, such is also the liturgy. So, instead of asking ourselves *what* the liturgy is, I propose to approach the matter from a radically different angle and to ask instead: *where* is the liturgy, and *when* is the liturgy? This means that a logic of definitions, classifications and categorizations is left behind and that we make time and space for a topography and chronography of liturgy.[12]

To refuse to start from a definition of the liturgy is in a way to deviate, albeit slightly but nonetheless deliberately, from a method that was often applied in the bosom of the Liturgical Movement. Major representatives of that movement have come up with intriguing and encompassing definitions of the Church's liturgical worship, but thereby inscribed themselves into a logic of division-making which I think the liturgy itself actually challenges. There was of course an urge for predominantly pastoral and contextual reasons to distinguish between private prayer and collective devotional

---

[11] For an interesting conceptual exploration of this concept, see Arie L. Molendijk, 'In Pursuit of the Postsecular', *International Journal of Philosophy and Theology* 76 (2016): 100–15. Also the other contributions to this special issue are devoted to the issue of the post-secular as a challenge for contemporary theology and worth reading.

[12] In addition, this enterprise is more heuristic and metaphysical than hermeneutic and phenomenological. Within the scope of the present article, however, it is not possible to further elaborate on this.

practices on the one hand and the 'official' liturgy of the Church on the other hand.[13] However, instead of making subtle distinctions, many theoreticians of the liturgy ended up in drawing harsh demarcations and thereby, sadly, created separations. Today I think that the problem is no longer the difference between liturgy and devotions, but the question is how spiritual exercises, individual as well as collective ones, and other genuine expressions of Christian worship can be reconnected again, so that the *spiritus liturgicus*[14] continues to infuse all the segments of the people of God's occupations.

The propensity to understand what liturgy is through normative descriptions and other attempts at conceptual adequacy is related to a certain scope and focus which has long dominated theology, especially in the West and particularly at universities. To be sure, there is nothing wrong with endeavours to clarify and analyse, and darkness and opacity obviously need to make room for transparency and illumination everywhere, but one should not forget the narrow-mindedness of an intellectual culture which has systematically preferred cognition over other human faculties in its pursuit of truth and comprehension. In particular when it comes to grasping the mystery which drives the liturgy and the liturgy which embodies the mystery, passions, desires, impressions, emotions and – probably above anything else – the imagination are to play a prominent role as well.

It may not be an exaggeration to assert that the West has suffered from a certain *epistemologism*, which is the tendency to systematically yield the priority to knowledge and to the justification of the standards and the criteria according to which it is acquired and applied. Epistemologies and speculations about *Letztbegründung* are fine, but only if it is not to the detriment of sapiential and experiential accounts of understanding. The complexity of the topics with which theologians deal requires that one ultimately overcomes binary oppositions, for one will never sense the profound interwovenness of God, the world, culture and the human being, unless deductions and conclusions are embedded in a broad field where both wisdom and experience, tradition and community, *Vernunft* and *Einbildungskraft* have an equal share.

In this sense, one could justifiably say that the biggest problem with modernity and secularism is not that many people no longer believe in God, as if this were one opinion among a myriad of other possible convictions. To believe in God is not so much to have an explanatory idea about things but to be willing and prepared to live an exploratory life. So, rather, the biggest problem with secularism and (post-) modern cultures is indifferentism and a mentality that says to be tolerant and pluralist but ultimately blurs any difference. One does not know anymore which attitude to take on *coram Deo*, or how to behave in the overwhelmingly various presence of God: the possibility that there can be something like real presence does no longer make, and mark, a difference. One has to agree with Charles Taylor, then, when he lucidly observes that 'in Western modernity the obstacles to belief are primarily moral and spiritual, rather than epistemic'.[15] It is my conviction that the liturgy is the key, not to

---

[13] An exemplary description of the liturgy in accordance with these presumptions can be found in the renowned handbook *The Church at Prayer – Volume I: Principles of the Liturgy*, ed. Aimé-Georges Martimort et al. (Collegeville, MN: Liturgical Press, 1987).

[14] Second Vatican Council, Constitution on the Sacred Liturgy *Sacrosanctum Concilium* (4 December 1963), no. 37.

[15] Taylor, 'A Catholic Modernity?', 177.

solve the problem, but to make sure that the access to mystery is continuously offered, 'always and everywhere'.[16]

Instead of an 'epistemologistic' approach to liturgy I additionally think that a soteriological one is much more productive: one that takes its point of departure in the communication of the saving mysteries of the Lord, and, in so doing, immediately engages both the immanent and the economic Trinity, doxology,[17] and sacramentality. *Where is the liturgy?* The liturgy is everywhere where the mystery of redemption is actualized, enacted, offered, performed, transmitted and implemented. It is wherever assemblies gather to praise the Lord in communion with the angels and the saints and in accordance with the apostolic witness. *When is the liturgy?* The liturgy is any time when the Church is doing what she is supposed to do, that is, when she works through her 'agenda' and when she listens to and speaks the Word of God. The liturgy is when the Body of Christ is sacramentally seen and ecclesially realized,[18] and when the people of God actually become what they are supposed to be: 'a chosen race, a royal priesthood, a holy nation, God's own people' (1 Pet. 2.9). Liturgy is when and where the grand transformative dynamics of being is taking place concretely (not abstractly), and when and where the traces of God's omnipresence become events of grace. Liturgy is when and where, at the crossroads of *anabasis* and *katabasis*, the Paschal Mystery, in its full or partial glory, including the entire history of salvation, becomes accessible for human bodies and their senses.[19]

It is evident that such a topography and chronography of liturgy cannot be easily encapsulated within the schemas and confines of an objectifying logic. This approach may additionally be puzzling for minds that can only function with empirical exactitude, methodological rigidity and absolute notional certainty. One can easily imagine hundreds of instances where there is a grey zone and where it is not clear whether a practice, a posture, an expression, a gesture, a prayer, an assembly, an experience, etc. is liturgy. But this is precisely the point: liturgy escapes yes-or-no questions. It is much more interesting and fruitful to ask *how much* liturgy there is in all these and many other instances. In other words, liturgy is best understood in terms of ecclesial and sacramental density.[20] Through a fascinating variety and an ingenious mutual entangledness of *legomena* and *drômena* (and *sigè*, not to forget) the Church communicates the very mysteries to which she owes her own existence, outlook, energy, and stability, and ensures the possibility for humanity to 'actively participate' in them.

---

[16] See in this context my ponderings in 'Meandering in Mystery: Why Theology Today Would Benefit from Rediscovering the Work of Dom Odo Casel', in *Mediating Mysteries, Understanding Liturgies: On Bridging the Gap Between Liturgy and Systematic Theology*, ed. Joris Geldhof (Leuven, Paris, Bristol, CT: Peeters, 2015), 11–32.

[17] Geoffrey Wainwright, *Doxology: The Praise of God in Worship, Doctrine and Life: A Systematic Theology* (London: Epworth, 1980).

[18] See in this context a famous expression from *Sermo* 272 of St. Augustine: 'estote quod videtis, et accipite quod estis' (*PL* 38,1247).

[19] See Catherine Pickstock, 'Sense and Sacrament', in *The Oxford Handbook of Sacramental Theology*, ed. Hans Boersma and Matthew Levering (Oxford: Oxford University Press, 2015), 657–74.

[20] Initial inspiration for this approach could be drawn from Louis-Marie Chauvet, *Le corps, chemin de Dieu: Les sacrements* (Paris: Bayard, 2010), 35–54, where he elaborates some examples.

It is important to stress that the proposed topographical (or chronographical) approach does not, and should not, give rise to any kind of relativism. It does relate (to) everything and is after relations and relatedness. And that is precisely the opposite of a relativistic attitude, which cuts off things and no longer puts them into the right perspective (orthodoxy). A topography of liturgy, which lays bare moments of ecclesio-sacramental density, continues to subscribe to an understanding of Christian worship according to a traditional triple threefold of registers: the one of the Eucharist, the sacraments and the *Liturgy of the Hours*, the one of the daily, weekly, and yearly cycles of the liturgical year, and the one of the universal Church, the local church and the household or domestic church. The universal economy of salvation is operative through all of them, simultaneously, everywhere and always. Liturgical theologians are called to explain how this magnificent *opus Dei* works.

3 The Sanctifying Mystery

It has become clear that a Christian theological understanding of sacramentality significantly differs from anthropological accounts of sacredness. The difference has above all to do with the operationality of grace and salvation, which are verbs rather than nouns. The problem with natural sacredness is indeed its substantiveness and massiveness. It *is* something rather than that it *does* something. It is the qualification of an atmosphere or area of being but not something that works upon, or into, that being. In other words, one needs to distinguish between sanctification as an ongoing dynamic energy originating in God which reaches out to the depths and heights of human existence in the cosmos on the one hand, and sacredness as a given state of affairs, a situation or a condition on the other hand.

Interestingly, it is nothing but the liturgy that prompts one to such an understanding of the sanctifying mystery, which penetrates the entirety of being. The liturgy constitutively shares in this overarching dynamics: it enacts, expresses and communicates it. It lets the sanctifying mystery radiate and reach out to any person of good will. And that is an activity that does never coincide with upholding, protecting and entertaining a sacred sphere. To be sure, the sanctifying mystery is by no means diametrically opposed to religious sacredness; it perpetually invites it only to its transformative activity and takes it up into its porous mysteriosity. Yves Congar rightly says that 'we must be vigilant to guide whatever there is of an instinctive religiosity or of a natural sense of the sacred back to the foundation of the faith, back to the facts of the history of salvation',[21] and for him, that means primordially an encounter with Jesus Christ, the Son of God.

According to Congar, then, for Christians, 'there is only *one* sacred reality, the body of Christ'.[22] However, this one sacred reality cannot be considered to be static; rather, it is something operative which exerts a real influence on the reality and realities

---

[21] Yves Congar, 'Where Does the "Sacred" Fit into a Christian Worldview?', in *At the Heart of Christian Worship: Liturgical Essays of Yves Congar*, trans. and ed. Paul Philibert (Collegeville, MN: Liturgical Press, 2010), 107–34, at 131.

[22] Ibid., 126.

around it. In a terminology that comes very close to Henri de Lubac's ponderings about Church and Eucharist,[23] Congar explains: 'Christ's personal body ... is *amplified* through what we call the Mystical Body, which is the church, something at once visible and yet surpassing what we are able to see.'[24]

Congar bases his reflections on meticulous investigations of the Scriptures. He reads the New Testament as testifying to the fact that, through the Christ event, a new relation to space and time emerged.

> God's presence and our communion with his holiness are no longer linked to a place. ... Christ offers a new sacrifice by way of the new priesthood (according to the heavenly order of Melchizedek), which is exercised outside the temple and even outside Jerusalem – indeed outside of any particular place specially set apart for it. This new worship is offered under the heavens, as though in the temple of the entire world.[25]

As additional evidence for his position, Congar refers to his fellow Dominican brother St Thomas Aquinas, who says in third part of the *Summa Theologiae*:

> For the church was not going to be limited to the territory of the Jewish people, but was going to be extended to the whole world; therefore Christ's Passion did not take place within the city of the Jews, but out in the open countryside, in order that the whole world might serve as a domicile for Christ's Passion.[26]

4 A Universal Transformative Dynamics

In other words, Jesus Christ, the Son of God and Saviour of humankind, establishes a universal extension of God's grace, which, as a gift to the Church, his Bride, can be distributed everywhere. This gift, however, is not something that can be stocked; it is like the manna in the desert, good food for the journey. This nourishment is the essential energy for the intrinsic liturgico-sacramental potential of changing everything in every culture; so that the world, secular or not, adapts itself increasingly to the vision of the kingdom. Aidan Kavanagh specifies:

> He [the God-Man] does not transform culture as such. He recreates the World not by making new things but by making all things new. He does this by divine power working upon all that is through the agency of a human nature he holds in solidarity with us. He summons all into a restored communion with his Father, not in spite of matter but through matter, even spit and dirt, thereby clarifying the

---

[23] Henri de Lubac, *Corpus Mysticum: The Eucharist and the Church in the Middle Ages: Historical Survey*, ed. Lawrence P. Hemming and Susan F. Parsons (London: SCM Press, 2006).

[24] Congar, 'Where Does the "Sacred" Fit', 123.

[25] Ibid., 114–15.

[26] Congar, 'Where Does the "Sacred" Fit', 115. The quotation is from *Summa Theologiae* III, q. 83, a. 3, ad 1: 'Et quia Ecclesia non erat concludenda sub finibus gentis Iudaicae, sed erat in universo mundo fundata, ideo passio Christi non est celebrata intra civitatem Iudaeorum, sed sub divo, ut sic totus mundus se haberet ad passionem Christi ut domus.'

true meaning of the material world itself. He summons all to his Father in time, thereby renewing both time and its spatial functions. He addresses all people not only in mind and soul but in body as well, thereby renewing the human person in his and her relation to matter, to time and space, and to the whole created world.[27]

This peculiar way in which the mystery of salvation is crocheted into the universe – moreover, in such a way that the threads orient one towards the ultimate fulfilment – needs some further refinement. The universal transformative dynamics of the sanctifying mystery, as it is embodied in the liturgy of the Church, allows one to look at common differences and oppositions *differently*. For the sake of brevity, I will only develop four antagonisms which should not be that. Both their agony and their being 'anti' can and should be transformed, or liberated or renewed, when they are touched by 'the Body of Christ'.

4.1 Church and World

The relation between Church and world is always a complex and multifaceted one, and secularism makes no fundamental difference in this respect. The Church is in the world with the vocation of making it into a better place to live. Inasmuch as secularist ideologies are obstacles to that vocation, critical discernment is obviously needed. However, inasmuch as secularist ideas are harmless or, maybe paradoxically, inasmuch as they provide a stimulating environment for the flourishing of the Gospel and the communities living from it, the partnership with their proponents needs to be continuously researched and evaluated as well. A continuous dialogue is not an option; it is a necessity.

In this context, Aidan Kavanagh has come up with a healthy disarming hermeneutical key, which is based on the conviction that secularism may not, or at least not always, be equalled with worldliness. For the consequence of secularism may be that one is not worldly enough: in other words, that one has detached or alienated too radically from engagement in the world and from the care for its inhabitants. According to Kavanagh, secularism runs the risk of producing

> people who are awash in an oceanic ideology of shifting intimacy which is replete with uncontrolled, unanchored, and undirected sacralities. It is unworldly to the point of being creepy, for what it amounts to is the effacement of the *res publica* by the preference to believe that social meanings are generated only by the feelings of individual human beings.[28]

In particular, if secularism goes hand in hand with a libertarian view on human autonomy, with an idealization of the bonds between science, technology and the manipulation of creation, as well as with an economic paradigm of endless commercial commodification, it may direly need a liturgical corrective and regain a concrete footing in the earth. There are contexts in which not secularism but the church and

---

[27] Aidan Kavanagh, *On Liturgical Theology: The Hale Memorial Lectures of Seabury-Western Theological Seminary, 1981* (Collegeville, MN: Liturgical Press, 1992), 50.

[28] Ibid., 28.

her official worship preserve the connection of humankind with the cosmos. We need thinkers who can make this point convincingly and who do that on all kinds of fora, well aware that a persuasive strategy based on the assumption that 'I am right and the others are wrong' will not only not work but also is opposed to liturgical and human wisdom.

4.2 Heaven and Earth

It was modern cosmology which was no longer able and willing to see the intricacies of the interaction between heaven and earth. Basically, because of its being impregnated by epistemologism it drew sharp dividing lines instead of noticing connections. To the extent that the images of heaven and hell were used to superintend masses of people, and that an elite shamelessly profited from maintaining a culture of culpability, what was said and believed about heaven needed critical treatment. However, as is so often the case, one tended to throw the baby out with the bathwater and did no longer talk at all about heaven.

Nevertheless, from a soteriological and sacramental point of view, heaven is where the choirs of the angels sing and, as we on earth celebrate the liturgy, we join in their eternal song of praise. That is not only a comforting thought or image but also an ecclesial action that bears a symbolic meaning of the utmost importance. It is constitutive of the Church's eternal call to divine worship and, as such, of the necessarily doxological dimension of liturgy. In his thoughtful reflections about a new liturgical culture, Cardinal Kasper rightly notes: 'Die Liturgie ist Gottesverehrung ('cultus divinus') oder sie ist nicht mehr Liturgie.'[29]

Furthermore, in his ground-breaking reflections on the Church's 'true piety', aptly translated by Virgil Michel as *Liturgy the Life of the Church*, Dom Lambert Beauduin recalls: 'Between the Church of heaven and the Church of the earth there exists an intimate union which shall one day become perfect.'[30] One could consider the liturgy as the motor towards that perfection. A secularist ideology is actually not able to shut down that motor. It may make it difficult to drive around the car, but the engine will run as long as the economy of salvation provides the fuel.

4.3 Cult and Culture

Cult and culture have the same etymological origin and there is some evidence that they also came into being simultaneously. However, the Christian cult can never coincide with any culture. Charles Taylor is very firm on this, and I think he is right: 'There can never be a total fusion of the faith and any particular society, and the attempt to achieve it is dangerous for the faith.'[31] From a historical perspective, it is definitely true

---

29 Walter Kasper, 'Aspekte einer Theologie der Liturgie: Liturgie angesichts der Krise der Moderne – für eine neue liturgische Kultur', in *Die Liturgie der Kirche*, Gesammelte Schriften, vol. 10 (Freiburg – Basel – Vienna: Herder, 2012), 15–83, at 42.

30 Lambert Beauduin, *Liturgy the Life of the Church*, trans. Virgil Michel (Collegeville, MN: Liturgical Press, 1929), 22.

31 Taylor, 'A Catholic Modernity?', 170.

that we are still trying to come to terms with the effects of Christendom, 'the attempt to marry the faith with a form of culture and a mode of society',[32] which was moreover transplanted into many other cultural environments.

The Christian liturgy may again assist to try to develop a better balance between faith and culture. Through the grand vision it maintains it may help undermine secular ideologies – from nationalism, ethnocentrism, populism, racism, libertarianism, anti-Semitism, ageism, sexism, communism, homophobia and xenophobia to the many illusions that we can create and manage absolute security with military means and an increase of police powers. The liturgy should play in full its desacralizing role vis-à-vis the many taboos and utopias of contemporary culture.[33] And then it can calmly propose its heterotopia and heterochronia: a world of cult, prayer, rite and worship which actually and actively participates in Christ's salvific work and thereby anticipates humanity's divinization.

It will require a lot of effort to show that this is about so much more than adding (again) some spirituality in a materialist culture. One must avoid any tendency to fall back into Manichaean representations of reality and realize that there is indeed an intrinsic threat of a 'gnostic return in modernity'[34] and, for that matter, also in Christianity. Liturgy itself, however, offers an intelligent alternative way of dealing with matter, for it is precisely through materiality and corporeality that our salvation has been achieved. Lambert Beauduin has this to say:

> To depreciate ritual piety because it is not purely mental, to diminish one's participation in liturgical acts under the pretext of fostering a more interior life, is to withdraw oneself from the adoration and prayer of the Spouse of Christ, to lessen the influence of the priesthood of our Lord upon the soul.[35]

In addition, I think that a renewed sensitivity for symbols is at stake. The mediations of cult and culture cannot be beneficial for Christian liturgy, and reversely, unless a symbolic conversion takes place, that is, a shift from semiotics to an ontology of language, or, from sign and signification theories to a metaphysics of symbolicity. For this suggestion I find Louis Dupré on my side, when he says: 'Without an innate capacity to reach out to what lies beyond itself the religious mind would be incapable of receiving, understanding, and much less of articulating a transcendent message.'[36] This unreservedly applies to liturgy in cultures of the present day. Dupré also says: 'A truly symbolic relation must be grounded in Being itself. Nothing exposes our religious impoverishment more directly than the loss of the ontological dimension of language.'[37] Again, this insight applies to our topic: liturgy is exactly the place where culture can learn (again) what a capacity for symbols and its corollary, a receptivity for transcendence, are.

---

[32] Ibid.

[33] For an elaboration of the idea that the liturgy has a desacralizing dimension, see my article 'Liturgy: From Desacralisation to Sanctification in Secular Environments', *Yearbook for Liturgical and Ritual Studies* 31 (2015): 117–31.

[34] Cyril O'Regan, *Gnostic Return in Modernity* (Albany, NY: State University of New York Press, 2001).

[35] Beauduin, *Liturgy the Life of the Church*, 15.

[36] Dupré, *Symbols of the Sacred*, 125.

[37] Dupré, *Religion and the Rise*, 116.

4.4 Religion and Politics

At an institutional level, it is best that State and Church make practical arrangements so that the one does not directly interfere with the daily business and the infrastructure of the other. But this does not imply that one has to undertake exceeding efforts to prevent that religion and politics interact. As a matter of fact, they do it anyway, whether or not the most committed defenders of *laïcité* like it or not. Moreover, if it is true, as Alexander Schmemann famously suggested, that the Church, her 'orthodoxy' and her sacraments are there 'for the life of the world',[38] then it follows that the liturgy has severe political consequences.

First of all, it follows from both a reflection about and an experience of the liturgy, that there is no place whatsoever for individualism. Beauduin decidedly contends:

> From the very first centuries to our own day, the Church has ever given to all her prayer a character profoundly and essentially collective. By means of living the liturgy wholeheartedly, Christians become more and more conscious of their supernatural fraternity, of their union in the mystic body of Christ.[39]

Liturgy does not tolerate the whimsical preferences and allegedly free choices of the individual as the highest criterion for the organization neither of itself nor of society. Rather, it supposes and promotes deeply human and personal qualities which give evidence of veritable solidarity, connectedness and empathy. Romano Guardini expounds:

> The requirements of the liturgy can be summed up in one word, humility. Humility by renunciation; that is to say, by the abdication of self-rule and self-sufficiency. And humility by positive action; that is to say, by the acceptance of the spiritual principles which the liturgy offers and which far transcend the little world of individual spiritual existence.[40]

Second, whatever initiative Christians take or support in the public arena must be guided by catholicity and apostolicity. This does not mean that the prerogatives of the Catholic Church must be defended against all odds, but that the things that the apostles received and passed on continue to work positively for people throughout the world (*kath'holon*). Kavanagh sketches the contours of this 'agenda' in his typical prose as follows:

> The World sets the City's agenda, an agenda which is then executed in the City's workshop, the Church. The scope of this agenda is such that the Church must first of all be and act in a manner which is catholic, that is, Citywide and Worldwide in its nature and ends. Catholicity is a quality endowed upon Church by City and World. It is not a quality which the Church generates for itself, in its own

---

[38] Alexander Schmemann, *For the Life of the World: Sacraments and Orthodoxy* (Crestwood, NY: St Vladimir's Seminary Press, 1973).

[39] Beauduin, *Liturgy the Life of the Church*, 23–4.

[40] Romano Guardini, *The Spirit of the Liturgy*, Milestones in Catholic Theology, trans. Ada Lane (New York: Crossroad, 1998), 39.

self-interest according to criteria which are the Church's own. ... The Church and sectarianism are thus antithetical entities, and that the Church Catholic is one denomination among others, a sort of religious boutique in the suburbs, is an unthinkable proposition. When the Church fails at being catholic, it begins to fail at being one, holy, and apostolic as well.[41]

5 Concluding Observations

Our reflections have shown that it is impossible to let the liturgy be absorbed in the many polarizations that characterize contemporary cultures. If secularism is considered to be the fundamental evolution that gave rise to many opposing modern and postmodern ideologies, the liturgy is incommensurable with *all* of them. Not that it remains unaffected, but its very core cannot be caught. By consequence, if secularism is considered to be one among the plethora of ideologies, the same analysis stands. Therefore, I think it is important to nuance Schmemann's harsh statement that secularism is the 'negation' of Christian worship.[42] While there is definitely some truth in his underlying assertion that secularism is an anthropological heresy, the liturgy is, metaphysically, not of such a kind that it can be negated. To the contrary, it is posited, that is, both revealed and public, *offenbar*, '*propter nostram salutem*'.

In line with the incarnation, the liturgy dwells among us so that we can dwell in her, and she embraces us before we can even start to love and cherish her. The liturgy establishes the between from where the beyond becomes visible. This is exactly what the Church's sacramental liturgy *does*: she moves with us from the between to the beyond, she carries us up (*anaphora*) from finitude towards the Infinite, from within spatiotemporal conditions to the Eternal. She ensures that, as the Letter to Diognetus indicates, for Christians, every country is a homeland, but every homeland is a foreign country.[43] In other words, Christians are at home everywhere, also in secular societies, but ultimately, they do not belong there. As many of their liturgical prayers indicate, their perspective is *per omnia saecula saeculorum*.

---

[41] Kavanagh, *On Liturgical Theology*, 43.
[42] Schmemann, *For the Life of the World*, 118.
[43] See the interesting reflections of Gordon W. Lathrop, 'Every Foreign Country a Homeland, Every Homeland a Foreign Country: On Worship and Culture', in *Worship and Culture: Foreign Country or Homeland*, ed. Gláucia Vasconcelos Wilkey (Grand Rapids, MI: William B. Eerdmans, 2014), 10–25.

8

'Especially in Mission Territories' (SC 38): New Evangelization and Liturgical (Reform of the) Reform

Stephen Bullivant

This chapter will sketch out a specific historical and theological argument concerning both the intent and interpretation of *Sacrosanctum Concilium*.[1] This has, I think, clear implications for the contemporary role of the sacred liturgy within the ambit of the new evangelization, and vice versa.

The argument will proceed in two main movements. In the first, my basic contention is that the liturgical reforms mandated by the Second Vatican Council were themselves manifestly motivated, and justified, by neo-evangelistic thinking and concerns. Furthermore, a concern for the new evangelization guided the interpretation and implementation of the reforms (in all their diversity, and to all their varying effects). This all may *sound* strange, since of course the phrase itself, 'new evangelization', did not appear until some decades later. However, as we will see, what the magisterium *means* by that phrase – 'a "new evangelization" or a "re-evangelization" … of those peoples who have already heard Christ proclaimed', in the words of St John Paul II[2] – was demonstrably at the forefront of many of the council fathers' and *periti*'s minds long before the term was coined. The second part of the argument, however, will be that this recognition is far from simply a historical observation about the reform of the liturgy. Rather, it opens up considerable possibilities – indeed, perhaps *demands* – for the reform of the reform. In brief, *if* the original liturgical reforms were motivated and justified by neo-evangelistic concerns, then they must also be judged by them. 'Pastorally efficacious to the fullest degree' (SC 49) is, I suggest, quite a demanding benchmark.

---

[1] Second Vatican Council, Constitution on the Sacred Liturgy *Sacrosanctum Concilium* (4 December 1963). References will be made in the body of the paper with the abbreviation SC followed by the paragraph number. All quotations of magisterial documents, not least those from *Sacrosanctum Concilium* itself, are given according to the English translations available on www.vatican.va, unless stated otherwise.

[2] John Paul II, Encyclical Letter on the Permanent Validity of the Church's Missionary Mandate *Redemptoris Missio* (7 December 1990), nos. 33 and 30.

1 What is So New About the New Evangelization?

First, the easy part: what do we (or perhaps, *should we*) actually mean when we talk about the new evangelization? Or rather, if indeed the Church 'exists in order to evangelize',[3] then what is or can be 'new' about the new evangelization?

In his 1990 Encyclical Letter, *Redemptoris Missio*, St John Paul II distinguishes between three kinds of situation. The first consists of 'peoples, groups, and socio-cultural contexts in which Christ and his Gospel are not known, or which lack Christian communities sufficiently mature to be able to incarnate the faith in their own environment and proclaim it to other groups'.[4] Necessary here, of course, is what he calls *missio ad gentes* – proposing the good news about Jesus Christ and the Church he founded to people who have never heard, or heard much, about it, and carefully nurturing it once it is established. This is the primary mode of evangelization throughout Christian history (and it is, of course, still of pressing need in much of the world today); so much so that we might term it 'classic evangelization'.

The second situation is, essentially, that of cultures where classic evangelization has been successful; where Christianity has taken root, matured, and is ticking along nicely (including to the extent of sending missionaries elsewhere). These are 'Christian communities with adequate and solid ecclesial structures. They are fervent in their faith and in Christian living. They bear witness to the Gospel in their surroundings and have a sense of commitment to the universal mission'.[5] Here, the *primary* task is not evangelization per se, but rather 'pastoral care' of the faithful.

The third situation, and the critical one for our purposes, is where this kind of solidly established Christianity is beginning to crumble within a culture: 'countries with ancient Christian roots, and occasionally in the younger Churches as well, where entire groups of the baptized have lost a living sense of the faith, or even no longer consider themselves members of the Church, and live a life far removed from Christ and his Gospel'.[6] St John Paul specifically calls this 'an intermediate situation'; and in context, it is clear that the meaning here is *intermediate between the second and first situations*, that is, a situation in which a culture where the Church has been firmly established is in the process of lapsing back into a position where, for the most part, 'Christ and his Gospel are not known'. It is *here* that what is needed is 'a new evangelization of those peoples who have already heard Christ proclaimed'.[7] The newness, then, refers primarily to a difference of sociocultural context. And it is this *difference of context*, which requires a different evangelistic approach.

So, the *concept* of new evangelization refers to the Church's missionary activity in sociocultural contexts where a long-established Christian (we might go so far as to say specifically Catholic) culture is significantly weakening: Western Europe is the classic case here, of course. The *phrase* itself is naturally a handy label, or shorthand

---

[3] Paul VI, Apostolic Exhortation *Evangelii Nuntiandi* (8 December 1975), no. 14.
[4] John Paul II, *Redemptoris Missio*, no. 33.
[5] Ibid.
[6] Ibid.
[7] Ibid., 30.

description, to have. But obviously, it is perfectly possible for the concept to have existed before the coining of the phrase.[8]

2 The Old New Evangelization

And so it did. Albeit *avant-la-lettre*, the Second Vatican Council's documents are shot through with the new evangelization. And in fact, this is true of the very rationale for calling a council in the first place. Why, after all, would one embark upon so vast an undertaking – perhaps 'the biggest meeting in the history of the world'[9] – if everything was already going perfectly? In his opening address, St John XXIII spoke of a need to 'introduc[e] timely changes … [to] really succeed in bringing men, families and nations to the appreciation of supernatural values'. He further urged that, while 'never for an instant los[ing] sight of that sacred patrimony of truth inherited from the fathers', the Catholic Church must nevertheless 'keep up to date with the changing conditions of this modern world, and of modern living'.[10] Even in the early 1960s, these were far from idle concerns.

Permit me to give just a few examples here. In 1943, two French priests published a sociological report entitled *La France – Pays de Mission?* ('France – A Mission Field?'), in which they designated large areas, primarily around industrial cities like Paris, Lyons and Marseilles, as 'Pagan areas. Missionary areas'.[11] The following year, 1944 – the same year, note, that the future John XXIII was named as nuncio to France – Cardinal Emmanuel Suhard, archbishop of Paris, launched the worker-priest experiment, precisely as a means of *re*-evangelizing large sections of the French population.[12] Whatever else the short-lived worker-priest experiment may have been, it was assuredly a bold *attempt* at new evangelization. Similar trends are discernible elsewhere in Europe too. In England and Wales, the Catholic Missionary Society, founded in 1910 to convert non-Catholics, increasingly in the post-war period, turned its attentions to lapsed Catholics. This was initially under the leadership of Fr John Heenan, who would go on to be archbishop of Westminster from 1963 and cardinal from 1965 until his death in 1975.[13] In 1950s Germany, Joseph Ratzinger worried in

---

[8] Incidentally, it is worth remarking here that John Paul's *original* coinage of the phrase does not necessarily correlate with the concept he would later, and definitively, attach it to. For example, the first recorded instance appears to have been in Poland in 1979 (*Homily at Shrine of the Holy Cross*, Mogiła, 9 June 1979), and the second in Haiti in 1983 (*Discourse to the XIX Assembly of CELAM*, Port-au-Prince, 9 March 1983). Neither time and place would seem to be a particularly fitting example of a neo-evangelistic heartland, at least not in light of what the phrase would *come to mean* in the pope's own teaching.

[9] John W O'Malley, 'Vatican II: Did Anything Happen?', *Theological Studies* 67 (2006): 3–33, at 10.

[10] John XXIII, Opening Address to the Council *Gaudet Mater Ecclesia* (11 October 1962). English translation available online: https://www.catholicculture.org/culture/library/view. cfm?RecNum=3233 (accessed 30 June 2015).

[11] Henri Godin and Yvan Daniel, 'France A Missionary Land?', in *France Pagan? The Mission of Abbé Godin*, ed. Maisie Ward (London: Sheed and Ward, [1943] 1949), 65–191, at 69.

[12] See Stephen Bullivant, *The Salvation of Atheists and Catholic Dogmatic Theology* (Oxford: Oxford University Press, 2012), 55–9.

[13] See James Hagerty, 'The Conversion of England: John Carmel Heenan and the Catholic Missionary Society, 1947–1951', *Recusant History* 31 (2013): 461–81.

print that Catholicism was increasingly becoming 'a Church of pagans who still call themselves Christians but in truth have become pagans'.[14] Meanwhile, Karl Rahner could describe, apparently as a readily recognizable and common figure, the Christian who 'lives in a family circle whose members although originally Catholic, not only are not zealously "practising," but if the truth is to be told have become completely without faith, sometimes to the point of being actively hostile, of officially leaving the Church'.[15]

3 The Liturgical Reform

When viewed against this background, the impulses towards reform at Vatican II, and more to the point, the willingness to interpret and implement those reforms in ways that pushed up against (and, in some cases, went far beyond) the limits of even what the council *permitted*, perhaps start to make more sense. So much was risked; and why? This question brings us, finally, to the liturgical reform, and especially to *Sacrosanctum Concilium* itself: 'the firstfruit and the ultimate theological-pastoral expression of Vatican II'.[16]

The Constitution on the Sacred Liturgy is perfectly upfront about its evangelistic, and indeed neo-evangelistic, inclinations.[17] Indeed, its very opening sentence affirms that, among the council's four main aims, two of them are 'to impart an ever increasing vigour to the Christian life of the faithful' and 'to strengthen whatever can help to call the whole of mankind into the household of the Church' (SC 1). The task of 'undertaking the reform and promotion of the liturgy' (ibid.) is then explicitly linked to fulfilling these aims. Moreover, the text's expressed desire of imbuing the liturgical rites with 'new vigour to meet the circumstances and needs of modern times' (SC 4) is a clear admission that the rites, as they currently stood, were felt to be somewhat less than optimally 'vigorous' for achieving these ends. And of course, this same impulse is clear in the document's leitmotiv – that is, in its repeated insistence on 'fully conscious, and active participation' (SC 14) which, albeit emphasizing an idea already present in the magisterium of St Pius X (e.g. *Tra le Sollecitudini*, 1903) and of Ven. Pius XII (e.g., *Mediator Dei*, 1947), is strikingly asserted here to be 'In the restoration and promotion of the sacred liturgy … *the aim to be considered before all else*' (ibid.; emphasis added).

It is these pastoral and evangelistic motivations – a desire, indeed, that 'that the sacrifice of the Mass, even in the ritual forms of its celebration, may become pastorally efficacious to the fullest degree' (SC 49) – which undergird and justify many of *Sacrosanctum Concilium*'s most distinctive reforms: the simplification of the Mass, removing repetitions and accretions (SC 50); the greater involvement of the people through responses, singing, actions and so on (SC 39); allowing the use of the laity's

---

[14] Joseph Ratzinger, 'Die neuen Heiden und die Kirche', *Hochland* 5 (1958): 1–11, at 1.

[15] Karl Rahner, 'The Christian Among Unbelieving Relations', in *Theological Investigations: Volume III: The Theology of the Spiritual Life*, trans. Karl-Heinz Kruger and Boniface Kruger (London: Darton, Longman and Todd, [1954] 1967), 355–72, at 355.

[16] Massimo Faggioli, *True Reform: Liturgy and Ecclesiology in* Sacrosanctum Concilium (Collegeville, MN: Liturgical Press, 2012), 155.

[17] See Timothy P. O'Malley, *Liturgy and the New Evangelization: Practicing the Art of Self-Giving Love* (Collegeville, MN: Liturgical Press), 22–34.

'mother tongue' (SC 36); the permission of vernacular musical styles and a wider range of instruments (SC 119-20); even the call for new norms for 'the worthy and well planned construction of sacred buildings, the shape and construction of altars, [and] the proper ordering of sacred images, embellishments, and vestments' (SC 128). Such reforms did not, naturally enough, come out of nowhere. In fact, from as early as 1943 there are impressed testimonies from French worker-priests about the experiments by German Dominicans with such things as the vernacular and altars facing the people.[18] The latter practice, though not itself mandated by *Sacrosanctum Concilium*, soon became folded into 'the reforms', and justified for the same reasons as the rest.

While the reforms as a whole are motivated largely by (neo-)evangelistic considerations, this general pattern becomes all the sharper where *Sacrosanctum Concilium* speaks explicitly on the topic of 'mission territories' (SC 38, 40, 65, 68, 119). Article 40, for instance, acknowledges that 'in some places and circumstances, however, an even more radical adaptation of the liturgy is needed'. Although what 'places and circumstances' these might be is not clearly defined, it is later implied that these are to be found 'especially in mission territories (*praesertim in Missionibus*)' (SC 40). Elsewhere, the council states that 'provisions shall also be made, when revising the liturgical books, for legitimate variations and adaptations to different groups, regions, and peoples, *especially in mission territories*' (SC 38; emphasis added). And while Gregorian chant is to be given 'pride of place in liturgical services' (SC 116) and 'the pipe organ is to be held in high esteem' (SC 120), other possibilities are permitted. And once again, this applies 'in certain parts of the world, especially in mission territories, [where] there are peoples who have their own musical traditions, and these play a great part in their religious and social life' (SC 119).

Now, if my reading of *Sacrosanctum Concilium* is correct, then these specific comments about 'mission territories' are not *exceptions* to the overall thrust of the document's liturgical theology, but are rather the logical outworking of it. They are, in short, simply particularly clear instances, as per article 14, where the 'full and active participation by all the people', 'demanded by the very nature of the liturgy', is indeed 'the aim [being] considered before all else' (SC 14). Furthermore, while the primary referents of the document's references to *terrae Missionum* are undoubtedly 'classic' mission territories (i.e. areas where the *missio ad gentes* is the Church's primary task, as per *Redemptoris Missio*), it cannot have escaped the notice of the council fathers and *periti*, including those directly involved in drafting it, that – as we have noted above – large areas of Western Europe, the very heart of Christendom, were already, and with good reason, being described as mission territories in their own right.

This, I believe, is critical for understanding the ways in which *Sacrosanctum Concilium* was then interpreted and implemented – very often in ways that surely went far beyond what the council fathers had in mind, even as they near-unanimously approved what was itself, not necessarily a radical text per se, but rather a conservative text that permitted (with good reason) some radical things. The document itself devolves a huge degree of latitude to the 'competent territorial bodies of bishops legitimately established' (the forerunners of our modern bishops' conferences) on the question of

---

[18] E.g. Henri Perrin, *Priest-Workman in Germany*, trans. Rosemary Sheed (London: Sheed & Ward, 1947), 51.

how, precisely, to apply the liturgical vision of the council (SC 22). For example: 'It is for the competent territorial ecclesiastical authority ... to decide whether, and to what extent, the vernacular language is to be used' (SC 36). It is accordingly very difficult here to distinguish sharply between 'the letter' of the council and its implementation.

This is most clearly the case with respect to liturgical music.[19] As has been often remarked, the *bulk* of the conciliar statement on music constitutes a stirring promotion of traditional Church music as 'a treasure of inestimable value, greater even than that of any other art' (SC 112).[20] But, as we have noted above, the text also permits the use of 'other kinds of sacred music ... so long as they accord with the spirit of the liturgical action' (SC 116), even to the point of allowing, 'especially in mission territories', 'a suitable place' to the introduction of vernacular musical styles (SC 119). Along with this, the authority to sanction the use of instruments other than the organ in the liturgy is granted to 'the competent territorial authority', albeit '*only on condition* that the instruments are suitable, or can be made suitable, for sacred use, accord with the dignity of the temple, and truly contribute to the edification of the faithful' (SC 120; emphasis added).

Now we have here a clear case where the council's notably guarded *opening up of possibilities* was, almost immediately, taken up and run with in parishes across Western Europe and North America. Presumably, this was because these were regarded as akin to mission territories, and that there were specific neo-evangelistic reasons for doing so, in the interests of leading 'all the faithful ... to that fully conscious, and active participation in liturgical celebrations which is demanded by the very nature of the liturgy' (SC 14). I say 'presumably' here since this is the only possible justification that one could make for these experiments on the basis of the council's texts themselves.

The early 'folk Mass' experiments in the United States, for instance, were interesting in this regard. There were, for instance, some quite serious attempts to compose works in the authentic spirit of traditional American religious music; for instance, the work of Fr Clarence Rivers, the first African American priest to be ordained for the Archdiocese of Cincinnati, is clearly influenced by the negro spiritual tradition.[21] This kind of endeavour has clear parallels with the nineteenth-century work of, say, Sabine Baring-Gould or Ralph Vaughan-Williams in constructing an English hymn repertoire drawing extensively on traditional folk tunes. And these are both instances where one could certainly construct a case, albeit a problematic one, regarding 'peoples who have their own musical traditions, and these play a great part in their religious and social life' (SC 119).

The difficulty, however, was in where to draw the line. What if 'people who have their own musical traditions' is interpreted to include the great mass of teenagers (remembering that the liturgical reforms were being implemented at precisely the same moment as baby boomers were becoming young adults) whom pastors were already, and with good reason, beginning to fret about losing? Explicitly or not, that

---

[19] See, for example, Joanna Bullivant and Stephen Bullivant, '*Actuosa participatio*: Vatican II and the Vernacular', unpublished paper given at the conference, '*Psallite Domino*: Sacred Music and Liturgical Reform after Vatican II', Liverpool Metropolitan Cathedral, 20 June 2015; Joanna Bullivant and Stephen Bullivant, 'Sing an Old Song to the Lord', *Pastoral Review* 7 (2011): 58–65.

[20] See Christopher McElroy, '"*Actuosa participatio*" vs "*Thesaurus Musicae sacrae*": Towards a synthesis?', draft paper, 2016.

[21] See Ken Canedo, *Keep the Fire Burning: The Folk Mass Revolution* (Portland, OR: Pastoral Press, 2009), 36–8.

is precisely how the conciliar phrase was soon interpreted. And, no doubt with good neo-evangelistic *intentions*, the young people of a parish were often enough not only allowed, but actively encouraged, to introduce to Masses music that indeed played 'a great part in their religious and social life'. Hence the infamous intrusion of, say, Bob Dylan's *Blowin' in the Wind*, Pete Seeger's *If I Had a Hammer* and even the Beatles' *Hey Jude* into the liturgical oeuvre.[22]

No doubt such music did, sometimes, 'truly contribute to the edification of the faithful' (SC 120).[23] Although for most people, I suspect, it had precisely the opposite effect. Furthermore, such experiments in vernacular music were, from the start, fraught with difficulties. Chief among these, of course, is: *Whose vernacular?* A certain style of non-traditional vernacular music might, among a limited group, truly aid 'active participation' (something which, incidentally, the Sacred Congregation of Rites' 1967 instruction *Musicam Sacram* rightly stresses to be primarily 'interior'[24]). But in Western societies, at least, this is certainly not the case in, say, a typical parish congregation. This general problem is exacerbated where the vernacular music of, say, (some) young people thirty, or forty or fifty years ago is *still* being offered up. My wife and I were, for example, once present at a 'youth Mass' at a Berlin parish where a group of teenagers had somehow been persuaded to perform 'The Last Supper' song from *Jesus Christ Superstar* – a musical which, even laying aside serious doctrinal and liturgical concerns, came out over a decade before any of them had been born.

4 The Reform of the Reform

So far in this paper, I have argued that the reforms proposed in *Sacrosanctum Concilium*, in harmony with much of the overarching rationale for the council itself, are, in large measure, an attempt at *new evangelization*. At least, insofar as a large proportion of the council fathers and experts were coming out of, and concerned for, the state of the Church in Western Europe – and elsewhere – where there were already longstanding pastoral and missionary concerns. And I have further argued that the interpretation and implementation of those reforms, in all their diversity and (at times) radicality, were motivated and justified by similarly neo-evangelistic concerns. In fact, very rapidly the 'competent territorial authorities' across Europe and America either encouraged or tolerated a vast latitude (if not laxitude) of liturgical practices: a latitude which the council itself, by and large, reserves for extreme cases ('especially in mission territories'), and even then with a good dose of caution and circumspection. I have offered, albeit rather sketchily, liturgical music as a clear example here, though I think the basic point applies across the board. This too, I contend, was motivated by the same sorts of concerns the Church would, within a few decades, characterize as new evangelization.

---

[22] Ibid., 75.

[23] See, for instance, the testimony in Lisa Middendorf Woodall, 'This Old Church: Confessions of a Guitar-Mass Catholic', *America* (15–22 August 2016): 30–2.

[24] Sacred Congregation of Rites, Instruction on Music in the Liturgy *Musicam Sacram* (5 March 1967), 17.

Careful readers, I hope, will have noticed that I have spoken, more or less exclusively, of neo-evangelistic *intentions*, *motivations* and *justifications*. I have not, note well, spoken of neo-evangelistic *successes*.

This is not a point I wish particularly to labour. A few examples should suffice. Among cradle Catholics in England and Wales, only 56 per cent now even identify as Catholic and 40 per cent 'never or practically never' attend a place of worship of *any* religion or denomination, other than for funerals, baptisms or weddings.[25] Among American cradle Catholics, according to the General Social Survey, around a third no longer tick the Catholic box on surveys. In both countries, moreover, baby boomers – that is, those who come of age around the time of the council, and for whose specific benefit many of the most radical liturgical adaptations were justified – are particularly likely to have lapsed or disaffiliated altogether. Now, there are assuredly a large number of complex reasons for these kinds of trends. But even so, it is extraordinarily difficult to see how the liturgical reforms and/or how they were interpreted and implemented *up until now* have succeeded in their explicit aims: 'to impart an ever increasing vigour to the Christian life of the faithful' and 'to strengthen whatever can help to call the whole of mankind into the household of the Church' (SC 1). I should say here, however, that I confine this judgement only to Western Europe and North America (I have seen it argued, for example, that the liturgical reforms have borne very serious fruit in other parts of the world, and I have no reason to contradict these claims[26]). Equally, even in Western Europe and North America, I am referring here only to the 'big picture' (there are undoubtedly many particular success stories – in certain parts of the charismatic renewal, or within certain ecclesial movements, for instance – countering the prevailing trend). Those qualifications aside, however, I think the general case is a strong one.

This is of the utmost importance, not least in terms of what has sometimes been termed 'the reform of the reform' (a phrase I use here in a broad sense). The same criteria which inspired, motivated and justified the conciliar reforms not only permit, but demand, that the liturgy be re-reformed if the anticipated results have not been achieved. In the explicit words of the council itself, the Christian faithful 'should be drawn day by day into ever more perfect union with God and with each other' (SC 48), and it is thus: '*For this reason* the sacred Council … has made the following decrees in order that the sacrifice of the Mass, even in the ritual forms of its celebration, may become pastorally efficacious to the fullest degree' (SC 49; emphasis added). An ongoing commitment to – if, as and when necessary – continually revisit the concrete applications of the reform is not, therefore, something opposed to *Sacrosanctum Concilium*, but is rather an authentic fulfilment of both its letter and spirit.

Here, it is important to remember that a good number of the council's so-called 'reforms' are deliberately non-specific. In large part, *Sacrosanctum Concilium* opens up possibilities, usually with some caution (as we have seen with regard to vernacular

---

[25] Stephen Bullivant, *Contemporary Catholicism in England and Wales: A Statistical Report Based on Recent British Social Attitudes Data*, Catholic Research Forum Reports 1 (Benedict XVI Centre for Religion and Society, 2016), 11, 14. Available online: http://www.stmarys.ac.uk/benedict-xvi/docs/2016-may-contemporary-catholicism-report.pdf (accessed 30 May 2016).

[26] For example Alexander Lucie-Smith, 'Africa is where Vatican II has really worked', *Catholic Herald*, 4 June 2015. Available online: http://www.catholicherald.co.uk/commentandblogs/2015/06/04/africa-is-where-vatican-ii-has-really-worked/ (accessed 3 July 2016).

musical styles and instrumentation). Actual, concrete changes are, often enough, devolved to national bishops' conferences (or rather their forerunners). This is clear, for example, in what is almost certainly the most significant of the council's decrees, SC 36, which I reproduce here with my own emphases added:

1. Particular law remaining in force, the use of the Latin language is to be preserved in the Latin rites.
2. **But since the use of the mother tongue**, whether in the Mass, the administration of the sacraments, or other parts of the liturgy, **frequently** *may be* **of great advantage to the people, the limits of its employment** *may be* **extended**. This will apply in the first place to the readings and directives, and to some of the prayers and chants, according to the regulations on this matter to be laid down separately in subsequent chapters.
3. These norms being observed, **it is for the competent territorial ecclesiastical authority** mentioned in Art. 22, 2, **to decide** *whether, and to what extent,* **the vernacular language is to be used**; their decrees are to be approved, that is, confirmed, by the Apostolic See. And, whenever it seems to be called for, this authority is to consult with bishops of neighbouring regions which have the same language.
4. Translations from the Latin text into the mother tongue intended for use in the liturgy must be approved by the competent territorial ecclesiastical authority mentioned above.

Even here, the most distinctive and far-reaching hallmark of the Vatican II liturgy, we have permission for the use of the vernacular (and the document seems to presume, even then, a limited use), and not a demand for it.

My point here is not to argue against vernacular in the liturgy; far from it. Rather, it is simply to point out that the specific way (or rather, specific set of range of ways) that the liturgy was reformed in light of the council was not the only inevitable one. Rather, what soon became the post-conciliar 'new normal' was, and could only have been, the product of a diverse array of separate decisions. These, in a notable number of cases, opted for the extreme edges of possibilities opened up by the council (plus a number of other changes – *versus populum*, Communion in the hand – upon which it had been silent). As noted above, this in itself suggests that a quite drastic refashioning of the liturgy was thought to be pastorally and evangelistically necessary. In the great majority of cases, though, these decisions were all perfectly *compatible* with the council's teachings.[27] Although, at the risk of labouring the point, they only *remain* compatible with the council's teaching to the extent that they truly are 'pastorally

---

[27] Of course, genuine abuses can and do occur; but then, they always have. To cite just one: at the Field of Cloth of Gold, the summit between Henry VIII of England and Francis I of France held in 1520, a huge, flaming effigy of a dragon – perhaps some form of kite – appeared in the skies during the final Mass. As my colleague, the eminent Tudor historian Professor Glenn Richardson, has written: 'The appearance of a "dreadful monster, of immoderate size" with its flames, blazing eyes and hissing noises, would surely have been at the very least a distraction from the ceremony on the high altar if not a cause of alarm among some spectators. ... The dragon's appearance was surely inconsistent with the reverential decorum usually expected at the high point of the celebration of the Eucharist.' Glenn Richardson, *The Field of Cloth of Gold* (New Haven, CT: Yale University Press, 2013), 173–4.

efficacious to the fullest degree' (SC 49). Where this is not the case, then the overall thrust of *Sacrosanctum Concilium's* liturgical vision is quite plain: those original decisions should, indeed must, be revisited.

To what extent do our liturgies, as they are concretely, *genuinely* fulfil the neo-evangelistic intentions of the Second Vatican Council? This is a question that should be asked at all levels: from the Congregation of Divine Worship right down to the individual parishes, and at all stops – international language-group commissions (such as ICEL), national bishops' conferences – in between.

5 Conclusion

On two occasions, *Sacrosanctum Concilium* advises the undertaking of 'studies and necessary experiments' (SC 44; also 40) before any drastic liturgical decisions are taken. True to this, a number of now-standard features of Masses were originally rolled out *'ad experimentum'.*[28] Generally speaking, immediate feedback on many of liturgical changes in the 1960s was reportedly positive (though this was *not* unanimous, and it would perhaps be fair to say that those with negative views tended to be ignored or worse). A few months, or even years, is however a very short period of experimentation for undertaking something so significant as a large-scale liturgical reform. And in any case, even I would admit that 'be[ing] drawn day by day into ever more perfect union with God and with each other' (SC 48) is a difficult thing to measure by the means of survey questions.

Nevertheless, fifty years on, it is at the very least an open question as to whether the liturgical reform, as it has actually been undertaken, has indeed lived up to its promise. And it is not enough here simply to focus our thinking on *current* and *regular* Mass-goers. The really hard question will come if we ask ourselves how well our liturgies 'impart an ever increasing vigour to the Christian life' (SC 1) of that by-now very large proportion of the faithful who have been *staying away* from Mass, in increasing numbers, for many decades now. (A trend that, though it certainly began *before* the council, rapidly accelerated after it. Though of course, *post Concilium* need not imply *propter Concilium*.) It is these 'entire groups of the baptized [who] have lost a living sense of the faith, or even no longer consider themselves members of the Church, and live a life far removed from Christ and his Gospel'[29] who are the primary objects of the new evangelization.

To recap: this chapter has attempted to sketch out a particular argument, with two main movements. In the first, I argued that once one focuses on the *meaning* of the phrase 'new evangelization', then it becomes clear that the council's liturgical reforms, in common with the overarching purpose and vision of the council itself, were in large measure motivated by straightforwardly neo-evangelistic concerns. Furthermore, this explains the precise ways in which the reforms were interpreted and implemented in

---

[28] Alana Harris, *Faith in the Family: A Lived Religious History of English Catholicism, 1945-82* (Manchester: Manchester University Press, 2013), 98.
[29] John Paul II, *Redemptoris Missio*, no. 30.

much of Europe and North America: in a way commensurate with a conviction, explicit or implicit, that these are indeed 'mission territories', as had been argued, at least in Western Europe, for several decades prior. In the second, my argument was simply that these neo-evangelistic criteria remain in full force today, and, insofar as we hope to be true to the council, are the measure against which our liturgical practices, both historically over the past fifty years, and today, must be judged; and in light of which, if deemed necessary, must be revised. This is, indeed, an ongoing process. Even if we do succeed in creating 'pastorally efficacious to the fullest degree' (SC 49) liturgies for a particular group – in a particular parish, at a particular time, say – whether they will remain so forever is a moot point. *Perhaps* in the early 1970s incorporating repertoire from *Jesus Christ Superstar* into Mass managed, I know not how, to 'add delight to prayer, foster unity of minds, or confer greater solemnity upon the sacred rites' (SC 112). But *if* it once did, it certainly no longer does.

In short, if it is the case – and prima facie, there are good grounds for thinking it is – that our liturgies often fail both 'to impart an ever increasing vigour to the Christian life of the faithful' and 'to strengthen whatever can help to call the whole of mankind into the household of the Church' (SC 1), then it is *Sacrosanctum Concilium* itself that demands that the reforms be reformed.

9

The Tridentine Liturgical Reform in Historical Perspective

Uwe Michael Lang

1 The Study of Liturgy in Context

In this paper I propose to consider the liturgical reform initiated by the Council of Trent (1545–63), in particular the post-Tridentine edition of the *Missale Romanum* (1570), from a wider historical perspective. My intention is to look at some of the questions associated with this important phase in the history of the Western liturgy in the context of early modern Christianity. Such a broader approach can provide a corrective to a forceful strand of liturgical scholarship, which has understood itself as a highly specialized discipline with a proper methodology that at times appears 'set apart from the general trends of theological and historical research'.[1] This is the observation of Yitzhak Hen, a noted historian of early medieval liturgy, to which he adds: 'Scholars who submerged themselves in the study of liturgy too often tend to ignore the context in which the liturgy evolved, as if liturgical texts were produced in a political and cultural vacuum'.[2]

In his seminal work on the interpretation of cultures, Clifford Geertz describes religion as a 'system of symbols', by which he means 'any object, act, event, quality or relation which serves as a vehicle for a conception'. Symbols are thus 'tangible formulations of notions, abstractions from experience fixed in perceptible forms, concrete embodiments of ideas, attitudes, judgments, longings, or beliefs'.[3] By means of such symbols, a religion shapes and directs the dispositions, attitudes, ideas and incentives of its adherents. As a system of symbols, religion articulates and communicates conceptions about the whole cosmos. In doing so, it proposes a model *of* reality as well as a model *for* reality, that is, it claims to represent things as they are and to show how they should be.

---

[1] Yitzhak Hen, 'Key Themes in the Study of Medieval Liturgy', in *T&T Clark Companion to Liturgy*, ed. Alcuin Reid (London: Bloomsbury T&T Clark, 2016), 73–92, at 73.

[2] Ibid.

[3] C. Geertz, 'Religion as a Cultural System', in *The Interpretation of Cultures: Selected Essays* (New York: Basic Books, 1973), 87–125, at 90–1.

Geertz's description of religion as a system of symbols is particularly relevant for the medieval and early modern periods, when divine worship was an 'important indicator of cultural creativity and social development'[4] in European societies that identified themselves as a Christian commonwealth. Standard liturgical textbooks have portrayed the later medieval period (from about 1200 onwards) as an age of liturgical decadence: what used to be an expression of communal worship became an almost exclusively clerical exercise of a hypertrophied ritual system. The formation of national languages and cultures meant that Latin as the language of the liturgy became even more removed from the language of the people. Consequently, it is argued, lay participation largely disappeared, including even the reception of Holy Communion. The faithful would rather occupy themselves with private, largely visual devotions while the priest celebrated Mass at some distance, in a language they could not comprehend.[5]

More recently, however, other voices have made themselves heard. The focus on liturgical texts has been widened in favour of multidisciplinary approaches that include musical, artistic, literary, social and, more generally, religious perspectives. It has been argued that the use of Latin did not raise an impenetrable barrier to popular understanding of and participation in the Mass. In the Romance-speaking countries, where the vernacular developed from Latin, there was a basic understanding at least of the meaning conveyed in liturgical texts, and this was so even among the lesser educated, at least if they chose to follow attentively.[6] More importantly, as the (Lutheran) liturgical scholar Frank Senn argues, such a conclusion rests on a narrow understanding of participation that 'sees liturgy only as text and limits participation to speaking roles'. Senn continues:

> The laity have always found ways to participate in the liturgy, whether it was in their language or not, and they have always derived meaning from the liturgy, whether it was the intended meaning or not. Furthermore, the laity in worship were surrounded by other 'vernaculars' than language, not least of which were the church buildings themselves and the liturgical art that decorated them.[7]

The work of Eamon Duffy has shown the vitality of the late medieval liturgy in England even on a parish level.[8] The history of the Church's worship in this period is ripe for fresh scholarly approaches, and, it is important to question the conventional narrative.

---

[4] Hen, 'Key Themes in the Study of Medieval Liturgy', 73.

[5] See, for example, the devastating assessments of Theodor Klauser, *A Short History of the Western Liturgy: An Account and Some Reflections*, trans. John Halliburton, 2nd edn (Oxford: Oxford University Press, 1979), 97; Anscar J. Chupungco, 'History of the Roman Liturgy until the Fifteenth Century', in *Handbook for Liturgical Studies, Vol. I: Introduction to the Liturgy*, ed. Anscar J. Chupungco (Collegeville, MN: Liturgical Press, 1997), 131–52, at 150.

[6] See Augustine Thompson, *Cities of God: The Religion of the Italian Communes 1125–1325* (University Park, PA: The Pennsylvania State University Press, 2005), 239–41.

[7] Frank C. Senn, *The People's Work: A Social History of the Liturgy* (Minneapolis, MN: Fortress Press, 2006), 145.

[8] See Eamon Duffy, *The Stripping of the Altars: Traditional Religion in England 1400-1570* (New Haven, CT: Yale University Press, 1992).

2 From the Late Medieval to the Early Modern Period

The period of transition from the late medieval to the early modern period was a complex one. The historian Robert Bireley has identified five major factors that brought about profound changes in Church and society:[9]

1. The late medieval period saw the 'growth of the state; that is, the consolidation and centralization of political authority over a particular geographical area', which has been described as 'the establishment of sovereignty'.[10] This development had significant impact on the lasting areas of conflict between ecclesiastical and civil authority, above all questions concerning jurisdiction and taxation. As the identification with a united Christendom declined among European elites in favour of identification with their own nation, monarchs and princes took greater control over the church in their territories.

2. The period saw momentous social and economic changes. After the devastations of the Black Death, population was growing again. Cities were profiting from economic expansion, and an urban middle class emerged as a major player in society.

3. New horizons were opened by the expansion of European powers into Asia, America and, to a lesser extent, Africa. This expansion combined genuinely religious motives with profit-seeking and sheer desire for adventure. The Spanish and Portuguese colonial conquests helped to create a global Catholicism.

4. Renaissance humanism opened new intellectual, spiritual and artistic horizons. The Renaissance was by no means a monolithic movement, and its ideas were articulated in diverse ways. While elements of social and cultural continuity with the medieval world should not be overlooked,[11] the Renaissance introduced an optimistic understanding of man and of the world that saw as its point of reference the legacy of Greek and Roman antiquity. At the same time, humanism saw a revival of Christian antiquity, marked by a renewed interest in the early Church fathers, especially the Greek. Christian humanists, above all Erasmus, offered a trenchant critique of contemporary Scholastic theology and advocated a return to a 'simpler' theology founded on the Bible (read in its original languages) and the patristic tradition. They also advanced the call for a reform of the Church 'in head and members', which came from the conciliarist movement as a response to the crisis of the papacy after its move to Avignon and the Western schism, which lasted from 1378 to 1417.

5. A major factor for the history of the Church is of course the Protestant Reformation, a religious rupture that profoundly changed European societies, with worldwide consequences. The Reformation did not come as an external onslaught, but as a radical internal transformation, and hence can only be understood within its historical context. There has been a strong 'revisionist' current in recent historical scholarship that has questioned long-held beliefs about the alleged decadence and decline of the late medieval Church and has successfully challenged the teleological narrative that the Protestant Reformation as the inevitable resolution of this period of

---

[9] See Robert Bireley, *The Refashioning of Catholicism, 1450-1700: A Reassessment of the Counter Reformation* (Basingstoke: Macmillan, 1999), 1–24.
[10] Ibid., 9.
[11] The art historian Erwin Panofsky, 'Renaissance and Renascences', *The Kenyon Review* 6 (1944): 201–36, at 202, speaks of 'a thousand ties' that connect the Renaissance with the Middle Ages.

crisis.[12] Johan Huizinga's evocation of the 'waning' or the 'autumn' of the Middle Ages is to some extent substantiated by a sense of disintegration in late medieval society, for reasons that were only partly religious.[13] At the same time, however, the Church was remarkably successful in its 'primary' role concerning the pastoral care of the people: leaving aside the radical claims of Jean Delumeau,[14] we perceive a thoroughly Christian religious culture shaping life from birth to burial. There were denunciations of abuses, especially regarding the failings of individual priests and religious, usually linked with calls for reform, but the sacramental system as such was not contested, except by the most radical dissidents. What made the Church vulnerable was its secondary role that resulted from the seemingly inseparable entanglement between spiritual and temporal spheres. Questions of jurisdiction, taxation and land ownership brought conflicts both with local communities and with princes and monarchs. The papacy in particular, ruling over a territorial state in central Italy, was involved in the politics and warfare between Europe's leading powers.

Religious practice in the later Middle Ages is characterized by diverse, if not contrary tendencies. On the one hand, there was an increasing internalization of man's relationship to God to such an extent that private forms of devotion came to be regarded as more important than public acts of worship. This tendency developed fully in the early modern period, in both Protestant and Catholic reform movements. The historian Christopher Dawson singles out the flowering of mysticism in Spain and Italy, and the ascetic spirituality as represented in the Ignatian *Spiritual Exercises*, with their roots in the *devotio moderna*.[15] On the other hand, Caroline Walker Bynum shows the sheer materiality of religious devotion, with its focus on miraculous phenomena, relics and pilgrimages.[16] It would not seem adequate to separate these divergent tendencies into the categories of elite and popular piety. Rather they are found across the social spectrum, as shown, for instance, in the tangible devotion to the Holy Face of Christ, which was shared equally among the populace, educated nuns and the Duke of Burgundy.[17]

---

[12] See the outstanding survey by Euan Cameron, *The European Reformation*, 2nd edn (Oxford: Oxford University Press, 2012), 1–98, and R. N. Swanson, *Religion and Devotion in Europe, c. 1215 – c. 1515* (Cambridge: Cambridge University Press, 1995).

[13] Johan Huizinga, *The Waning of the Middle Ages: A Study of the Forms of Life, Thought and Art in France and the Netherlands in the Fourteenth and Fifteenth Centuries*, trans. Frederik Hopman (London: Edward Arnold, 1924). The Black Death was still in living memory; the 'Little Ice Age' had adverse consequences for agriculture; the Hundred Years' War affected the population of England and France; Constantinople fell into the hands of the Ottoman Turks in 1453.

[14] Jean Delumeau, *Catholicism between Luther and Voltaire: A New View of the Counter-Reformation*, trans. Jeremy Moiser (London: Burns & Oates, 1977).

[15] Christopher Dawson, *The Dividing of Christendom* (San Francisco: Ignatius Press, 2009; originally published in 1965), 33.

[16] Caroline Walker Bynum, *Christian Materiality: An Essay on Religion in Late Medieval Europe* (New York: Zone Books, 2011).

[17] See the papers of the international conference on 'The European Fortune of the Roman Veronica in the Middle Ages', held at Magdalene College, Cambridge, 4–5 April 2016, which will be published in *Veronica, Saint Veronica and vera icona in Medieval Texts and Art*, ed. H. L. Kessler and A. Murphy (Turnhout: Brepols, 2017), forthcoming.

3 Western Liturgy in the Later Middle Ages

The situation of the Western liturgy in this period is also marked by diverse tendencies. A movement towards unification and standardization of liturgical books emerged from the reforming pontificates of the eleventh century, especially with Pope St Gregory VII (1073–85).[18] His policy succeeded in the abandonment of the Mozarabic rite and its substitution with the Roman rite in the reconquered parts of Christian Spain. Still, general conformity with Roman liturgical practice began to be spread throughout the Latin Church only with the rapid expansion of the Franciscan Order in the thirteenth century. The mendicant orders constituted a new type of religious life that did not have a vow of stability. Instead, friars would periodically move from house to house. With Latin as the common language of the Church, of higher education and culture, the friars enjoyed high mobility throughout Europe. It proved onerous for them to adapt to local liturgical variations and so the desire arose for a unified practice within the orders. The Dominicans adopted a proper use that was established in 1256 by the Master of the Order, Humbert de Romans.[19]

The Franciscans adopted the liturgical books of the Roman rite in the form used by the papal curia. The editions of these books were to some extent simplified by comparison with the full ceremonial observed in the major basilicas of Rome, because the papal court often travelled in this period and therefore liturgical practice was given a standard form that could also be celebrated in Anagni or Orvieto. Through the Franciscans a degree of unification of the missal and the breviary was achieved that previous popes may have demanded but were never able to implement effectively.

A momentous step in this history is the liturgical work of the Haymo of Faversham, who served as minister general of the Franciscans from 1240 to 1243, after the turbulent second tenure of Elias of Cortona (1232–9). At the order's chapter in Bologna in 1243, Haymo presented the ordinal known by its opening words *Indutus Planeta* ('Wearing the chasuble …'), which describes itself as an 'ordo agendorum et dicendorum', that is, an order regulating the ceremonies to be carried out and the texts to be recited, in the private Mass of a priest or the simple conventual Mass on a ferial day.[20] *Indutus Planeta* was based on the liturgical use of the Roman curia; its Order of Mass included the prayers at the foot of altar with Psalm 42 (*Iudica me …*) and the offertory prayers in their definitive Roman form. The ordinal was adopted by the Friars Minor and helped shape a unified Franciscan liturgy.

---

[18] See H. E. J. Cowdrey, 'Pope Gregory VII (1073-85) and the Liturgy', *Journal of Theological Studies* N.S. 55 (2004): 55–83.

[19] See the still unsurpassed work of William R. Bonniwell, *A History of the Dominican Liturgy 1215 – 1945*, 2nd edn edition revised and enlarged (New York: Joseph F. Wagner, Inc., 1945).

[20] The text of *Indutus Planeta* can be found in *Tracts on the Mass*, ed. J. Wickham Legg, Henry Bradshaw Society, 27 (London: Harrison, 1904), 181–8. See Stephen J. P. Van Dijk, O.F.M. and Joan Hazelden Walker, *The Origins of the Modern Roman Liturgy: The Liturgy of the Papal Court and the Franciscan Order in the Thirteenth Century* (Westminster, MD and London: The Newman Press – Darton, Longman & Todd, 1960), 292–301. Anna Welch, *Liturgy, Books and Franciscan Identity in Medieval Umbria*, Medieval Franciscans, 12 (Leiden: Brill, 2015), 77–8, holds that Haymo's authorship of *Indutus Planeta* is not beyond doubt; however, his decisive reform of the Franciscan order, including its liturgical practice, is certain.

Thus through the Friars Minor a standardization of the missal was achieved in the Latin Church to a degree that previous popes may have demanded but were never able to implement effectively. The Order of Mass 'secundum consuetudinem Romane curie' provided the model for missals of local dioceses and religious orders. It was codified in the first printed edition of the *Missale Romanum* in 1474. *Indutus Planeta* was incorporated into the Order of Mass compiled by the papal master of ceremonies Johannes Burckhard (first edition 1498, second, more widely received, edition 1502). Burckhard's Order of Mass in turn formed the basis for the *Ritus servandus* of the 1570 *Missale Romanum*.

This standardization of the missal (and the breviary), for which the Franciscan Order acted as a catalyst, did not happen overnight, but in a long process. Variations in the missals of dioceses and religious orders remained and could be considerable: in the liturgical calendar, above all the sanctoral cycle; in the formal presentation of Mass formularies (such as the technical terms for prayer and chant texts); and in the structure and sequence of parts within the liturgical books. Even where the Order of Mass followed essentially the Roman pattern, there were differences in the ceremonies and texts of the introductory rites and of the concluding rites. Likewise, the ritual form and the prayers of the offertory were by no means uniform. Rubrics often originated from private annotations, as a practical help for priests to celebrate Mass; they did not have an official character and varied both in quality and in usefulness.[21] Liturgical diversification increased with the addition of new saints' feasts, the proliferation of prefaces, tropes and sequences of uneven quality, and the multiplication of votive Masses, some of them attached to questionable practices, such as the use of a symbolic number of candles for specific Masses: seven for the Mass of St Sophia along with seven orations, 12 for the twelve apostles, and 24 for the elders of the Apocalypse.[22]

Local bishops did apparently not have an effective control over the production of liturgical books in their dioceses. A case in point is the largely unsuccessful effort of Cardinal Nicholas of Cusa, who as the bishop of Brixen tried to enforce the correction of missals in use according to approved normative manuscripts at diocesan synods in 1453 and 1455.[23] The invention of printing could have given the ecclesiastical authorities the opportunity to prune this rank growth by insisting on a previous approbation of liturgical books. However, only a few ordinaries used this chance for an official revision

---

[21] See Hubert Jedin, 'Das Konzil von Trient und die Reform der liturgischen Bücher', *Ephemerides Liturgicae* 59 (1945): 5–38, at 5–7. The desire for a codification of rubrics and the focus on the written text is often connected with increasing literacy and with book production, especially with printing. See Aidan Kavanagh, *On Liturgical Theology: The Hale Memorial Lectures of Seabury-Western Theological Seminary, 1981* (Collegeville: Liturgical Press, 1984), 103–7, and Anthony J. Chadwick, 'The Roman Missal of the Council of Trent', in *T&T Clark Companion to Liturgy*, ed. Alcuin Reid (London: Bloomsbury T&T Clark, 2016), 107–31, at 108.

[22] See the still valuable work of Adolph Franz, *Die Messe im deutschen Mittelalter: Beiträge zur Geschichte der Liturgie und des religiösen Volkslebens* (Freiburg im Breisgau: Herder, 1902), esp. 268–91.

[23] Hubert Jedin, 'Das Konzil von Trient und die Reform des Römischen Meßbuches', *Liturgisches Leben* 6 (1939): 30–66, at 40–1.

of missal and breviary.[24] Leaving aside the core of the Order of Mass and the temporal cycle of the liturgical year, the actual composition of a diocesan missal seems to have been largely in the hands of the printers themselves, as the eminent historian of the Catholic Reform and Counter-Reformation Hubert Jedin noted.[25] Rather than leading towards uniformity, the possibility of printing missals introduced an even greater variety. Amato Pietro Frutaz has drawn attention to the categorical differences in the sanctoral calendars of early printed editions of the *Missale Romanum* from the last quarter of the fifteenth century, most of them coming from Italy. The *editio princeps*, printed by Antonio Zarotto in 1474, simply lists a saint or a group of saints for almost each day of the year. Other early printed missals use a version of the Franciscan calendar, with a motley addition of saints.[26]

The proliferation of votive Masses and the important role assumed by printers can be illustrated with the example of the liturgical veneration of the Holy Face, which stemmed from the increasing devotion to the Roman Veronica, the sacred cloth upon which the suffering Christ was believed to have imprinted his face.[27] The collection of early printed missals from the Diocese of Passau in the Bavarian State Library (*Bayerische Staatsbibliothek*) in Munich allows us to reconstruct a timeline for the addition of a Mass formulary of the Holy Face. Three editions of the *Missale Pataviense* between 1491 and 1503, printed with the mandate of Christoph von Schachner, bishop of Passau from 1490 to 1500, do not have such a formulary.[28] The *Missale secundum chorum Pataviensem*, printed in Augsburg by Erhard Ratdolt in 1503, does not contain the Mass either.[29] However, another edition of the same missal, printed also in Augsburg in 1503 by an unidentified printer, includes a formulary with the title '*Officium sancte Veronice: hoc est de facie Iesu Christi*' in a section with votive Masses,[30] which is introduced with the rubric: 'The printer added the following special Masses to incite a greater love of God, and for the glory of his work.'[31] A subsequent edition of the *Missale Pataviense* printed in Augsburg by Erhard Ratdolt in 1505, with the mandate of Wiguleus Fröschl von Marzoll, bishop of Passau from 1500 to 1517, does not include

---

[24] Examples are given by Jedin, 'Das Konzil von Trient und die Reform der liturgischen Bücher', 9. Jedin, 'Das Konzil von Trient und die Reform der liturgischen Bücher', 12, mentions the provincial synod of Bourges in 1528, under the presidency of Cardinal Tournon, which stipulated that henceforth breviaries, missals and rituals could be printed only with the previous approbation of the competent bishops. This would imply that such had not been done before. The synod also recalled that a reduction of feast days was the remit of ordinaries.

[25] Jedin, 'Das Konzil von Trient und die Reform des Römischen Meßbuches', 41, notes pointedly: 'Die gedruckten Missalien waren allzuhäufig Privatunternehmungen tüchtiger Drucker'.

[26] *Missale Romanum Mediolani, 1474. Vol. I. Text*, ed. Robert Lippe, Henry Bradshaw Society, 17 (London: Harrison and Sons, 1899), xiii–xxiv. See Amato Pietro Frutaz, 'Contributo alla storia della riforma del Messale promulgato da san Pio V nel 1570', in *Problemi di vita religiosa in Italia nel Cinquecento: Atti del Convegno di storia della Chiesa in Italia (Bologna, 2-6 sett. 1958)*, Italia Sacra, 2 (Padova; Editrice Antenore, 1960), 187–214, at 201–3.

[27] See my paper 'Origins of the Liturgical Veneration of the Roman Veronica', in *Veronica, Saint Veronica and vera icona in Medieval Texts and Art*, forthcoming.

[28] *Missale Pataviense* (Passau: Johann Petri, 1491); *Missale Pataviense* (Augsburg: Erhard Ratdolt, 1494); *Missale Pataviense* (Vienna: Johann Winterburger, 1503).

[29] *Missale secundum chorum Pataviensem* (Augsburg: Erhard Ratdolt, 1503), shelfmark Rar. 1739.

[30] *Missale secundum chorum Pataviensem* (Augsburg: s.n., 1503), shelfmark 4 Liturg. 400, f. 306v–8r.

[31] 'Subsequentes missas speciales per maiori divini amoris incentivo et operis decore subiunxit impressor'. Ibid., f. 305r.

these additional votive Masses. However, the *Missale Pataviense* printed in Vienna by Johannes Winterburger in 1509, has an appendix entitled '*Missae speciales*', introduced by the printer with the same rubric as mentioned above, and includes the formulary of the Holy Face.[32]

While the liturgical life of the Western Church was not in a general state of decay and decadence, there were aspects of it that were in real need of reform. For instance, the '*missa sicca*' ('dry Mass') was a form of devotion where a complete Mass formulary was used except the offertory, the Canon of the Mass and Communion. It was used, for instance, for funerals or marriages held in the afternoon, when (because of fasting rules) no Mass could be celebrated. In the '*missa bifaciata*' or '*trifaciata*', the priest said the parts of the Mass from the Introit to the Preface two or three times, and then continued with the Canon. This was done with the idea of fulfilling several Mass intentions, after Pope Innocent III had prescribed in 1206 that a priest should say only one Mass a day (except on Christmas, when he could offer the three different Masses of the feast).[33] These practices were denounced as signs of greed on the part of the clergy. It was also observed that priests exhibited lack of preparation, carelessness in liturgical functions or disregard for rubrics. Such phenomena can be seen as part of the general critique of the state of the clergy and the appeals for reform, which were concerns widely shared at the time.

Calls for greater liturgical unification were heard long before Trent. In the early period of the Council of Constance (1414–18), the anonymous author of a treatise calling for a reform of the Church lamented the '*discordia et discordancia magna*' of different liturgical uses and called for a conformity to the practice of the Roman Church.[34] About a century later, in 1513, the *Libellus* addressed to Pope Leo X by two hermits of Camaldoli, Bl. Paolo Giustiniani and Pietro Quirini, included among its considerations for Church reform an appeal for a unified celebration of Mass and other ceremonies.[35]

The profound rupture of the Protestant Reformation had a significant impact on liturgical life. Martin Luther offered a radical critique of the sacrificial character of the Mass and rejected the Roman Canon. However, he changed the ritual structure of the Mass only gradually and in many Lutheran church orders, some ceremonies that had a popular appeal were kept, including traditional Mass vestments and the elevation of the consecrated species.[36] In central and northern Europe an even greater liturgical diversification ensued, which would often but not always reflect doctrinal differences. The Western liturgy had entered a period of veritable confusion.

---

[32] *Missale Pataviense* (Vienna: Johann Winterburger, 1509), f. 254v and 255v–6v.

[33] See Franz, *Die Messe im deutschen Mittelalter*, 73–86.

[34] *Acta Concilii Constantiensis*, ed. Heinrich Finke, 4 vols. (Münster: Regensbergsche Buchhandlung, 1896–1928), vol. II, p. 591.

[35] Stephen M. Beall has published a revised version of the text from *Annales Camaldulenses Ordinis Sancti Benedicti*, ed. Giovanni B. Mittarelli and Anselmo Costadoni, vol. IX (Venice: Monasterium Sancti Michaelis De Muriano, 1773), 612–719, as well as an English translation, on https://marquette.academia.edu/StephenBeall (accessed 12 December 2016). See Jedin, 'Das Konzil von Trient und die Reform der liturgischen Bücher', 8–9.

[36] See Bryan D. Spinks, *Do This in Remembrance of Me: The Eucharist from the Early Church to the Present Day* (London: SCM Press, 2013), 246–71.

4 The Council of Trent

The rivalry between the Kingdom of France and the House of Habsburg, which ruled Spain and held the throne of the Holy Roman Empire, delayed the convocation of a general council for several years. When the council finally assembled in the city of Trent, which was part of the Empire but on Italian soil, its twofold agenda was shaped by the doctrinal challenges of the Protestant Reformers and the need for reform of the Church's discipline. This included a reaffirmation of Catholic doctrine on the sacraments and the Mass, as well as the demand to address liturgical abuses. As it had been decided early on to deal with questions of doctrine and of Church reform in parallel, the need for renewed liturgical discipline was articulated already during the council's first period from December 1545 to March 1547. However, the question was resumed in earnest only in its last period, from January 1562 to December 1563, alongside the deliberations about the decree on the sacrifice of the Mass.

As Hubert Jedin has observed, there were strong calls for a unified missal coming from the nations that were represented at the council.[37] The item was included in the substantial list of petitions submitted in 1561 by Bl. Bartholomew a Martyribus (1514–90), archbishop of Braga in Portugal.[38] In March 1562, a memorandum from a group of Italian prelates close to the Augustinian Cardinal Girolamo Seripando (1493–1563) recommended the reform and standardization of liturgical books.[39] A clear statement came from the Spanish bishops in early April 1562. In a memorandum presented to the legates of the council, they suggested a unified breviary and missal 'used in all churches' with a separate proper of saints for each diocese.[40] The emperor Ferdinand I had a *libellus reformationis* sent to the assembly, in which he supported the revision of liturgical books and the removal of apocryphal elements, as well as the introduction of German psalm- and hymn-singing.[41] The emperor's intervention is significant in that it signals the failure of attempts to reform the liturgy on a local and regional level, by means of provincial councils and imperial diets. The matter was handed over to the initiative of the General Council. A contrasting voice came from France: in January 1563 the French representatives at Trent presented their own *libellus reformationis* with a list of liturgical reform measures, which included the demand for more extensive use of the vernacular in the Mass and in the administration of the sacraments, but said nothing about a reform of missal or breviary.[42] The French bishops evidently wanted to keep the oversight over liturgical books for themselves rather than relinquish it to the council or to the pope.

---

[37] The following discussion is based on Jedin, 'Das Konzil von Trient und die Reform des Römischen Meßbuches', 37–45, and 'Das Konzil von Trient und die Reform der liturgischen Bücher', 28–30.

[38] *Concilium Tridentinum: Diariorum, Actorum, Epistularum, Tractatuum Nova Collectio*, ed. Societas Goerresiana (Freiburg: Herder, 1901–), vol. XIII/1, 544: 'Sacerdotes celebrant iuxta missale romanum, nihil addentes vel minuentes, et quae alta voce et intelligibili et quae secrete dicenda sunt, [ita] dicant.'

[39] Ibid., 610: 'Tam breviaria quam missalia reformanda essent et a multis ineptiis purganda.'

[40] Ibid., 627: 'Videatur, an expediret unum breviarium et unum missale fieri, quod ad omnes ecclesias deserviret, exceptis sanctis cuiusque dioceseos, de quibus in brevi libello posset notari varietas.'

[41] Ibid., 671.

[42] See Jedin, 'Das Konzil von Trient und die Reform des Römischen Meßbuches', 39–40, and 'Das Konzil von Trient und die Reform der liturgischen Bücher', 29–30.

The conciliar debates on the doctrine of the sacrifice of the Mass were accompanied by a consideration of concrete steps towards liturgical reform. At a general congregation of the council on 20 July 1562 a commission was instituted to study this question. The commission produced a dossier on liturgical issues,[43] the contents of which can broadly be distinguished into three categories:

First, there were observations of a doctrinal character. For instance, the question was raised whether it was correct to refer to the unconsecrated elements of bread and wine as '*immaculata hostia*' (spotless victim) and '*calix salutaris*' (chalice of salvation) in the offertory prayers. Likewise, the legitimacy of making the sign of the cross over the consecrated species after the Words of Institution in the Canon of the Mass had been discussed.

Secondly, there were comments that reflected the new historical consciousness of Renaissance humanists, who promoted a return *ad fontes*, to the biblical and patristic sources of the Catholic tradition. The concrete proposals for reform include the purging of liturgical texts from apocryphal material that was clearly not historical, and of texts that were considered superstitious, especially in votive Masses. These concerns reflect the aspiration to give priority to the traditional order of the Roman liturgy over forms of private devotion and personal piety. The ideal of the *norma patrum*, the norm of the fathers, would later be enshrined in the bull promulgating the *Missale Romanum* of 1570.

Thirdly, there were indications of liturgical abuses on the part of the clergy, which had been denounced by reformers both Protestant and Catholic. These include neglect of sacred vessels, ignorance of or disregard for rubrics on the part of priests, and dubious practices, such as the *Missa sicca*. There can be no doubt that such abuses really happened, but it is hard to say how pervasive they really were. Any reformer is inclined to make the picture of the present situation as bleak as possible. Rhetorical emphasis, if not exaggeration, is often used as a tool to advance one's own reforming agenda.

The dossier on liturgical abuses was condensed to a compendium, which retained the demand for a unified missal and stated the need for standardized rubrics very clearly; it also claimed the project of reforming the missal for the agenda of the council itself, so that the local ordinaries would then have a secure foundation for their own particular reform measures.[44] However, even this shorter text did not make it to the council floor, because there was a concern that it would delay the current session and threaten its successful conclusion. There was a strong desire for the widest possible consensus among the council fathers, and hence the final *Decree concerning the things to be observed, and to be avoided, in the celebration of Mass* of 17 September 1562 was limited to addressing liturgical abuses in the narrow sense of the word and instructed diocesan bishops to show diligence in matters of divine worship and to correct errors, but did not mention an actual revision of liturgical books.[45]

A new impetus for reform was given, when after the death of the Cardinal legates Ercole Gonzaga and Girolamo Seripando in March 1563, Cardinals Giovanni Morone and Bernardo Navagero were appointed in their stead. The discussion on the liturgical books continued over the summer, and in October 1563, Charles de Guise, Cardinal

---

[43] *Concilium Tridentinum*, vol. VIII, 916–21.
[44] Ibid., 921–4.
[45] Ibid., 962–3.

of Lorraine, on a visit to Rome, procured the sending of a manuscript of the Gregorian Sacramentary from the Vatican Library to Trent. The Cardinal of Lorraine was not an official legate at the council, but was treated as such by Cardinal Morone, in order to ensure his support for Morone's energetic reform programme. The arrival of the manuscript on 25 October 1563 was a tangible symbol of the desire to prune and revise the existing missal in light of the ancient Roman tradition.[46] It is, however, extremely difficult to trace the progress of the conciliar discussions because of a lack of sources. The bishop of Salamanca, Pedro Gonçales de Mendoça, notes in his council diary that in the general congregation of 26–27 October 1563 deputies were appointed to produce a reformed missal and breviary, but this is not noted in the official acts. Jedin suggests that no special commission (*deputatio*) was instituted, but that the task of revising the liturgical books was entrusted to already existing commissions, either the one working on the index, or, more likely, the one working on the *Catechism*. These commissions did not leave any minutes; at least there is no record in the acts of the council.[47] In his diary Bishop Gonçales de Mendoça also expressed his apprehension that the work on the missal and the breviary could not be completed at the council, because it had been left so late. In fact, it seems to have been the prevailing view among the council fathers that they were not in a position to undertake the revision of liturgical books themselves. The council was concluded prematurely on 4 December 1563, because of alarming news about the ill health of Pope Pius IV. In the final session, it was decided that several reform measures, which the council was not able to complete, should be left to the pope, among them the reform of the breviary and of the missal.

To summarize, the discussions at Trent established two fundamental principles for this work: in the first place, the council fathers supported a unification of the Order of Mass and its rubrics; any celebration of Mass was meant to conform to this general standard. Secondly, there was a broad consensus to restore the ancient form and structure of the Roman rite, pruned from later accretions, especially those containing apocryphal material, those reflecting private devotions and those bordering on the superstitious.

5 The *Missale Romanum* of 1570

Soon after the council Pope Pius IV set up commissions for revising the liturgical books. Since a more pressing need for the reform of the breviary was seen, this work was undertaken first. However, work on the missal probably commenced in parallel, given the fact that its revised *Missale Romanum* of 1570 appeared only one and a half years after the revised *Breviarium Romanum* in 1568. Once again we face the difficulty that we do not have official records of this ongoing work, but are dependent on occasional information, found especially in personal correspondence. We have hardly any sources on the working principles and methods of the commission working on the missal.

---

[46] See Frutaz, 'Contributo alla storia della riforma del Messale', 188–9.
[47] Jedin, 'Das Konzil von Trient und die Reform der liturgischen Bücher', 35–7; see also Frutaz, 'Contributo alla storia della riforma del Messale', 188–92.

Amato Pietro Frutaz discovered a *Missale secundum morem Sancte Romane Ecclesie*, printed by Giovanni Battista di Sessa in Venice in 1497, with many annotations and corrections from the hand of Cardinal Guglielmo Sirleto (1514–85), who was a key collaborator in the post-Tridentine revision of the Vulgate text, the composition of the *Catechism* and the reform of the liturgical books. Sirleto's notes are found mainly in the calendar, where he deleted many feasts of saints, and in the Mass Propers, where he made various emendations. There are only few suggestions for changes in the Order of Mass. The annotations show a work in progress, and by no means all of Sirleto's proposals were accepted in the 1570 edition of the *Missale Romanum*.[48]

Frutaz also discovered two relevant handwritten documents in the Vatican Library: the first is an Italian memorandum of a few pages signed by Leonardo Marini, archbishop of Lanciano, with the title *Information for the Correction of the Missal*.[49] This document can be dated before 13 October 1568, when Marini's successor, Ettore Piscicelli, was appointed to the See of Lanciano. The author's first objective is the harmonization of the missal with the breviary, especially regarding the calendar and the biblical readings (there had been discrepancies in this regard in the existing liturgical books). The second document is an anonymous list of twelve questions in Latin presumably emerging from the reform commission.[50] There is scope for further research here, and the longer memorandum would suggest that a study of the reform of the breviary, for which more sources are available, could shed light on the reform of the missal. Within the limits of this paper, however, the actual work of reform will be elucidated by means of a comparison between the post-Tridentine missal and its pre-Tridentine ancestors.

Pope St Pius V's bull of promulgation *Quo primum* of 14 July 1570 states that the Missal has been restored 'to the original norm and rite of the holy fathers (*ad pristinam ... sanctorum patrum normam ac ritum*)'. This reflects the Renaissance humanist ideas that animated some of the proposals for reform at the council. However, caution is needed in interpreting this return to the fathers. As Josef Andreas Jungmann noted, the implicit assumption is that 'the development which had taken place meanwhile, separating the present from the *pristina sanctorum patrum norma* should not be put aside as long as it did not disturb the ground-plan but rather unfolded it'.[51] Moreover, we need to be aware that limiting the title '(Church) father' to normative theologians in the early centuries of Christianity is a late modern conception. The Benedictine scholar Jean Mabillon (1632–1707) still considered St Bernard of Clairvaux, who died in 1153, as the last of the fathers. Even in the nineteenth century, one of the great editorial projects of Jacques-Paul Migne (1800–75), the *Patrologia Latina*, concluded with the works of Pope Innocent III, who died in 1216.[52] It is consonant with the early

---

[48] Sirleto's annotations are presented by Frutaz, 'Contributo alla storia della riforma del Messale', 197–208.

[49] Ibid., 210–3.

[50] Ibid., 213–4.

[51] Jungmann, *The Mass of the Roman Rite: Its Origins and Development (Missarum Sollemnia)*, trans. Francis A. Brunner, C.SS.R., 2 vols. (New York: Benziger, 1951–5), vol. I, 137.

[52] See Hubertus R. Drobner, *Lehrbuch der Patrologie* (Freiburg i. Br: Herder, 1994), 3. On the question of *norma patrum* see also Stefan Heid, 'Tisch oder Altar? Hypothesen der Wissenschaft mit weitreichenden Folgen', in *Operation am lebenden Objekt: Roms Liturgiereformen von Trient bis zum Vaticanum II*, ed. Stefan Heid (Berlin: be.bra wissenschaft, 2014), 351–74, at 352–3 and 372–4.

modern understanding of *norma patrum* that the Missal of 1570 in essence follows the mixed Franco-Roman rite that had been established in the city of Rome since the pontificate of Gregory VII (1073–85) and had since then been spread gradually to most of the Western Church.

5.1 The Order of Mass

For the Order of Mass, the *Missale Romanum* of 1570[53] largely follows the missal of the Roman curia and Johannes Burckhard's Order of Mass in its second edition of 1502.[54] Rubrics are standardized, including those for the elevation in the consecrated species and the genuflexions of the celebrant (which were already found in earlier printed editions of the *Missale Romanum*).

The most significant changes concern the beginning and the conclusion of Mass.[55] The preparatory prayers of the celebrant are now made at the foot of the altar rather than Psalm 42 (*Iudica me*) being recited in procession to the altar, as in some medieval missals. The final blessing is given after the prayer *Placeat*, not vice versa, as in some earlier editions of the missal. The 'Last Gospel' is read at the altar rather than said sotto voce from memory as the celebrant returns to the sacristy. It would appear that the rationale for these changes was to focus on the sacred texts and their authentic meaning, and to avoid a perfunctory recitation.

In liturgical books from the later Middle Ages we find a wide use of tropes, that is, texts (in both poetry and prose) added to embellish or augment chant from the Order or from the Proper of the Mass. The missal of 1570 specifically proscribed the troping of the Introit, the Kyrie and the Gloria.

The offertory follows the custom of the Roman curia. However, the offertory procession that is still included in Burckhard's *Ordo Missae* of 1502, is not retained.[56] Anthony Chadwick suggests that this was 'probably for fear of pecuniary abuses on the part of the clergy'.[57]

5.2 Calendar and Mass Propers

Considerable work was done on the liturgical calendar.[58] The very full sanctoral cycle of the pre-Tridentine books was substantially reduced, with the aim of bringing the temporal cycle to the fore again. The Roman calendar of 1568 and 1570 has 157 ferial

---

[53] *Missale Romanum: Editio Princeps (1570)*, ed. Manlio Sodi and Achille Maria Triacca, Monumenta Liturgica Concilii Tridentini, 2 (Vatican City: Libreria Editrice Vaticana, 1998).

[54] Burckhard's *Ordo Missae* can be found in Wickham Legg, *Tracts on the Mass*, 121–74.

[55] See Chadwick, 'The Roman Missal of the Council of Trent', 115–16.

[56] Ibid., 110: 'When the gifts were brought to the altar, the celebrant was directed to go to the Epistle corner, to take off his maniple and to accept the offerings. Each of the faithful kissed the priest's hand and made the offering. The celebrant would say: *Acceptabile sit sacrificium tuum omnipotenti Deo* or *Centuplum accipias: et vitam aeternam possideas*. Having accepted the oblations, the priest put on his maniple and went to the middle of the altar. He then proceeded with the offering of the host. The rest of this offertory rite was exactly reproduced in the 1570 missal.' See Burckhard, *Ordo Missae*, in Wickham Legg, *Tracts on the Mass*, 149.

[57] Chadwick, 'The Roman Missal of the Council of Trent', 115.

[58] See ibid., 116–17 for a concise overview.

days, not counting the octaves (which were much simplified). Especially in the months of March and April, many feasts of saints were removed to keep Lenten ferias as free as possible. The new sanctoral is focused on the early Christian centuries, especially martyrs. Among the later saints added are mainly popes, doctors of the Church and founders of religious orders.[59]

There were no alterations in the structure of the temporal cycle of the liturgical year, which had been established in the early Middle Ages, and few modifications in its prayers, chants and readings. The most substantial change was the purging of the poetic sequences to be sung before the Gospel, except those for Easter, Pentecost and Corpus Christi (as well as the Requiem Mass).

The Common of Saints was laid out more systematically, with complete Mass formularies. The number of votive Masses was reduced; their use was strictly regulated and restricted to weekday ferias.

The pruning of the sanctoral cycle and the restoration of ferial days meant that ordinarily on weekdays the Mass formulary of the preceding Sunday would be used, including its scriptural readings. The memorandum of Archbishop Leonardo Marini reports a proposal to select three passages each from the Epistles of St Paul and from the Gospels, which are not contained in other Mass formularies, to be used every week on ferial days, in order to avoid repeating the Sunday readings.[60]

Many diocesan missals in the later Middle Ages contained specific readings for Wednesdays and Fridays during the liturgical year, unless the day had a proper Mass formulary. These ferial pericopes stem from the early Roman-Frankish lectionary tradition, which was consolidated in the Carolingian period. They were not included in the plenary missal of the Roman curia and hence in the early printed editions of the *Missale Romanum*.[61] The proposal may have been made with an awareness of the contents of diocesan missals. It goes beyond this earlier tradition, however, by recommending the selection of scriptural passages that would not be read otherwise. The intention is obviously to present the treasury of Holy Scripture more fully in the course of the liturgical year. This proposal was not heeded in the 1570 edition, which rather followed the pre-Tridentine curial missals.

---

[59] There has been some discussion about the archetype chosen for the revision of the calendar. Theodor Klauser, with two of his disciples, argued that the idea was to restore the calendar of the *Ordo officiorum ecclesiae lateransis* compiled by Prior Bernard around the year 1145, that is, the calendar used in the cathedral church of Rome around the time of the Gregorian Reform, with the addition of more recently canonized saints. By contrast, Frutaz argues, on the basis of Sirleto's annotations, that the direct model for the work of the commission was rather the Franciscan calendar of the thirteenth century, which in turn is based on the *Ordo* from the Lateran Basilica from the middle of the twelfth century. See Frutaz, 'Contributo alla storia della riforma del Messale', 203–5.

[60] See Frutaz, 'Contributo alla storia della riforma del Messale', 211–2.

[61] See Antoine Chavasse, *Les lectionnaires romains de la messe au VIIe et au VIIIe siècle: sources et dérivés*, Spicilegii Friburgensis Subsidia 22, 2 vols. (Fribourg Suisse: Editions Universitaire, 1993), and the summary of Cyrille Vogel, *Medieval Liturgy: An Introduction to the Sources*, rev. and trans. William G. Storey and Niels Krogh Rasmussen, O.P. (Washington, DC: The Pastoral Press, 1986), 349–55.

6 The Shape of the 'Tridentine Mass'

The *Missale Romanum* of Pope Pius V thus stands in strong continuity with the plenary missals of the Roman rite in the form used by the Roman curia, which go back to the thirteenth century. This continuity extends even further to the time of the Gregorian Reform in the eleventh century, and, in the essential structure and contents of the rite, to the early medieval papal stational Mass.[62] Perhaps the most significant change concerns the form of celebration, or the 'shape' of the Tridentine Mass. The *Ritus servandus* ('Rite to be observed') that is placed at the beginning of the 1570 missal would seem to presuppose that the simple 'low Mass' of a priest is the normative form of the rite.

In the early Middle Ages, the ideal that each priest should offer Mass daily for the spiritual benefit of the living and the dead, which originated from monastic houses, became more and more widely adopted by the secular clergy. The ritual shape of such daily celebrations was greatly simplified and would foresee only one or two servers in assistance. In what came to be known as 'private Masses'[63] the liturgical parts that the solemn Mass assigned to the deacon, subdeacon, lector or the choir were performed by the priest himself. Gradually, these parts came to be recited rather than sung. The wide diffusion of the private Mass is often connected with the formation of the plenary missal, which contained all the texts the priest had to recite, along with instructions on ceremonial. Until then, various books were used in liturgical celebrations for those who had a particular ministry or role. Jungmann sees in the plenary missal 'the product not indeed of the predominance of the private Mass (which had long been in use), but at least of its general extension and its increased acceptance'.[64] On the other hand, Stephen van Dijk and Joan Hazelden Walker observe that the plenary missal 'grew in popularity among the clergy along with the development of pastoral care'.[65] A single manuscript that contains all the texts of the Mass is obviously easier to use and better suited to the network of rural parish churches and chapels that were established in most parts of Europe in the course of the later Middle Ages.

The Solemn High Mass with the assistance of deacon and subdeacon, and the participation of the *schola cantorum*, would still remain the normative form of celebration. This can be inferred from the fact that St Thomas Aquinas, when he discusses on the rite of Mass both his commentary on the *Sentences* and in the *Summa Theologiae*, chooses precisely this form.[66] In his *Letter to the Entire Order* (1225–6) St

---

[62] See Johannes Nebel, *Die Entwicklung des römischen Meßritus im ersten Jahrtausend anhand der Ordines Romani: Eine synoptische Darstellung*, Pontificium Athenaeum S. Anselmi de Urbe, Pontificium Institutum Liturgicum, Thesis ad Lauream, 264 (Rome, 2000).

[63] The term is infelicitous for various reasons, and there was some confusion about its precise meaning during the discussions at the Council of Trent; see Reinold Theisen, *Mass Liturgy and the Council of Trent* (Collegeville, MN: St. John's University Press, 1965), 87–107. Terminological difficulties are also found in twentieth-century liturgical scholarship; see Van Dijk and Hazelden Walker, *The Origins of the Modern Roman Liturgy*, 47–8.

[64] Jungmann, *The Mass of the Roman Rite*, 107.

[65] Van Dijk and Hazelden Walker, *The Origins of the Modern Roman Liturgy*, 65; the second chapter of the volume, with the subheadings '1. The Private Mass' and '2. The Complete Missal', ibid., 45–66, remains an indispensable treatment of this topic.

[66] Thomas Aquinas, *Super Sent.*, lib. 4 d. 8 q. 2 a. 4 qc. 3 expos.; *Summa Theologiae*, III, q. 83, a. 4 co.

Francis of Assisi commanded that in the houses of his order only one Mass a day should be celebrated. If there was more than one priest in a house, he should rather assist at the solemn conventual Mass. This instruction is consistent with Francis' utmost care for the beauty and dignity of the sacred liturgy.[67]

The priority given to the simple form of Mass in the *Missale Romanum* of 1570 may partially be explained with practical and pastoral considerations, but it ratified the gradual shift documented in the thirteenth-century ordinal *Indutus Planeta* (see above) towards the understanding that the Mass ceremonial was 'based on low Mass rather than low Mass being a reduction of the normative pontifical Mass'.[68] Subsequently, in the post-Tridentine period, the gap widened between the 'official' liturgy that was performed by the priest at the altar and the devotional exercises the laity used to follow it.

7 Conclusion

The Council of Trent's decision to leave the reform of the missal and breviary in the hands of the pope (and therefore also of his curia) inaugurated a period of unprecedented liturgical standardization. In 1588, Sixtus V created the Sacred Congregation of Rites, which was to give authentic interpretations of questions arising from the new liturgical books and ensure the observance of liturgical norms. Clement VIII promulgated the *Pontificale Romanum* (1596) and the *Caeremoniale Episcoporum* (1600) for pontifical celebrations, and in 1614 Paul V issued the *Rituale Romanum* for all those sacraments and sacramentals not reserved to bishops.[69] It should be recalled, however, that the *Missale Romanum* of 1570 was not compulsory for dioceses or religious orders that could legitimately claim a particular liturgical tradition older than 200 years (for instance, Milan and Toledo, or the Dominican order). As a matter of fact, the desire to strengthen the visible unity and cohesion of the Church, which had already been felt at Trent, led to the adoption of these books in many places where an older tradition existed. This was not forced by the papacy, but was seen as an appropriate step taken for the good of the Church at the time. Even the English polymath Adrian Fortescue (1878–1923), who was not altogether happy with this course of events, conceded that 'the Protestant revolt of the sixteenth century had its natural result in increased centralisation among those who remained faithful'.[70]

---

[67] 'Most likely, with the growing number of clerics and the facilitation of the daily Masses by the privilege of portable altars, Franciscan celebration of the liturgy was becoming routine and sloppy, the very sin that Francis had so abominated in the clergy. ... Rather than waiting line to rush through their own private Mass in assembly-line fashion, or even to mumble Mass at a side altar while the other brothers are chanting the Office (a not-uncommon solution to the multiplying of Masses), friar priests were to take turns celebrating the solemn sung community liturgy with deacon, subdeacon, and all the proper ministers and rites.' Augustine Thompson, *Francis of Assisi: A New Biography* (Ithaca, NY: Cornell University Press, 2012), 120–1.

[68] Chadwick, 'The Roman Missal of the Council of Trent', 108–9; see also Jungmann, *The Mass of the Roman Rite*, 106.

[69] Note that the *Rituale Romanum* was never imposed as such, like the other liturgical books of the post-Tridentine reform, but was rather intended as a model to be adapted in local rituals.

[70] Adrian Fortescue, *The Early Papacy to the Synod of Chalcedon in 451*, 4th edn by Alcuin Reid (San Francisco: Ignatius Press, 2008), 36.

10

On the Council Floor: The Council Fathers' Debate of the Schema on the Sacred Liturgy

Alcuin Reid

1 Introduction

On 29 October 1962, at the ninth general congregation of the Second Vatican Council, the council fathers began their discussion of the second chapter of the *Schema Constitutionis de Sacra Liturgia*.[1] This included article 37 on the reform of the *Ordo Missae*. It proposed:

> The Order of Mass is to be reviewed, either in general or in its individual parts, so that it may be more clearly understood and so that it may render the actual participation of the people easier.[2]

Given the centrality of the Order of Mass in the life of the Church, this article generated considerable comment. Some fathers saw these words as a licence for revolution and protested strongly: the interventions of Francis Cardinal Spellman (1889–1967)[3] and of Alfredo Cardinal Ottaviani (1890–1979)[4] are noteworthy for their criticisms; and those of Archbishop Frederico Melendro SJ (1889–1978)[5] and Bishop George Patrick

---

[1] For a synopsis of the texts (Pontificia Commissio de Sacra Liturgia praeparatoria Concilii Vaticani II, *Constitutio de Sacra Liturgia*, Textus approbatus in sessione plenaria 11–13 January 1962; *Schema Constitutionis de Sacra Liturgia*, 23 July 1962 and 22 October 1962; *Schema Constitutionis de Sacra Liturgia textus emendatus*, 3 October 1963 and *Constitutio de Sacra Liturgia*, 4 December 1963), see Francisco Gil Hellín, *Concilii Vaticani II Synopsis: Constitutio de Sacra Liturgia Sacrosanctum Concilium* (Vatican City: Liberia Editrice Vaticana, 2003).

[2] 'Ordo Missae ita recognoscatur, sive in generali dispositione sive in singulis partibus, ut clarius percipiatur et actuosam fidelium participationem faciliorem reddat'; Gil Hellín, *Concilii Vaticani II Synopsis*, 151–2.

[3] 29 October 1962. See *Acta Synodalia Sacrosancti Concilii Oecumenici Vaticani II*, vol. I, part I (Vatican City: Typis Polyglottis Vaticanis, 1970), 598–9; Gil Hellín, *Concilii Vaticani II Synopsis*, 541–2. English translation [ET]: *American Participation at Vatican II*, ed. Vincent A. Yzermans (New York: Sheed & Ward, 1967), 155–6. It should be noted that Yzermans' book erroneously titles the Constitution on the Sacred Liturgy as a 'Dogmatic' Constitution.

[4] 30 October 1962. See *Acta Synodalia Sacrosancti Concilii Oecumenici Vaticani II*, vol. I, part II (Vatican City: Typis Polyglottis Vaticanis, 1970), 18–20; Gil Hellín, *Concilii Vaticani II Synopsis*, 552–5.

[5] 30 October 1962. See *Acta Synodalia*, vol. I, part. II, 30–2; Gil Hellín, *Concilii Vaticani II Synopsis*, 561–3. Melendro is not opposed to a reform of the Order of Mass, but wishes to specify what this would mean in practice.

Dwyer (1908–87)[6] called for the article's clarification. Bishop Alberto Devoto (1918–84) argued that 'the renewal of the Order of Mass without doubt is at this moment of great importance; on account of this, this article lacks the requisite precision'.[7] The coadjutor bishop of Strasbourg, Léon-Arthur Elchinger (1908–98), sought a solution:

> I propose that the entire text of this article be conserved but that it may be clarified by the publication of the complete *declaratio* prepared by the preparatory commission under this article. So as to 'calm the spirits' of those who fear a complete revolution of the Order of Mass and the death of the Roman rite. This *declaratio* does not propose for us a revolution but only an evolution – a pastoral evolution – something sound and prudent.[8]

The *Declarationes* were the explanatory notes that had accompanied articles of the *Schema* in the various stages of redaction so as to specify the drafters' intentions.[9] While they formed part of the drafts tabled in the work of the preparatory commission, they were not included with the text of the *Schema Constitutionis de Sacra Liturgia* distributed to the council fathers. The resultant lack of specificity contributed to the anxiety of some fathers and fuelled the calls for clarification by others.

In the next session Bishop Henri Jenny (1904–82) intervened. A member of the liturgical preparatory and conciliar commissions, Bishop Jenny set forth the content of the *declaratio* on the reform of the Order of Mass asked for by Bishop Elchinger. Before outlining the specific reforms, the assurance was given that 'Hodiernus Ordo Missae, qui decursu saeculorum succrevit, *certe* retinendus est'. ('The current *Ordo Missae*, which has grown up in the course of the centuries, *certainly* is to be retained.')[10] The

---

[6]   30 October 1962. See *Acta Synodalia*, vol. I, part. II, 37–9; Gil Hellín, *Concilii Vaticani II Synopsis*, 602–3.

[7]   31 October 1962. 'Instauratio Ordinis Missae est sine dubio res magni momenti, propterea hoc articulum debita precisione indiget.' *Acta Synodalia*, vol. I, part. II, 71–3; Gil Hellín, *Concilii Vaticani II Synopsis*, 617–19.

[8]   31 October 1962. 'Propono ut textus huis numeri omnino servetur sed ut clarificetur publicatione integrae declarationis a commissione praeparatoria sub isto numero elaboratae. Ita mente reficerentur qui timent universam Ordinis Missae revolutionem et mortem ritus romani. Haec declaratio etenim nobis proponit non revolutionem sed tantum evolutionem – evolutionem pastoralem – et quidam sanam et prudentem.' *Acta Synodalia*, , vol. I, part. II, 80; Gil Hellín, *Concilii Vaticani II Synopsis*, 624.

[9]   For the development of the *Schema* presented to the council fathers, including the various *declarationes*, see Angelo Lameri, *La 'Pontifica Commissio de sacra liturgia preparatoria Concilii Vaticani II' – Documenti, Testi, Verbali* (Rome: Centro Liturgiche Vincenziano, 2013).

[10] 5 November 1962. *Acta Synodalia*, vol. I, part II, 121; Gil Hellín, *Concilii Vaticani II Synopsis*, 653. The council's press bulletin for that day states: 'The need was again stressed of using caution in revising words, gestures and prayers which have acquired great nobility in the passing of the centuries without losing anything of their original significance. It is considered, therefore, that the order of the Mass be retained in its substance, while admitting partial changes for the purpose of making the active participation of the faithful in the individual Rites [*sic*] easier. ... It was insisted that the Canon of the Mass especially should remain intact because of its solemnity and for literary, liturgical, historic and juridical reasons known to all'. *Council Daybook – Vatican II: Session 1, Oct 11 to Dec 8 1962, Session 2, Sept 29 to Dec. 4 1963*, ed. Floyd Anderson (Washington, DC: National Catholic Welfare Committee, 1965), 63. Somewhat ironically, 5 November 1962 also saw the intervention and press conference of Bishop Wilhelm Duschak (discussed below).

word 'certainly' was emphasized. The French Dominican *peritus* Yves Congar noted in his council diary that Jenny 'was listened to very attentively'.[11]

Was the Order of Mass that had developed in the course of the centuries retained? Did the *Ordo Missae* promulgated by Bl. Paul VI (1897; 1963–78) on 3 April 1969 respect this assurance given to the council fathers *in aula* when there was disquiet on the council floor, in the council's first session, as to whether an evolution or a revolution was being proposed?[12] We know that Cardinal Ottaviani and Antonio Cardinal Bacci (1885–1971) protested very strongly to Paul VI in September 1969 in what has become known as the 'Ottaviani Intervention', that the new Order of Mass 'represents, both as a whole and in its details, a striking departure from the Catholic theology of the Mass as it was formulated in session 22 of the Council of Trent'.[13]

But this takes us far ahead. Our task here is to remain on the council floor in 1962 and 1963 to study the debate of the text that would be promulgated on 4 December 1963 as the *Constitution on the Sacred Liturgy*, having received the approbation of no fewer than 2,147 council fathers, with only four voting against it,[14] and to ask what did the fathers think they were approving? What was their intention, to borrow Bishop Elchinger's words, 'a revolution' or 'an evolution – a pastoral evolution – something sound and prudent'?

In examining this question I propose to remain with article 37 of the *Schema* and to track its development into article 50 of the constitution. The constitution comprises some 130 articles and there is material enough for many studies of the development and redaction of most if not all of them. But, as Bishop Devoto affirmed, 'the renewal of the Order of Mass is ... a matter of great importance', and we shall begin here.

2 Some Hermeneutical Observations

Before doing so it is important to make some hermeneutical observations. First, what do we know about the liturgical profile or background of the more than 2,600 council fathers? What might they have been intending when they arrived *in aula* to debate the *Schema* on the Sacred Liturgy?

An adequate answer would need to begin by examining the responses to the June 1959 questionnaire sent to the world's bishops, major religious superiors and Catholic institutes of higher learning soliciting suggestions as to what should be discussed at the council. The resulting responses (*vota*) fill eight volumes and to date have been

---

[11] Yves Congar, *My Journal of the Council*, ed. Denis Minns (Collegeville, MN: Liturgical Press, 2012), 147.

[12] See *Missale Romanum ex decreto Sacrosancti Oecumenici Concilii Vaticanum II instauratum auctoritate Pauli PP VI promulgatum: Ordo Missae*, editio typica (Vatican City: Typis Polyglottis Vaticanis, 1969).

[13] *The Ottaviani Intervention: Short Critical Study of the New Order of Mass*, ed. Anthony Cekada (Rockford, IL: TAN Books and Publishers, 1992), 27.

[14] See *Acta Synodalia Sacrosancti Concilii Oecumenici Vaticani II*, vol. II, part VI (Vatican City: Typis Polyglottis Vaticanis, 1973), 407.

the subject of little scholarly enquiry.[15] It is not our place to examine them here,[16] but in passing it may be of interest to note that in his study of the returns of the bishops of the British Isles, Brian W. Harrison observes that 'only one in five of the British bishops expressed ... the expectation that changing the existing rites would prove to be pastorally or spiritually beneficial in any significant way'. According to Harrison, liturgical reform was a 'low-priority issue' for these bishops before the council.[17]

That is not to say that the world's bishops did not expect that further liturgical reform would ensue, or fail to make proposals for what such reform might encompass. Indeed, they had lived through the various reforms enacted in the 1950s,[18] and Pope John XXIII himself expressed the expectation that the council would decide the necessary orientation for liturgical reform in his July 1960 *Motu proprio* approving the reform of the rubrics of the breviary and the missal:

> We therefore, having under divine guidance, decreed that an Ecumenical Council should be convened, have given much thought as to what could be done about this initiative of our Predecessor. After long and mature consideration we have reached the conclusion that the higher principles for a general liturgical restoration (*altiora principia, generalem liturgicam instaurationem respicientia*) should be referred to the Fathers of the forthcoming Ecumenical Council, but that the correction of the rubrics of the breviary and missal should not be postponed any longer.[19]

The council fathers did, then, expect further reforms and knew that their role was to consider the principles upon which they should be based. From what we do know of their pre-conciliar *vota* it is reasonable to assume that most anticipated further moderate reform with an increased use of the vernacular, an expansion of the lectionary, and probably some ritual simplification along the lines of the previous reforms. For example, it could have been foreseen that just as the priest's illogical duplication of Scripture readings at solemn Mass had been abolished in the 1960 reform of the rubrics,[20] so too his duplication of the common of the Mass at sung or solemn Mass – the Kyrie, Gloria, Sanctus and Agnus Dei – would similarly have been abolished in future reforms. But there is no evidence, I submit, that the greater part, or even a significant minority, of the council fathers arrived *in aula* expecting 'a revolution', even if individual fathers would express such desires during the council.

---

[15] See *Acta et Documenta Concilio Vaticano II apparando,* Series 1, Antepraeparatoria (Vatican City: Typis Polyglottis Vaticanis, 1960).

[16] I attempt to examine the liturgical content of existing studies of the *vota,* and some relevant *vota* themselves, in the chapter 'Towards the Council' in *Continuity or Rupture? A Study of the Second Vatican Council's Reform of the Liturgy* (forthcoming).

[17] Brian W. Harrison OS, 'A Reform of the Mass? Britain has Other Priorities', *Apropos* 18 (1996): 69–74, at 73.

[18] See further the presentation of the *Schema* on the council floor in the fourth general congregation on 22 October 1962 by the secretary of the conciliar liturgical commission, Fr Ferdinando Antonelli OFM: *Acta Synodalia,* vol. I, part II, 305–6.

[19] John B. O'Connell, *The Rubrics of the Roman Breviary and Missal* (London: Burns & Oates, 1960), 2–3. Translation modified.

[20] See Alcuin Reid, 'Holy Week Reforms Revisited: Some New Material and Paths for Further Study', in *Liturgy in the Twenty-First Century: Contemporary Issues and Perspectives,* ed. Alcuin Reid (London: Bloomsbury, 2016), 234–59, at 236–7.

The second hermeneutical observation I would make is that we need an appropriate methodology in examining the articles of the constitution, indeed the whole of the constitution itself, in seeking an answer to the question: what did the fathers of the council intend the liturgical reform to be? This question is fundamental if we are to assess the work of the *Consilium ad exsequendam Constitutionem de Sacra Liturgia* established by Paul VI on 25 January 1964 to implement *Sacrosanctum Concilium*. Knowing the mind of the council fathers and assessing the fidelity or otherwise of the *Consilium* to it are necessary if decisions about liturgical reform today, and even the consideration of a possible 'reform of the reform', are to be both sufficiently informed and increasingly faithful to the wishes of the most recent ecumenical council of the Church.

Therefore, the study of the debate and redaction of the text at the council itself is crucial, for whatever the intentions of those who prepared the *Schema*, it is the pope and the council who gave the text its ultimate meaning and authority. That is to say, regardless of what experts may have hoped that the council would approve, or may even have read it as approving – then or afterwards – an accurate reading of the constitution is one that is in accord with the council fathers' intentions expressed *in aula* and the consequent explanations and redactions of the conciliar liturgical commission, which were again considered by the fathers before the text was finally approved and promulgated.

One example: At the very beginning of the debate on the *Schema* on the Sacred Liturgy, a council father intervened at length. In the midst of his intervention he asserted that 'in truth the liturgy is established for men, not men for the liturgy'.[21] This phrase became something of a slogan and was widely popularized in the coming decade.[22] Given that its author was the then archbishop of Milan who was elected Pope Paul VI in June 1963, it could even have been asserted that this phrase reflected the stance of the pope whose responsibility it became to complete and implement the council and its liturgical reform.

There is no doubt that such a slogan is capable of distracting from, if not obscuring the fact that, man is made primarily for the worship of Almighty God, as the first commandment of the Decalogue teaches. So too it could easily fuel an unduly anthropocentric implementation of liturgical reform, both officially and at a local level, with the risk of resultant liturgies in which it is 'modern man' who seems to be worshipped almost to the exclusion of Almighty God. Indeed, these words of Cardinal Montini are still cited by scholars in support of positions that, I would argue, neither the council fathers nor Paul VI held or would recognize as authentic, including a tendency to instrumentalize the sacred liturgy so that it becomes 'the main way for the announcement of the Gospel'.[23] Indeed, one father would use Montini's words as just such a slogan in concluding his intervention some two days later.[24]

---

[21] 'Liturgia nempe pro hominibus est instituta, non homines pro liturgia'. 22 October 1962. *Acta Synodalia*, vol. I, part I, 315; Gil Hellín, *Concilii Vaticani II Synopsis*, 403.

[22] 'Liturgy is for men, not men for the liturgy'. Joseph M. Champlin, *The Priest and God's People at Prayer: The Priest in a Flexible Liturgy* (London: Geoffrey Chapman, 1972), 65.

[23] Massimo Faggioli, *True Reform: Liturgy and Ecclesiology in Sacrosanctum Concilium* (Collegeville, MN: Liturgical Press, 2012), 55.

[24] Bishop Joseph Descuffi (1884–1972), 24 October 1962. *Acta Synodalia*, vol. I, part I, 416; Gil Hellín, *Concilii Vaticani II Synopsis*, 452.

And yet, if one reads Cardinal Montini's intervention – all of it – one finds that his assertion that the liturgy is established for men, not men for the liturgy, has a precise meaning and context: that is, his support for an increased use of the vernacular. In his use of the phrase 'the liturgy is established for men, not men for the liturgy', Montini was arguing that the people should easily be able to understand the instructive parts if the liturgical rites (principally what we now call 'the Liturgy of the Word'). Furthermore, we find that this much-misused phrase follows Cardinal Montini's assertion that 'the use of the ancient language given to us by the fathers, namely that of the Latin language for the Latin Church, should be firm and stable in [the] parts of rite that are sacramental or properly and truly priestly'.[25]

This council father was, along with a great many others, doing nothing other than arguing for the stance which would be articulated in the promulgated constitution with its insistence that 'the use of the Latin language is to be preserved in the Latin rites' while permitting that the limits of the use of the vernacular 'may be extended' (see no. 36). While it is clear that Montini's stance changed later, and that as pope he accepted what he called in November 1969 the 'sacrifice' of Latin in the liturgy,[26] it is a historical fact that on the council floor he was neither arguing for the complete vernacularization of the liturgy (which later, as pope, he permitted), nor was he arguing that the sacred liturgy was something to be refashioned so that that indefinable entity 'modern man' could take centre stage, nor indeed that it was to be instrumentalized as a catechetical or missionary tool.

Certainly what happened in the interpretation and implementation of the constitution is an important and potent area for study, but we shall not have sufficient grounding to do that accurately if we do not read the constitution in a manner that is consistent with the minds of the council fathers. We must be good historians; understanding the historical context of the principles and measures they laid down is crucial.[27] An a

---

[25] '… usus linguae antiquae et a maioribus traditae, videlicet linguae latinae pro Ecclesia latina, firmus sit ac stabilis in iis partibus ritus quae sunt sacramentales ac proprie vereque sacerdotales'. *Acta Synodalia*, vol. I, part I, 314–15; Gil Hellín, *Concilii Vaticani II Synopsis*, 402–3.

[26] See Paul VI's General Audience address of 26 November 1969, no. 8: 'It is here that the greatest newness is going to be noticed, the newness of language. No longer Latin, but the spoken language will be the principal language of the Mass. The introduction of the vernacular will certainly be a great sacrifice for those who know the beauty, the power and the expressive sacrality of Latin. We are parting with the speech of the Christian centuries; we are becoming like profane intruders in the literary preserve of sacred utterance. We will lose a great part of that stupendous and incomparable artistic and spiritual thing, the Gregorian chant'. *L'Osservatore Romano: Weekly Edition in English*, 4 December 1969, 1 and 12. See also the recollections of Rembert G. Weakland OSB, *A Pilgrim in a Pilgrim Church: Memoirs of a Catholic Archbishop* (Grand Rapids, MI: William B. Eerdmans, 2009), 130–1, where he recounts Paul VI's *volte face* in respect of his Apostolic Letter to the supreme moderators of clerical religious institutes obliged to the choral recitation of the Divine Office, *Sacrificium Laudis* of 15 August 1966, which reasserted 'the mandate of preserving the age-old solemnity, beauty and dignity of the choral office, in regard both to [the Latin] language, and to the chant'.

[27] It is to be expected that bodies charged with the implementation of a reform may well find that some measures not originally envisaged may serve the overall purpose to hand. No one thought that the council's work was to itself lay down every single detail of the reform that would follow. However, in the implementation of the Constitution on the Sacred Liturgy any such measures should, surely, serve its fundamental aims articulated in article 14, and respect the principles for development laid down in article 23.

posteriori isogesis of the constitution, as is fashionable in some circles, is simply bad scholarship.[28]

Thirdly, I would make some brief observations on the sources available for the study of the debate of the *Schema* on the Sacred Liturgy.

The Constitution on the Sacred Liturgy promulgated by Paul VI in 1963 was the product of drafting, discussion, debate and further redaction from the first draft of the preparatory liturgical commission in August 1961 to the text promulgated by Paul VI in 1963. There are eight principal redactions of the text, all of which are published.[29]

Following the presentation of the *Schema* at the council in October 1962, two further redactions were made: the *Schema Constitutionis de Sacra Liturgia textus emendatus* of 3 October 1963 and the text as finally promulgated on 4 December 1963. These redactions were the work of the conciliar liturgical commission in the light of the fathers' interventions on the council floor, as well as the written interventions they submitted when it was not possible to make them aurally. For these the four 'parts' of volume I of the *Acta Synodalia Sacrosancti Concilii Oecumenici Vaticani II* and the six 'parts' of volume II are a necessary reference tool, containing the chronological acts of the daily congregations as well as texts of written submissions, etc. These are now available online.[30]

To these fundamental references we should add chapter seven of Nicola Giampietro's book,[31] which gives informative accounts of the meetings of the conciliar liturgical commission of which Father Antonelli (1896–1993) was the secretary – an appointment which, it is true to say, Father Annibale Bugnini CM (1912–82) might have reasonably expected to be given in the light of his work as secretary of the preparatory commission, but, significantly and controversially, was not. Of this Bugnini himself would write 'This was the first sign that the new president of the liturgical commission, Arcadio

---

[28] See, for example, the assertion of Faggioli, *True Reform*, 54–5 that '*Sacrosanctum Concilium* was never supposed to be a legal document to be read by itself, that is, out of the hermeneutical context of other council documents'. Similar assertions appear on page 3. The fact is that neither the fathers of the council, the *Consilium,* nor Paul VI held this position. The implementation of the constitution began immediately following its promulgation, as the constitution instructed, without waiting for any reflection on its hermeneutical context in respect of the other documents. It is true that spirits and orientations attributed to later documents influenced the implementation of the reform, but it is historically untenable to assert that this was intended by the fathers when the constitution was promulgated.

[29] 1. Pontificia Commissio de sacra Liturgia praeparatoria Concilii Vaticani II, *Constitutio de Sacra Liturgia fovenda atque instauranda,* 10 August 1961; 2. Pontificia Commissio de sacra Liturgia praeparatoria Concilii Vaticani II, *Emendatio Capitis I Constitutionis de Sacra Liturgia,* 11–13 October 1961; 3. Pontificia Commissio de sacra Liturgia praeparatoria Concilii Vaticani II, *Constitutio de Sacra Liturgia,* Schema transmissum Sodalibus Commissionis, 15 November 1961; 4. Pontificia Commissio de sacra Liturgia praeparatoria Concilii Vaticani II, *Documenta Sessionis Plenariae,* January 1962; 5. Pontificia Commissio de sacra Liturgia praeparatoria Concilii Vaticani II, *Constitutio de Sacra Liturgia,* Textus approbatus in Sessione Plenaria, 11–13 January 1962; 6. *Schema Constitutionis de Sacra Liturgia,* 23 July and 22 October 1962; 7. *Schema Constitutionis de Sacra Liturgia textus emendatus,* 3 October 1963; 8. *Constitutio de Sacra Liturgia,* 4 December 1963. The first four texts are published in Lameri, *La 'Pontifica Commissio de sacra liturgia praeparatoria Concilii Vaticani II'.* The latter are published in Gil Hellín, *Concilii Vaticani II Synopsis.*

[30] *Acta Synodalia Sacrosancti Concilii Oecumenici Vaticani II,* Available online: https://archive.org/search.php?query=subject%3A%22acta+synodalia%22 (accessed 6 December 2016).

[31] Nicola Giampietro, *The Development of Liturgical Reform: As Seen by Cardinal Ferdinando Antonelli from 1948-1970* (Fort Collins, CO: Roman Catholic Books, 2009), 73–141. Clearly the unpublished *Verbali delle riunioni della Commissione Conciliare di Sacra Liturgia* from which Giampietro draws are an important primary source.

Cardinal Larraona, was following a different course from that of the commission that had drawn up the schema',[32] giving a clear indication that the politics in play are another legitimate area for study. Bugnini's own chapter 'The Liturgical Constitution at the Council', though much shorter and not based on direct experience of the conciliar commission, is a necessary referent given his importance.[33]

During the council the fathers and their *periti* gave numerous interviews and conferences. These, together with the impressions of journalists and other observers can help in an understanding of the period certainly, though I would emphasize that they are at least at one remove from the activity of the council itself and cannot necessarily be used as a basis for establishing the intentions of the council. The later recollections of council fathers are themselves of import, though again it is their words and work at the council itself which is of primary importance in interpreting its meaning.[34]

3 On the Floor of the Council

And so, we return to the council's debate of article 37 of the *Schema* as presented to the fathers.[35] The text presented *in aula* on 22 October 1962 read:

> Ordo Missae ita recognoscatur, sive in generali dispositione sive in singulis partibus, ut clarius percipiatur et actuosam fidelium participationem faciliorem reddat.

> The Order of Mass is to be reviewed, whether in a general way or in the individual parts, so that it may more clearly be understood and so that it renders actual participation of the faithful more straightforward.[36]

As this article was the first of Chapter II, it was not discussed in the coming days, which were themselves devoted to chapter I, although the intervention of Dom Benedict Reetz (1897–1964), abbot president of the Beuronese Benedictine Congregation, raised an issue closely related to the structural reform of the *Ordo Missae*. He asked what would happen to Gregorian chant, which itself contains something sacred and which is proper to the Roman Church, if, as proposed by many, the first part of the Mass (up to the offertory) were to be solely in the vernacular: would chant be condemned to death or become a remnant solely in one or other monastery, as if it were conserved in a museum?[37] The conciliar discussion of the use of the vernacular is itself vast, and

---

[32] Annibale Bugnini, *The Reform of the Liturgy 1948-1975*, trans. Matthew J. O'Connell (Collegeville, MN: Liturgical Press, 1990), 30. Yves Congar, *My Journal of the Council*, 158, noted in his diary that Larraona 'is against the schema and has said so publicly to the Spanish bishops'.

[33] See Bugnini, *The Reform of the Liturgy*, 29–38.

[34] See Alcuin Reid, 'The Fathers of Vatican II and the Revised Mass: The Results of a Survey', *Antiphon* 10 (2006): 170–90.

[35] Space here permits only a brief examination of the conciliar debate itself. I hope to complete this picture in *Continuity or Rupture: A Study of the Second Vatican Council's Reform of the Liturgy* (forthcoming).

[36] *Acta Synodalia*, vol. I, part I, 279.

[37] 'A multis proponitur ut prima pars Missae usque ad Offertorium in lingua vulgari dicuntur. Quid tunc? Cantus gregorianus, qui aliquid sacri in se continet et qui proprius est Ecclesiae Romanae, ad mortem damnabitur, vel in uno vel alio monasterio sicuti in museo conservabitur'. 26 October 1962. *Acta Synodalia*, vol. I, part I, 469–70; Gil Hellín, *Concilii Vaticani II Synopsis*, 477.

we must leave that aside – while remaining conscious that in any assessment of the council's work or of the reform that followed, questions of sacred and vernacular language, of liturgical music, sacred art and architecture, etc. are of great importance: liturgical rites are much, much more than simply ink on paper.

Another father called for various simplifications to the rite of Mass in his intervention on Chapter I, including the reduction of the number of times *Dominus vobiscum* was said, the abolition of signs of the cross over the Sacred Species, and for the universal abolition of the amice and maniple which he claimed 'no longer have any meaning or benefit for the Christian people'.[38]

Two fathers did refer to the reform of the *Ordo Missae* in their written *animadversiones* (observations) on chapter I submitted to the secretariat but not read *in aula*. Bishop José de Jesús Clemens Alba Palacios (1909–97) submitted that, just as the council wished to reform the Church and restore it to its original purity, the Order of Mass should be reformed accordingly.[39] Conversely, in an extensive and considered submission which rejected a radical reconstruction of the Mass, Bishop Smiljan Franjo Cekada (1902–76) argued that the renewal of the Order of Mass should include only small modifications – those truly necessary to render actual participation more straightforward.[40]

When the debate on Chapter II opened on 29 October it was Cardinal Spellman who spoke first. While regarded even before the council as something of a 'liturgical dinosaur',[41] Spellman's intervention does not dispute the need for a truly pastoral renewal of the liturgy. He states:

> In chapter two 'On the Most Holy Mystery of the Eucharist' there is enunciated the highest pastoral goal to be attained in the liturgy, namely, that the faithful be present at this mystery of faith not as inert and mute spectators, but that they participate in the rites and prayers consciously, actively and piously.
>
> The question that arises is only about the means most appropriate to attain this end, and not about the end itself. Therefore, in this regard, it must be accurately recalled that what was said in chapter one about true pastoral usefulness as the highest norm,[42] about the greatest prudence and circumspection in introducing

[38] Bishop Fidel García Martínez (1880–1973): 'quorum pro populo christiano nulla iam manet nec utilitas nec significatio'. 29 October 1962. *Acta Synodalia*, vol. I, part I, 582; Gil Hellín, *Concilii Vaticani II Synopsis*, 532.

[39] 'Quoad s. Liturgia instaurationem, etiam in ordine Missae, attendendum in finem celebrationis Concilii, reformanda nempe Ecclesiam et reducendi ad puritatem primigeniam vultum eius'. *Acta Synodalia*, vol. I, part I, 386.

[40] 'ut in ordine quoque Missae quaedam instaurentur, sed haec fiant pauca: tantum ea, quae maxime necessaria sunt, ut actuosam participationem fidelium faciliorem reddant'. *Acta Synodalia*, vol. I, part I, 388.

[41] See Alcuin Reid, *The Organic Development of the Liturgy: The Principles of Liturgical Reform and Their Relation to the Twentieth Century Liturgical Movement Prior to the Second Vatican Council*, 2nd edn (San Francisco: Ignatius Press, 2005), 219.

[42] See Spellman's intervention in the fourth general congregation, 22 October 1962, *Acta Synodalia*, vol. I, part I, 316–19; Gil Hellín, *Concilii Vaticani II Synopsis*, 404–6. ET: Yzermans, *American Participation at Vatican II*, 149–51.

innovations and about avoiding an exaggerated 'historicism' and a zeal for novelties.[43]

Specifically, in respect of article 37 Spellman observed:

> It is proposed: 'The rite of the Mass is to be so revised ... that it may be more clearly understood and that it may render easier the [actual] participation of the faithful.' This principle, as such, cannot be disputed. It is asked, however, what does 'to revise the rite of Mass' mean? It does not seem that it should be admitted as the only primary principle that those rites which first appeared in the Roman missal in the sixteenth century are to be renewed. Such a principle, if admitted and rigidly applied, would easily lead to revivifying only rites already obsolete. In the fifth or the sixteenth or the twentieth century, the Church, always the same, lives and grows with the mission divinely given her and forms her liturgical structure, at least in part, in every age from her experience of the necessities and benefit of the faithful.
>
> In the same article it is proposed: 'The rite of Mass is to be so revised ... in each of its parts.' This seems to leave the way wide open for every sort of innovation. There are those who would wish that there be fewer signs of the Cross, kisses of the altar, genuflections and bows during the Mass. Again it is asked whether these innovations would be made for the true benefit of the faithful? Sometimes there is talk of a shorter formula for the distribution of Holy Communion, for example, 'The Body of Christ. Amen.' But we must be on our guard lest reverence for the Most Holy Sacrament be lessened. On the other hand, they can do away with all restrictions by which the faithful are kept from receiving Holy Communion at certain Masses.[44] This would be a truly pastoral consideration.[45]

Cardinal Ottaviani intervened on October 30:

> One reads in article 37 of this Chapter: The Order of the Mass, whether in its general disposition or in its singular parts, should be reviewed. What do these words mean? Now, is it a certain revolution of the whole Mass that is desired? Because if the Order of the Mass must be reformed either in its general disposition or in its singular parts, what will remain? What are these words that are so ample and large, that they can freely authorize a reformation? It seems to me that these words ought to be wholly extirpated, or at least clarified. The Order of the Mass has been such for many centuries; the Mass is the centre of the whole of liturgical worship; a most holy thing, well known to each of the faithful who know, especially now thanks to the pastoral work on the liturgy, its singular parts, and the danger is not of causing surprise, but rather that of scandal due to excessive change. It is about a most holy thing that cannot freely be changed during one age. It is about

---

[43] *Acta Synodalia*, vol. I, part I, 598; Gil Hellín, *Concilii Vaticani II Synopsis*, 541–2. ET: Yzermans, *American Participation at Vatican II*, 155.

[44] This was a clear concern of Cardinal Spellman in the wake of the 1955 Holy Week reforms. See Reid, 'Holy Week Reforms Revisited', 242–7.

[45] *Acta Synodalia*, vol. I, part I, 598–9; Gil Hellín, *Concilii Vaticani II Synopsis*, 42. ET: Yzermans, *American Participation at Vatican II*, 155–6.

a most holy thing that should be treated in a holy and venerable manner, and only with difficulty it ought to be touched. At this moment the words of God come to mind given to Moses when approaching the burning bush: 'Take the sandals off your feet for the place on which you stand is holy ground.' In the same way we ought to be careful about proposing changes to the Mass.[46]

Accounts of the council frequently dismiss Spellman and Ottaviani as troglodytes opposed to all progress. But the fact is they articulate reasonable and serious concerns. Furthermore, Spellman's clarity that the principle of enhancing actual participation in the liturgy 'cannot be disputed', and Ottaviani's recognition of the positive effect of 'the pastoral work on the liturgy' gives the lie to those who would malign them. Whatever of these fathers' concerns about future reform, they were not opposed to genuine progress in people acquiring 'the true Christian spirit' through fruitful participation in its 'foremost and indispensable fount' namely 'the public and solemn prayer of the Church'.[47]

Lest we think that Spellman and Ottaviani, with their concerns of undue innovation and revolution, were indulging in the setting up of a straw man, the intervention of Bishop Wilhelm Duschak SVD (1903–97) in the twelfth general congregation (5 November 1962) should be examined. The fifty-nine-year-old Vicar Apostolic of Calapan in the Philippines proposed:

If in our times from this council, and from the whole history of the Church, what is most desired and expected is the renewal of the Mass, and also the greatest of means and guidance that conduces to the active participation of the faithful, then the best method that must be chosen seems to be to go back to the first and original Mass that Christ himself instituted during the Last Supper and just as he ordered that that this be done and repeated in memory of him. …

According to the motto 'to renew all things in Christ' (*omnia instaurare in Christo*) how can we return to the first and most venerable form of the Mass instituted by Christ himself? …

Christian brothers that are not Catholic, but believe in the Eucharistic Christ, will not accept the Latin rite nor any other historical rite, but perhaps are ready to accept an invitation of cooperating, having been aided by experts of all the rites and also of the churches that hold Eucharistic faith, in the composition of the Mass that can truly be called ecumenical Mass or 'Mass of the world' (*Missa orbis*), the Mass would follow the rite of the Lord's Supper and the principles generally and by all enumerated above.

So we would be able to have a truly ecumenical Mass, a Mass of the world, and with it this much desired unity, at least in the Eucharistic remembrance of the Lord. Let the highest authorities of the Church take notice, let the practical and

---

[46] *Acta Synodalia*, vol. I, part II, 18; Gil Hellín, *Concilii Vaticani II Synopsis*, 552–3. For the charged context of this intervention, which famously ended with the presiding Cardinal, Bernard Jan Alfrink (1900–87), interrupting Cardinal Ottaviani after his allotted time had expired, to the applause of the assembled fathers, see Xavier Rynne, *Letters From Vatican City: Vatican Council II (First Session) Background and Debates* (London: Faber & Faber, 1963), 116–17.

[47] St Pius X, Motu Proprio on the Restoration of Sacred Music *Tra le sollecitudini* (22 November 1903); see also *Sacrosanctum Concilium* 14.

theoretical experts take notice. The people of God will have rejoiced in this perfect and intimate Supper that the Apostles rejoiced in. The conception and proposition of the 'Mass of the world' boldly emits an odour, but not of temerity, because we follow the example and precept of Christ the Lord.

It also helps to remember that this council is to be the greatest in the history of salvation and the council known as the council of union.

The conception and proposition of the Mass of the world perhaps is like that mustard seed, which is indeed the smallest (Mt. 13.32-32) but if we would have faith (Mt. 17.19), it will give fruit (Mt. 13.8) and nothing will be impossible (Lk. 17.19).[48]

That evening Bishop Duschak gave a press conference in which he amplified his proposal. The text was promptly translated and published in the journal *Worship*. This elucidation of his intervention *in aula* is of interest:

> It seems to me that, with the exception of the fore-Mass, the Latin Mass could not be greatly modified, with a view to making it more effective liturgically, without fundamental alterations to its characteristic structures. The saying of the Lord about putting a new patch on an old (venerable) garment would seem to apply here. This is true of low Mass, and all the more of the Latin high Mass. We seem to be confronted here with a form of liturgy which has reached its final, essentially immutable stage of development. ...
>
> Basically, what I wish to suggest is that if the Christians of the past centuries could freely create their own rites of the Mass and choose their liturgical languages, then could not the present ecumenical Council, the greatest ever in the number of participants, authorise the creation, with all due reverence, of a new Mass liturgy? A new Mass in accord with the intellectual attainments, the aspirations and the mores of contemporary man? An ecumenical Mass designed for a world which is constantly becoming smaller and more unified?[49]

In his dialogue with journalists on this occasion Duschak went further and asked: 'Why shouldn't the greatest ecumenical council in the Church's history create a new rite – an ecumenical or world Mass – to which Catholics could invite their Protestant brothers who retain a love for the Eucharist?'[50]

In the conciliar debate on the sacred liturgy Bishop Duschak's proposal is singular in its radicalism and is in no sense representative of the more than forty other aural or written interventions concerning article 37 of the *Schema*. One father, the Chilean bishop Ceasar Vielmo (1914–63), made a written submission detailing various, and at times radical, reforms of the *Ordo Missae*. But his proposals were not accompanied by

[48]   *Acta Synodalia*, vol. I, part II, 109–2; Gil Hellín, *Concilii Vaticani II Synopsis*, 643–6.
[49]   Wilhelm Duschak, 'An Ecumenical Mass Liturgy', *Worship* 37 (1962–3): 538–46, at 539–40.
[50]   Anderson, *Council Daybook*, 64.

either the rhetoric or publicity of Duschak,[51] and given that they were contained in a written intervention, would have not been widely known about by the other fathers.[52] Duschak's stance does, however, serve to justify the concerns of some fathers that a liturgical revolution – what one might call, with apologies to Aldous Huxley (1894–1963), a 'brave new liturgical world' – was desired by a small minority.

Of the other interventions, that of Bishop Dwyer, at that time bishop of Leeds and from 1965 to 1981 archbishop of Birmingham, is significant given his role in the implementations of the liturgical reforms throughout England and Wales. On 30 October he took the floor to say:

> Probably enough among us are content with the Order of Mass that we know from our youth. Nevertheless, stirred by the words of many fathers, especially of those from the Church of silence, whose pastoral reasons urge (us) as to why a new order of the Mass is to be established, I am ready to put aside personal desires so as to not impede the work of Holy Spirit in the apostolate.[53]

Yet, he continued: 'If every nation is permitted to make up its own proper Mass, we will not have the reconstruction of the Roman rite, but rather its destruction. And for my part I do not wish to stand at this council at the deathbed of the Roman rite.'[54] Accordingly, he proposed that 'this new order is restricted to the Mass of the Catechumens, so that from the offertory until the end the *Ordo* remains unchanged, and certainly in the Latin language, except for privileges'.[55] Adding that 'the Order of Mass of the Catechumens, however it is changed, and even if it is arranged completely in the vernacular, would be common and the same for everyone who use the Roman rite'.[56]

It is difficult to see in Dwyer's openness and his concern lest the Roman rite die anything other than the universally accepted principle articulated in article 18 of the *Schema* (which would become article 23 of the promulgated constitution) 'that sound tradition may be retained, and yet the way remain open to legitimate progress'.[57] While

---

[51] Bishop Duschak was clearly engaging on a carefully planned media offensive. The report of the archbishop of Canterbury's official observer at the council, Bernard Pawley, relayed: 'The substance of this speech was relayed to my wife on the telephone by the BBC correspondent in Rome, before it was delivered in S. Peter's. ... So much for the "secrecy" of the Council's deliberations!' *Observing Vatican II: The Confidential Reports of the Archbishop of Canterbury's Representative, Bernard Pawley, 1961-1964*, ed. Andrew Chandler and Charlotte Hansen (Cambridge: Cambridge University Press, 2013), 153. In his report on the debate on the *Schema* on the Sacred Liturgy dated 29 October 1962 Pawley records 'For the most part, the suggestions ... are eminently reasonable and acceptable by us. As the Bishop of Ripon remarked, "If they go on like this, they'll find they've invented the Church of England." We often comment that the general principles are similar to those of the Preface of the Book of Common Prayer'. Ibid., 140.

[52] See *Acta Synodalia*, vol. I, part II, 279–85, Gil Hellín, *Concilii Vaticani II Synopsis*, 715–20. Only those working on the conciliar liturgical commission – and significantly, not the other fathers – studied the written interventions.

[53] 30 October 1962. *Acta Synodalia*, vol. I, part II, 37; ; Gil Hellín, *Concilii Vaticani II Synopsis*, 602.

[54] *Acta Synodalia*, vol. I, part II, 38; Gil Hellín, *Concilii Vaticani II Synopsis*, 602.

[55] Such as in Croatia, where the use of the vernacular had a long and authorized history. See further: Reid, *The Organic Development of the Liturgy*, 133.

[56] *Acta Synodalia*, vol. I, part II, 38; Gil Hellín, *Concilii Vaticani II Synopsis*, 602.

[57] 'Ut sana traditio retineatur et tamen via legitimae progressioni aperiatur'. This wording remained unchanged; see Gil Hellín, *Concilii Vaticani II Synopsis*, 76–7.

it is impossible to continue a detailed examination of all the interventions here,[58] what they make clear is twofold. First, that even the fathers labelled as more 'conservative' accepted the legitimacy of reform so as to achieve the aim of more fruitful participation of the whole of Christ's faithful in the sacred liturgy. To that end they widely supported the use of the vernacular in the first part of the Mass, the augmentation of the lectionary and of prefaces and some ritual simplifications.[59] Secondly, it is clear that the council fathers (with perhaps two or three exceptions among more than 2,000 fathers) neither asked for, nor intended, a radical reform of the Roman rite.[60] A revolution in the liturgical life of the Church was simply not on the agenda. Indeed, as we have seen, concerns were expressed lest this occur and do real damage to the spiritual life of the faithful and to the sound aims of the council itself.

[58] In addition to those already cited 'the following fathers' interventions are pertinent to a study of the debate on article 37 of the *Schema*: Augustine Cardinal Bea (1881–1968), *Acta Synodalia*, vol. I, part II, 22–6, Gil Hellín, *Concilii Vaticani II Synopsis*, 556–9; Paul Rush (1903–86), *Acta Synodalia*, vol. I, part II, 35–7, Gil Hellín, 565–7; Francis Cardinal König (1905–2004), *Acta Synodalia*, vol. I, part II, 58, Gil Hellín, 607; Placid Cambiaghi (1900–87), *Acta Synodalia*, vol. I, part II, 59–60, Gil Hellín, 607–8; Juan Carlos Aramburu (1918–84), *Acta Synodalia*, vol. I, part II, 88–90, Gil Hellín, 628–9; Charles Ferrari (1910–92), *Acta Synodalia*, vol. I, part II, 115–16, Gil Hellín, 648; Armand Fares (1904–80), *Acta Synodalia*, vol. I, part II, 116–17, Gil Hellín, 649; Andrew Perraudin (1914–2003), *Acta Synodalia*, vol. I, part II, 122–3, Gil Hellín, 653–4; Paul Estevan (1912–2008), *Acta Synodalia*, vol. I, part II, 123–6, Gil Hellín, 654–6; Eladio Vicuña Aránguiz (1911–2008), *Acta Synodalia*, vol. I, part II, 130–3, Gil Hellín, 659–62; Francis Zauner (1904–94), *Acta Synodalia*, vol. I, part II, 151–3, Gil Hellín, 682–3; Rufino Cardinal Santos (1908–73), *Acta Synodalia*, vol. I, part II, 198–9, Gil Hellín, 800; Francis Austregésilo de Mesquita (1924–2006), *Acta Synodalia*, vol. I, part II, 203, Gil Hellín, 598; Críspulo Beníto Fontúrvel (1905–91), *Acta Synodalia*, vol. I, part II, 205, Gil Hellín, 732; Raphaël I Bidawid (1922–2003), *Acta Synodalia*, vol. I, part II, 206–8 (absent from Gil Hellín); Hugo Bressane De Araújo (1899–1988), *Acta Synodalia*, vol. I, part II, 210–1 (absent from Gil Hellín); Vincent Brizgys (1903–92), *Acta Synodalia*, vol. I, part II, 211–12, Gil Hellín, 539–40; John Baptist da Mota e Albuquerque (1909–84), *Acta Synodalia*, vol. I, part II, 216–17 (absent from Gil Hellín); Carlo Albert Ferrero di Cavallerleone (1903–69), *Acta Synodalia*, vol. I, part II, 223, Gil Hellín, 516; Anselm Giabbini (1908–2004), *Acta Synodalia*, vol. I, part II, 227, Gil Hellín, 669; Charles Heerey (1890–1967), *Acta Synodalia*, vol. I, part II, 235–6, Gil Hellín, 725; Clement Isnard (1917–2011), *Acta Synodalia*, vol. I, part II, 238–40, Gil Hellín, 711–12; Alexander Kovács (1893–1972), *Acta Synodalia*, vol. I, part II, 241 (absent from Gil Hellín); Antonio Kühner y Kühner (1914–91), *Acta Synodalia*, vol. I, part II, 241–3, Gil Hellín, 1049–50; Simon Landersdorfer (1880–1971), *Acta Synodalia*, vol. I, part II, 243–5, Gil Hellín, 604–5; Hanibal Fleitas (1917–76), *Acta Synodalia*, vol. I, part II, 246–7, Gil Hellín, 1050–1; John McEleney (1895–1986), *Acta Synodalia*, vol. I, part II, 249–50, Gil Hellín, 675–7; Sergio Méndez Arceo (1907–92), *Acta Synodalia*, vol. I, part II, 251–4, Gil Hellín, 729–32; Demetrius Moscato (1888–1968), *Acta Synodalia*, vol. I, part II, 254–5, Gil Hellín, 714–15; Francis Muguzera (1921–69), *Acta Synodalia*, vol. I, part II, 256, Gil Hellín, 740; Dragutin Nežic (1908–95), *Acta Synodalia*, vol. I, part II, 257–8, Gil Hellín, 1040–1; Leo Nigris (1884–1964), *Acta Synodalia*, vol. I, part II, 258, Gil Hellín, 600; Marijan Oblak (1919–2008), *Acta Synodalia*, vol. I, part II, 258–9, Gil Hellín, 722–3; Alexander Olalia (1913–73), *Acta Synodalia*, vol. I, part II, 259–60, Gil Hellín, 723–4; René-Georges Pailloux (1902–88), *Acta Synodalia*, vol. I, part II, 260–2 (absent from Gil Hellín); Augustine Sépinski (1900–78), *Acta Synodalia*, vol. I, part II, 272, Gil Hellín, 671–2; José Souto Vizoso (1893–1973), *Acta Synodalia*, vol. I, part II, 274–5, Gil Hellín, 747–8.

[59] The aforementioned (written) interventions of Archbishop Da Mota e Albuquerque and of Bishops Isnard, Kühner y Kühner, Fleitas, Méndez Arceo and Oblak outline proposals for the reform of the Order of Mass in some detail, largely in accordance with the moderate reforms envisaged *in aula*.

[60] The English-language summary of the *Schema* prepared for the English bishops by the *peritus* Lawrence McReavy on 19 October 1962 says that the *Schema* states, uncontroversially, that 'there should be a revision of the Ordo Missae to facilitate understanding and active participation'. *Vatican II As I Saw It: Letters, Journal, Diary and Papers of Lawrence Leslie McReavy*, ed. Cuthbert Johnson (Farnborough: St Michael's Abbey Press, 2015), 325. McReavy's also provides brief notes on the debate on article 37; ibid., 334–5.

4 Redaction by the Conciliar Commission and the Council's Second Session

From the accounts given of the work of the conciliar liturgical commission by Antonelli and Bugnini, there appears to have been no great controversy in the examination of the fathers' observations on article 37. While the questions of extending the use of the vernacular and of the introduction of some form of concelebration seem to have generated much angst,[61] that the Order of Mass was to be revised seems, largely, to have been accepted as an uncontroversial given.

In the council's second session (September to December 1964) the text of Chapter II of the *Schema* as revised by the conciliar liturgical commission was distributed to the fathers on 8 October 1963 with an explanatory introduction by Giacomo Cardinal Lercaro (1891–1976), an elected member of the commission.[62] The numeration of article 37 was changed to 50. It now read:

> Ordo Missae ita recognoscatur, ut singularum partium propria ratio necnon mutua connexio clarius pateant, atque pia et actuosa fidelium participatio facilior reddatur.
>
> Quamobrem ritus, probe servata eorum substantia, simpliciores fiant; ea omittantur quae temporum decursu duplicata fuerunt vel minus utiliter addita; restituantur vero ad pristinam sanctorum Patrum normam nonnulla quae temporum iniuria deciderunt, prout opportuna vel necessaria videantur.
>
> The rite of the Mass is to be reviewed in such a way that the intrinsic nature and purpose of its several parts, as also the connection between them, may be more clearly manifested, and that devout and actual participation by the faithful may be more easily achieved.
>
> For this purpose the rites are to be simplified, due care being taken to preserve their substance; elements which, with the passage of time, came to be duplicated, or were added with but little advantage, are now to be discarded; other elements which have suffered injury through accidents of history are now to be restored to the vigour which they had in the days of the holy fathers, as may seem useful or necessary.[63]

The printed copy of the amendments given to each of the fathers included the full text of the *declaratio* added to the *Schema* by the preparatory commission and referred to by Bishop Jenny and other fathers in the first session, but not hitherto made available in its entirety.[64] The *declaratio* opened with the 'Hodiernus Ordo Missae, qui decursu saeculorum succrevit retinendus est'. It then went on to specify that a distinction would be made between the two parts of the rite, the 'liturgy of the Word' which would properly be celebrated from the chair and the ambo (as hitherto in the pontifical rites) and the 'liturgy of the Eucharist' which would properly be celebrated at the altar. Later

---

[61] On concelebration, see Alcuin Reid, 'Concelebration Today, Yesterday and Tomorrow', in Joseph de Sainte-Marie OCD, *The Holy Eucharist – The World's Salvation* (Leominster: Gracewing, 2015), xvii–xxxix.

[62] See *Acta Synodalia*, vol. II, part II, 276–9.

[63] Ibid., 284.

[64] See ibid., 289.

Germano-Gallic rites were to be reviewed with a view to giving priority to earlier traditions.

Specifically, the *declaratio* stated that signs of the cross, kissing of the altar, bows and other similar rites were to be simplified; the prayers at the foot of the altar were to be shortened and simplified; the readings were to be read facing the people towards whom they were to be announced; an offertory procession was to be introduced as in the Ambrosian rite; the offertory prayers were to be revised and to be more sensitive to the offering of the gifts after the Consecration; the *super oblata* prayer was to be prayed aloud; prefaces were to be increased; the doxology at the end of the Canon was to be prayed aloud with the people responding 'Amen'; the signs of the cross in the doxology were to be abolished and reduced throughout the Canon itself; the embolism following the *Pater noster* was to be said aloud as was the fraction prayer and its conclusion; the fraction and the *pax* were to be rearranged in a more logical manner; restrictions on which faithful may receive Holy Communion in what Masses were to be abolished; Holy Communion was to be distributed with the formula from the Ambrosian rite: 'Corpus Christi. Amen.' The end of Mass was to finish with the blessing followed by the 'Ite missa est'. A simplification of the rubrics, including in pontifical rites, was foreseen, as was the extension of the possibility of sung Mass with a deacon (without a subdeacon) beyond the Holy Week ceremonies for which this practice had been authorized in the 1950s.

Bishop Jesús Enciso Viana (1906–64), another elected member of the conciliar liturgical commission, presented a *relatio* to the fathers. In speaking to this he highlighted the three areas that were widely disputed: the use of the vernacular, the reception of Holy Communion under both species, and concelebration.[65] The printed text, however, deals with each article revised giving details of the commission's rationale and its responses to various proposals made by the fathers. In respect of article 37 (50) the *relatio* specifically recalls Bishop Dwyer's proposal that

> this new order is restricted to the Mass of the Catechumens, so that from the Offertory until the end the *Ordo* remains unchanged, and certainly in the Latin language, except for privileges. The Order of Mass of the Catechumens, however it is changed, and even if it is arranged completely in the vernacular, would be common and the same for everyone who use the Roman rite.[66]

The commission's response was that 'it was not possible to establish the desired distinction between the first and the second part of the Mass absolutely, since even in the second part of the Mass there were some things, albeit of minor importance, which, it was held, be revised, for example, certain signs of the cross'.[67] Certainly, this

---

[65] See ibid., 290–308.

[66] 'Hic novus ordo restringatur ad Missam catechumenorum, ita ut ab Offertorio usque ad finem Ordo Missae immutatus maneat, et quidem lingua latina, salvo privilegio. Ordo Missae catechumenorum, utcumque mutatus et etiam si totus in lingua vulgari instructus, communis et idem sit pro omnibus, qui rito romano utuntur'. Ibid., 300.

[67] 'distinctio desiderata inter primam et secundam partem Missae non potest nimis absolute statui, quia etiam in secunda parte Missae aliqua sunt, etsi minores momenti, quae revidenda dicuntur, v. gr., quaedam crucissignationes'. Ibid., 301.

response accords with the intention of the pre-conciliar commission articulated in the *declaratio*.

As is evident, the revised text of article 50 had a new second sentence which included the statement that the 'rites are now to be restored to the vigour which they had in the days of the holy fathers', borrowing the language used by St Pius V in his Bull *Quo Primum* (14 July 1570) promulgating the *Missale Romanum* of 1570.[68] This sentence is somewhat ambiguous and is capable of being read in many ways. Bishop Duschak might have read it as an approbation of his 'ecumenical Mass of the World', whereas Cardinal Ottaviani may have seen it as a licence for the very revolution he feared. Others still, like Bishop Dwyer, may have read it and have resigned themselves to losing some precious elements of the rite for an apparent pastoral good.

How are we to interpret it? The addition of a phrase taken from the bull promulgating the 1570 missal was hardly likely to be seen as a statement of revolutionary intent.[69] It caused no comment *in aula* and did not prevent the smooth passage of the revised texts in the second session. And if we do read the fathers' interventions – all of them – it is simply not possible to assert that a revolution (Duschakian or otherwise) was what they called for or intended. Indeed, the debate on article 37 (50) proves the opposite. It shows that the fathers accepted the principle that, so as to achieve a greater *participatio actuosa*, a moderate reform of the Order of Mass was desirable, specifically along the lines of the *declaratio* given to them with the assurance that 'Hodiernus Ordo Missae, qui decursu saeculorum succrevit, *certe* retinendus est'. Thus one may assert that the only sound interpretations of this additional sentence are ones which accord with these fundamental intentions of the fathers,[70] regardless of what interpretations and uses this sentence may have had laid upon it subsequently.

Article 50 – and the other amendments proposed to Chapter II – were voted on immediately and received overwhelming approval: 2,278 in favour, 12 against, 1 in favour with modifications and 7 null votes.[71] This text underwent no further redaction and is the text promulgated by Bl. Paul VI in the Constitution on the Sacred Liturgy on 4 December 1963.

5 After the Promulgation of *Sacrosanctum Concilium*

It is worth noting two important but divergent events in respect of the Order of Mass following the promulgation of the Constitution on the Sacred Liturgy.

---

[68] See Reid, *The Organic Development of the Liturgy*, 41–2, 48.

[69] Even if some may see a strategic 'time bomb' here. Antonelli rather than Bugnini being the secretary of the conciliar liturgical commission would seem to discount this theory in the absence of further evidence. See Michael Davies, *Liturgical Time Bombs in Vatican II* (Rockford, IL: TAN Books and Publishers, 2003).

[70] It is interesting to note that the American *peritus* Frederick R. McManus (1923–2005) 'at a press conference following the council meeting [of 8 October 1963] gave the Last Gospel of the Mass as an example of an "addition." He said a sung Mass would be an example of the "duplications" where parts of the Mass are duplicated between the priest celebrant and the choir.' Anderson, *Council Daybook*, 171.

[71] See *Acta Synodalia*, vol. II, part II, 329.

The first is the appearance of the *Ordo Missae* jointly promulgated by the Sacred Congregation for Rites and the *Consilium* on 27 January 1965 prefaced by a decree mandating that it be adopted in new editions of the missal.[72] Of this 1965 Order of Mass, no less than Monsignor Klaus Gamber has written:

> The type of revision of the liturgy of the Mass envisioned by the Council was the *Ordo Missae* published in 1965. ... The revision made in 1965 did not touch the traditional liturgical rite. In accordance with the mandate of Article 50 of the *Consitution on the Sacred Liturgy*, it had been primarily concerned with removing some later additions to the Order of Mass.[73]

The sources make clear, though, that the *Consilium* charged with implementing the constitution, at least, regarded this as a merely provisional step,[74] as the second event, albeit at the time one that was utterly secret, makes clear.

Coetus or 'study group' 10 of the *Consilium* was itself, naturally enough, working on the reform of the Order of the Mass, for that was its mandate. Its *first* draft outline of a new rite of Mass is dated 22 October 1964.[75] A comparison of this to the *Ordo* promulgated in January 1965 is, however, illustrative. The proposal outlines a Mass with no preparatory prayers or *Confiteor* – the Introit, Kyrie, Gloria and Collect are all that occur in before the Epistle. It reduces the offertory prayers to a simple formula for the mixing of water and wine referring to the wedding at Cana followed by a joint holding up of the bread and wine accompanied by the words of the *Didache*: 'Even as this broken bread was scattered over the hills, and was gathered together and became one, so let your church be gathered together from the ends of the earth into your kingdom'; and followed by the prayer *In spiritu humilitatis*. The *Orate fratres* and other offertory prayers are abolished. The Canon is recited in a loud voice with many fewer ritual gestures and genuflections. The *Pater noster* is recited by all and the communion and concluding rites are reorganized, largely according to the *declaratio* mentioned earlier.

This document demonstrates a sharp disparity between the work of *Coetus* 10 of the *Consilium* in October 1964 and those responsible for the promulgation of the January 1965 Order of Mass. Clearly one must study the work of the *Consilium* in greater depth. Nevertheless this brief foray into its work – and by no means on an insignificant matter – suggests that

---

[72] *Ordo Missae: Ritus Servandus in Celebratione Missae et de Defectibus in Celebratione Missae Occurrentibus*, editio typica (Vatican City: Typis Polyglottis Vaticanis, 1965). While this *Ordo Missae* is declared to be an 'editio typica', it is to be noted that no such edition of a '1965 missal' exists. The closest typical editions are 1962 and 1970. The various and varying missals published from 1965 are the result of editorial choices made locally. Professor Hans-Jürgen Feulner of the University of Vienna has promoted research into the various missals published in the wake of the 1965 *Ordo Missae*.

[73] Klaus Gamber, *The Reform of the Roman Liturgy: Its Problem and Background* (San Juan Capistrano, CA and Harrison, NY: Una Voce Press and Foundation for Catholic Reform, 1993), 33–4. Gamber continues: 'The publication of the *Ordo Missae* of 1969, however, created a new liturgical rite. In other words, the traditional liturgical rite had not simply been revised as the Council had intended. Rather, it had been completely abolished.'

[74] See Alcuin Reid, '*Sacrosanctum Concilium* and the Reform of the *Ordo Missae*', *Antiphon* 10 (2006): 277–95, at 286–90.

[75] *Schemata* no. 44 *De missali* no. 9. See Marizio Barba, *La riforma conciliare dell' 'Ordo Missae'*, 2nd edn (Rome: Edizione Liturgiche, 2008), 365–9.

what Gamber regarded as 'the type of revision of the liturgy of the Mass envisioned by the Council' was, seemingly, dead in the water from the outset regardless of the aural and written interventions or indeed of the votes of the fathers of the council *in aula*.

6 Conclusion

On 31 October 1962 Bishop Elchinger sought to 'calm the spirits' of those fathers of the council who feared 'a complete revolution of the Order of Mass and the death of the Roman rite'. What was envisaged was 'not ... a revolution but only an evolution – a pastoral evolution – something sound and prudent', he assured them. In respect of such an evolution the written intervention from the first session of the council of the veteran archbishop of Salerno, Demetrius Moscato, advised that

> the penetration and interweaving of the words and the forms of our liturgy with divine things is such that if they are let go, it would have seemed to take away the soul from Christian piety or at least undermine it. Whence things must be managed with every reverence and like moderation. We even know that in the course of the centuries changes and accommodations have been made and to this extent are possible if the pastoral exigencies of souls require this.
>
> The cross stands while the world turns and also the cross advances as the world turns. And in fact, what is divine is irreformable and immutable; but what is immutable is not unmoving. Therefore, the cross advances in the newness of circumstances and of human life.[76]

Today, more than fifty years later, neither Archbishop Moscato nor Bishop Elchinger are here to assess the liturgical reform in the light of the conciliar debate *in aula*. Yet the question as to whether an evolution or a revolution in fact occurred remains. So too does the question of whether 'the highest pastoral goal' spoken of 'even' by Cardinal Spellman has been attained.

The answers to these questions are of more than historical or academic importance, for as the fathers knew only too well, the rite of the Mass is at the very heart of the life and mission of the Church – it involves, as Archbishop Moscato observed, 'the penetration and interweaving of the words and the [liturgical] forms ... with divine things'. If we have been the victims of a revolution, if we have taken away the soul from Christian piety or have in some way undermined it, or have jeopardized the noble pastoral goals of the council fathers, we must reconsider our recent liturgical history and our current liturgical practice as a matter of urgency. If this is indeed the case, to borrow Cardinal Sarah's words, 'let us ask the Lord to give us the love and the humility and wisdom so to do'.[77]

---

[76] *Acta Synodalia*, vol. I, part II, 255, Gil Hellín, *Concilii Vaticani II Synopsis*, 714.
[77] Robert Cardinal Sarah, 'Towards an Authentic Implementation of *Sacrosanctum Concilium*', Chapter 2, p. 10 in this book.

11

Sing a New Song to the Lord – Towards a Revised Translation of the *Liturgy of the Hours*

Alan Hopes

1 Some Initial Considerations

In some senses, the proposal of a revision of the translation of a liturgical text arises as soon as that translation is implemented. The recent new English translation of the *Roman Missal* was the first retranslation of the liturgical books issued after the Second Vatican Council.[1] In the case of the missal, the revised translation was almost forty years in coming. Its publication immediately drew attention to the need to revise all the liturgical books, which depend on the missal for some of their texts. Chiefly among these, is the *Liturgy of the Hours*, or as it is more commonly called in the UK, the *Divine Office*.[2]

It was the American Bishops' Conference (USCCB) that took the initiative in this respect and was the first to announce a proposed revision of their edition of the *Liturgy of the Hours*.[3] The Latin-rite bishops of the USCCB approved a 'scope of work' for the future second edition of the *Liturgy of the Hours* during their November 2012 plenary meeting. The scope of work was approved on a vote of 189 to 41 with one abstention.[4]

They have announced that in the revised edition the psalter will make use of the Revised Grail Psalter, which was approved for liturgical use in 2010.[5] The collects from the third edition of the *Roman Missal* will be put in place for Sundays, solemnities, feasts and memorials. Biblical texts will be taken from their current Lectionary for

---

1 *The Roman Missal: Renewed by Decree of the Most Holy Second Ecumenical Council of the Vatican, Promulgated by Authority of Pope Paul VI and Revised at the Direction of Pope John Paul II*, English translation according to the third typical edition (London: Catholic Truth Society, 2011).

2 *The Divine Office: The Liturgy of the Hours according to the Roman Rite, As Renewed by the Decree of the Second Vatican Council and Promulgated by the Authority of Pope Paul VI*, approved for use in Australia, England & Wales, Ireland, New Zealand, Scotland, 3 vols. (London: Collins, 1974).

3 *The Liturgy of the Hours according to the Roman Rite*, English translation prepared by the International Commission on English in the Liturgy, 4 vols. (New York: Catholic Book Publishing, 1986).

4 United States Conference of Catholic Bishops, Committee on Divine Worship, *Newsletter* 48 (2012): 41.

5 *The Revised Grail Psalms: A Liturgical Psalter*, Prepared by the Benedictine Monks of Conception Abbey (Collegeville, MN: Liturgical Press, 2012).

Mass approved for liturgical use.[6] Orations, hymns, new texts from the Proper of Saints, and additional antiphons for the canticles of Zechariah and Mary for use on Sundays and solemnities are being translated by the International Commission on English in the Liturgy (ICEL). The USCCB Committee on Divine Worship will also work with ICEL to determine the best course in regard to the retranslation of certain elements, such as the intercessions, the *Te Deum* and the General Instruction on the *Liturgy of the Hours*. It is envisioned that other elements, such as the texts of the Gospel canticles and the non-biblical readings of the Office of Readings, will remain in their current form.

The request from the USCCB for assistance in the production of a revised edition of the *Liturgy of the Hours* has resulted in a major translation project for ICEL, which will take several years. The USCCB seeks to publish a revised text which incorporates newly translated material alongside elements drawn from the current text. In undertaking this task, the conference has requested ICEL's assistance in providing the following elements for the revised edition:

- the complete selection of hymns as found in the *Liturgia Horarum*,
- *the Magnificat* and *Benedictus* antiphons for Sundays of the three-year cycle,
- the antiphons of the four-week psalter,
- the intercessions,
- the orations from the four-week psalter,
- the *Te Deum*,
- and the Marian antiphons for use at Compline.

You will understand, at once, that this is an enormous undertaking, as the sheer quantity of text puts this project almost on the scale of the *Roman Missal* translation in its magnitude. As ICEL prepares translations for potential use in all its member and associate conferences, these texts have to go through the established process of the appraisal of the bishops' conferences at the two levels of Green and Grey Books. It is envisaged that the *Liturgy of the Hours* project represents at least another four years' work before a text will be published for liturgical use.

There is much to be enthusiastic about in this proposed revised edition. The decision of the USCCB to incorporate the whole body of hymnody, as found in the Latin text, represents a massive recovery of a neglected element of this text. While it does not, in any way, preclude the use of other material, sourced either in an appendix or elsewhere, it does offer, in the body of the text, these jewels of our liturgical patrimony, hitherto unavailable in their entirety in the liturgical book in English.

Although many of these hymns are already available in English translations made from the nineteenth century onwards, the translators have tried to consider some of the very particular demands of their varied use in a twenty-first-century context. For this reason, the draft translations of these hymns do not rhyme but are in free verse which closely follows the metre and pattern of accentuation of the original Latin texts,

---

[6]   *Lectionary for Mass for Use in the Dioceses of the United States*, second typical edition, 4 vols. (Totowa, NJ: Catholic Book Publishing, 1998–2002).

enabling them to be sung either to the chant melody as given in the *Liber Hymnarius*[7] or a metrical hymn tune that might be more easily known.

ICEL is offering the chant melodies of these hymns at the Grey Book as it is recognized that their 'singability' is an important aspect of the reception of these texts. As many people pray the *Liturgy of the Hours* alone, there has also been an attempt to ensure that these texts have an integrity as spoken or read texts, avoiding wherever possible awkward inversions which are commonly used to preserve the rhyme scheme and have a tendency to obscure the sense.

The *Magnificat and Benedictus* antiphons follow the readings of the three-year cycle and are most often direct quotations from these Sunday gospels. Where this is not the case, they are often glosses on a Scriptural text or use older versions of the Scriptures particularly chosen to favour a Christological reading.

The preparation of these translations has taken into consideration majority readings of the versions most commonly used among ICEL conferences, although clearly in the United States, the resonances with the New American Bible Revised Edition texts of the Lectionary and the Revised Grail Psalter (Conception Abbey version) have also been taken into consideration. It is probably important at this point to state clearly that it lies with each Bishops' Conference to determine which version of the Scriptures is used in their territory. Currently at least half a dozen different versions are in use in English-speaking territories.

The intercessions as a body of text have probably generated more negative criticism than any other element of the *Liturgy of the Hours*. Their widely varying form and content reflect the fact that they were originally written by a number of different compilers, possibly working in a variety of languages and were only subsequently translated into Latin.

Translators have tried to equalize these discrepancies of style, while attempting to be faithful in transmitting the content of the Latin texts. There has also been an attempt to reinforce the litanic quality of this aspect of the text and to bear in mind that in some contexts they may also be sung. Once again, there has been care to identify the many Scriptural allusions and quotations which underpin these texts with reference to a range of Scriptural versions.

As yet, ICEL has not begun work on the *Te Deum* or the Marian antiphons. It is envisaged that, like the hymns, these will be presented with their chant melodies. The orations of the psalter are among the texts that were in draft form before the completion of the Missal translation. They are now being reviewed in the light of the Missal translation along which they will stand.

A further source of texts is the *Supplement to the Liturgy of the Hours,* which supplies proper texts for feasts that were added to the Universal Calendar since the last edition of the *Liturgy of the Hours.* This supplement is already at the stage of a Grey Book in the bishops' conferences and so will be available for use with current editions before the revised edition of the *Liturgy of the Hours* is in use.

Although the USCCB is in a sense the commissioning conference of this *Liturgy of the Hours* project, it is confidently expected that other conferences and groups of

---

[7] *Liber Hymnarius cum Invitatoriis et Aliquibus Responsoriis* (Solesmes: Abbaye St.-Pierre, 1983).

conferences will, in due course, wish to produce their own revised editions. At that time, they will have at their disposal all of the elements ICEL offers from which to assemble their revised edition. The bishops of the Commission have decided to issue *Liturgy of the Hours* material in seasonal fascicles, the first of which, containing texts for Advent and Christmas, is currently a Grey Book, Lent and Easter is a Green book, as is Ordinary Time and the four-week psalter. In order that there might be a greater appreciation of what might be expected in a revised edition, I would like to consider each of the individual elements of new translation that are being made available for inclusion in such a revision.

2 The Hymns

The following five basic principles or considerations have guided the work on the preparation of the translation of the Latin hymns:

2.1 Fidelity to the Latin Text

The Latin hymns focus on the theological and spiritual significance of the feasts of the liturgical year or the hours of the liturgical day. They are marked by a sobriety that is based on a solid and deep familiarity with Scripture, on the one hand, and with the liturgical tradition of the Church, on the other. Over time, individuals and communities learn to taste and appreciate the native sobriety of the Latin hymns; and once they are comfortable with this idiom that is the Church's heritage, then the theological and spiritual content of the hymns becomes anything but flat and lifeless. The hymns truly come to life, as one begins to understand that they are vehicles for the unveiling of the liturgical mystery. Expressed through rich and poetic imagery in a simple, yet elevated style, the hymns draw us into the flow of the unified thought that reveals the feast or the liturgical hour. Often, the Latin hymn will move with ever increasing richness and depth from a presentation of an historical event or an image from nature to the spiritual reality that stands behind the event or image to conclude with our participation in this spiritual reality. These texts provide a magnificent lesson and a beautiful impetus to fervent prayer.

In this undertaking, it has been recognized that the task of the translator is to produce a faithful rendering of the hymn text, not to rewrite it. The original thought should be retained, and if a hymn is written in the second or third person, plural or singular, English translations should respect the form, insofar as possible. Because Latin is a highly inflected language, many transitional words are not actually present in the Latin text of the hymns, but only implied, whereas English grammar requires more transitional words for clear expression, which must be taken into account in the work on the translation. The natural rules of English usage should be respected, while striving to be faithful to the original Latin. The goal of the translation, therefore, is to provide a careful and accurate rendering of the Latin text in natural and idiomatic English, so that the entire message of the original hymn may be understood and contemplated in a new idiom.

2.2 Nobility of Expression

Hymns are sung prayers in poetic form. They have a prominent part in the liturgy and must be respected first and foremost as prayers. The aspect of poetry and music adds an element of beauty to prayer. It has the power to move the soul, aids in chanting and facilitates memorization. Poetry, however, must not be allowed to dominate or obscure the meaning of the prayer.

Complicated, convoluted phrases should, whenever possible, be avoided. Worthy English should be employed throughout, and sentimental, colloquial or archaic expressions should be avoided, because liturgical prayer should bear an objective character which is suitable for all.

2.3 Rhyme

The patterns of accentuation in the English language are somewhat less regular when compared to many romance tongues, and, in the opinion of many, rhyme or assonance can soften and considerably enhance it. It is true that many Latin hymns do not strictly rhyme, though rhyme may occur merely as a function of the natural inflection of the language; for example, a series of words in the genitive and/or accusative case may all end in '-um'. For this reason, and others of a similar nature, the Latin language offers a pleasing, natural assonance. This natural assonance both facilitates the artistic use of rhyme in Latin poetry and also minimizes the impact of rhyme on the poetic metre of the verse. On the other hand, due to the heavy stress accent natural to English, and due to the fact that English is not an inflected language, the use of rhyme brings into a stanza of English verse a dominant element that controls the structure of the verse. This may easily lead to the imposition of a structure that is alien to the natural rhythm and assonance of Latin verse. It also may require the sacrifice of content and nuance in favour of words that rhyme in English.

2.4 Adaptability of the Hymn Texts to Various Uses

Particular attention has been paid to the rhythm and metre of each text, allowing for both the sung and spoken recitation of each hymn. When the hymns are sung, many communities desire to sing them to the traditional Gregorian chant melodies; other communities are accustomed to using more modern, strophic melodies. Since the translation should accommodate either style of singing these texts, in the process of translation each text has been sung to the Gregorian melody associated with it and also to a metrical hymn tune. For this reason, certain metrical tunes will favour the natural accentuation of the texts above other tunes of the same metre.

Each hymn is accompanied with a chant setting. The chant settings are taken from the *Liber Hymnarius*. In the case of texts which recur throughout the liturgical year, such as the hymns for Compline (Night Prayer), the melody given is the melody for weekdays in Ordinary Time. The other seasonal melodies for these texts will also be made available. It is envisaged that there will also be a suggested metrical hymn tune assigned to each text.

3 The Antiphons

The second typical edition (*editio typica altera*) of the *Liturgia Horarum* published in 1985 has provided new antiphons for the *Magnificat* and *Benedictus* for use on Sundays and some solemnities throughout the year.[8] These new antiphons reflect the three-year cycle of Gospel readings for Sundays and solemnities in the *Lectionary for Mass* and, for the most part, are derived from or based on these readings. The following four considerations have been brought to bear on the translation of these new antiphons.

3.1 Textual Considerations

The antiphon texts are not necessarily to be seen as quotations of Scripture passages but as 'texts of ecclesiastical composition'.[9] As such, they are texts constructed for liturgical use. Many of the antiphons have been *centonized*, consisting of a patchwork of two or more verses from different sections of the Gospel narrative upon which they are based. They almost always at least allude to, if not quote, Scriptural passages, sometimes combining and conflating terms and meanings from various sources. The translation should respect those associations, which are meant to evoke a sensibility that is both biblical and ecclesial and, consequently, liturgical. Therefore, in keeping with the nature of these texts, it is 'the text of the Latin *editio typica* itself that is to be translated'.[10]

Whereas most of the antiphon texts are derived from or based on the Neo-Vulgate text, some are derived from or based on the Vulgate text. Furthermore, of their nature these texts do not precisely replicate the content of the Hebrew or Greek originals and consequently contemporary translations of the Scriptures translated from critical editions of the ancient texts. Still the character of the antiphons also requires that those who recite or sing the translation recognize the familiar biblical passage on which the translation is based and that the translation be able to be used alongside any of the currently employed translations of the Scriptures.

For the sake of the appropriation of the texts, variant translations of a single term should be avoided, if and when possible. Because of the highly inflected nature of the Latin language, antecedents are readily perceived by those who know Latin. It is sometimes necessary in the English text, however, to introduce an element not explicit in the source text, for example, the name 'Jesus' when there is only a pronoun.

3.2 Oral and Aural Considerations

Particular attention should be paid to the rhythm of the translated text, since rhythm reinforces memory and the prayerful appropriation of the text. Insofar as possible,

---

[8] *Liturgia Horarum iuxta Ritum Romanum*, Editio typica altera, 4 vols. (Vatican City: Libreria Editrice Vaticana, 1985).
[9] Congregation for Divine Worship and the Discipline of the Sacraments, Fifth Instruction for the Right Implementation of the Constitution on the Sacred Liturgy *Liturgiam Authenticam* (28 March 2001), no. 23.
[10] Ibid.

awkward phrasing and syntax and difficult juxtaposition of consonant clusters should be avoided. Words or phrases that would be confusing or ambiguous when heard should likewise be avoided. In the process of translation, the texts should always be read aloud to test their suitability for proclamation.

3.3 Musical Considerations

Antiphons are by their very nature musical texts intended for singing.[11] Texts like the antiphons are lyrical in form and 'do not yield their fuller meaning, unless they are sung'.[12] In assessing the translation of the antiphons, close attention should be paid to the rhythm of these texts and to their oral proclamation both as spoken and potentially sung texts. The translation of these antiphon generally reflects the 'sprung rhythm' patterns which have characterized the various editions of the *Grail Psalter*.

3.4 Editorial Considerations

The Scriptural citations that appear above each antiphon are given as an aid to the appraisal of the texts and do not form part of the *editio typica* of the text and will not appear in the final version of the text. The citations also help to illustrate that many of the antiphons are *centonized* derivations from more than one Scriptural verse.

4 The Intercessions

The *Liturgia Horarum* provides different intercessory formularies (designated *preces* in the Latin text) for Vespers (Evening Prayer) and Lauds (Morning Prayer) of each day of the four-week Psalter in Ordinary Time, for Advent, Christmas Time, Lent and Easter Time in the Proper of Time, for certain feasts in the Proper of Saints, for the Common of Saints, and for the Office for the Dead. The term *preces,* translated in the *Liturgy of the Hours* as 'intercessions', applies to both the intercessions at Vespers (Evening Prayer) and to the invocations for dedicating the day to God at Lauds (Morning Prayer).[13]

    This prayer form of the *preces* is new to the history of the *Liturgy of the Hours*, and the texts themselves were newly composed by various members of the *coetus* (committee) on the Breviary of the *Consilium* for the Implementation of the Constitution on the Sacred Liturgy.[14] While petitions of this kind are new to the Divine Office, the *preces* for Vespers (Evening Prayer) always conclude with a petition for the dead, thus preserving the pre-conciliar tradition of a brief prayer for the dead at the end of the hour. Members of the *coetus,* who had provided sample vernacular translations of the intercessions, encouraged some freedom in the translation of these texts,[15] and this

---

[11] See *The Divine Office*, The General Instruction on the *Liturgy of the Hours*, no. 277.

[12] Ibid., no. 269.

[13] See ibid., no. 182.

[14] See Sacred Congregation for Divine Worship, *Preces: Ad Laudes Matutinas et ad Vesperas Officii Divini Instaurandi* (Vatican City: Typis Polyglottis Vaticanis, 1969).

[15] *Preces*, Introductio, no. 4.

same freedom was later referred to in the General Instruction on the *Liturgy of the Hours*, which states: 'Episcopal Conferences have the right to adapt the formulas of *The Divine Office* and approve new intercessions, keeping however the following norms [nos. 185 to 193]'.[16]

The new ICEL translation of these Latin texts attempts to render the whole sense of the Latin in English, but some minor syntactical accommodations had to be made in order to take into account those parts of the texts that either serve as a cue for the community's response or may be prayed by the entire community. It is also recognized that in several instances, the Latin texts of the intercessions were slightly altered or changed in the text given in the second typical edition.

The following considerations were taken into account in the preparation of the translation of the intercessions:

4.1 Scriptural and Patristic Considerations

All the intercessions allude to and rely heavily and frequently upon Scriptural texts and occasionally on patristic and conciliar texts. In the preparation of this translation special care has been taken to reflect these allusions and to ensure that the biblical text is recognizable and can readily fit alongside any of the currently approved translations of the Scriptures.

4.2 Liturgical Considerations

The intercessions consist of an introduction, followed by a response, then by four to six intentions, and conclude with the Lord's Prayer. If prayed in common, the introduction is said by the priest or minister, the response is said by the priest or minister and then repeated by the entire community, the intentions, which are divided into two parts, are said by the priest or minister in their entirety or are divided between the priest or minister, with the second part said by the community as an alternative response.

While the intercessions in the *Liturgy of the Hours* share some similarities with the sample texts of the Universal Prayer in the *Roman Missal*, there are significant differences between the two forms, not only in the way they are prayed in common, but also in their content. Unlike the intentions given in the missal, which contain a statement of what is being prayed for, the intentions in the *Liturgy of the Hours* directly address God.[17] Furthermore most of the intentions in the missal conclude with a cue, for example, 'let us pray to the Lord', which directly signals when the community is to say or sing the response. This cue is not present in the texts of the *Liturgy of the Hours*.

4.3 Linguistic and Stylistic Considerations

A review of the texts of the *preces* will show a somewhat wide variety of syntactical structures and content. In the translation, every attempt has been made to fully capture

---

[16] General Instruction on the *Liturgy of the Hours*, no. 184.
[17] See ibid., no. 191.

the content of the original, while at the same time the demands of the communal praying of these texts in English necessitated, insofar as possible, a regularity of syntactical pattern.

Thus, for example, many of the introductions to the response end with a verb in the present subjunctive (e.g. 'supplices quaeramus', translated as 'let us humbly ask') or with a present participle in Latin. To serve as a cue for the response, participles like 'dicentes' are translated 'as we say', rather than 'saying' (see also 'clamantes', 'deprecantes'). This is the same approach taken to the translation of all the present participles that conclude the Prefaces in the Missal (e.g. 'as we acclaim') and cue the *Sanctus*.

The intentions are divided into two parts, which allow for the first part to be said by the priest or minister and the second by the congregation, when this has been the customary way of praying them. To facilitate congregational participation, the syntax of the translation has been slightly simplified, even in the case of shorter intentions. For example, the intention 'Qui venisti contritis corde mederi – populi tui sana languores' is translated, 'You came to heal the contrite of heart – cure the weaknesses of your people' rather than 'You who came to heal the contrite of heart – cure the weaknesses of your people'.

5 The Scriptural Versions Used in Readings

The decision as to which version of the Scriptures is used lies with the Bishops' Conference in each territory. Their decision is then confirmed by the Holy See. Currently about half a dozen different translations are used in English-speaking conferences. Since the implementation of the new translation of the *Roman Missal*, several conferences have decided to adopt the Revised Standard Version (in its Catholic edition) as the basis of their Lectionary, given the fact that stylistically it complements the new Missal translation in vocabulary and register.[18] In such cases, one would presume that the same version might also be used in those conferences as the basis for a revised *Liturgy of the Hours*. In many places, this discussion is still under way and as yet, no conference, with the exception of the USCCB, has declared their hand in relation to a revised edition of the *Liturgy of the Hours*.

6 A Two-Year Cycle for the Office of Readings

There has been talk for many years now about the possibility of a two-year cycle of readings for the Office of Readings, which exists in several other languages.[19] While the

---

[18] *Lectionary: Revised Standard Version Second Catholic Edition with Grail Psalms*, For Use of the Holy See and the Dioceses of the Bishops' Conferences of Botswana, Ghana, Kenya, Lesotho, Nigeria, South Africa, Swaziland, Zimbabwe and of those countries where the Bishops have given approval, 3 vols. (San Francisco: Ignatius Press, 2012).

[19] See, for instance, the fascicles for the Office of Readings that are part of *Die Feier des Stundengebetes: Stundenbuch für die katholischen Bistümer des deutschen Sprachgebietes*, Authentische Ausgabe für den liturgischen Gebrauch (Einsiedeln: Benziger, 1978–).

current USCCB proposed that the revised version does not envisage or propose such a cycle, the Congregation for Divine Worship and the Discipline of the Sacraments has indicated that work is under way to provide the *editio typica* of a second year of readings as a fifth volume to the Latin text. We can only presume that such a development will be added to our revised editions in English in due course.

7 Digital Versions of the Text

One of the most revolutionary aspects of more recent developments in information technology is the availability of liturgical texts on handheld devices. It is probably a fact that an increasing number of those who pray the *Liturgy of the Hours* individually, do so using their phone or tablet rather than a breviary. There is a multiplicity of applications available that provides texts for the purpose in a diversity of languages and forms. When the newly translated texts are available for liturgical use, bishops' conferences will be the portal of these texts to all who publish in their territory, whether in hard copy or digital form. The USCCB have already declared their intention to produce their own app for this purpose. Other conferences may do likewise or enter into partnership with the 'publishers' of existing applications. Time will tell.

8 Some Concluding Thoughts

I hope that my presentation of some of the features of a revised translation of the *Liturgy of the Hours* helps to promote a greater understanding of why such an important project is desirable, while revealing some of the very considerable challenges implied in such an enterprise. The prayer of the Church is the primary way, together with our daily celebration of the Mass and the other sacraments, in which we consciously engage in the sanctification of time. I can do no better than to conclude with these words of the Constitution on the Sacred Liturgy of the Second Vatican Council:

> Christ Jesus, high priest of the new and eternal covenant, taking human nature, introduced into this earthly exile that hymn which is sung throughout all ages in the halls of heaven. He joins the entire community of mankind to Himself, associating it with His own singing of this canticle of divine praise.
>
> For he continues His priestly work through the agency of His Church, which is ceaselessly engaged in praising the Lord and interceding for the salvation of the whole world. She does this, not only by celebrating the eucharist, but also in other ways, especially by praying the divine office.[20]

---

[20] Second Vatican Council, Constitution on the Sacred Liturgy *Sacrosanctum Concilium* (4 December 1963), no. 83.

12

Divine Worship: The Missal and 'the Liturgical Books Proper to the Anglican Tradition' (Anglicanorum Coetibus, Art. III)

Andrew Burnham

Without excluding liturgical celebrations according to the Roman Rite, the Ordinariate has the faculty to celebrate the Holy Eucharist and the other Sacraments, the Liturgy of the Hours and other liturgical celebrations according to the liturgical books proper to the Anglican tradition, which have been approved by the Holy See, so as to maintain the liturgical, spiritual and pastoral traditions of the Anglican Communion within the Catholic Church, as a precious gift nourishing the faith of the members of the Ordinariate and as a treasure to be shared.[1]

Speaking of a pamphlet urging the creation of an Anglican Uniate body, Blessed John Henry Newman wrote to Ambrose de Lisle in 1876: 'Nothing will rejoice me more than to find that the Holy See considers it safe and promising to sanction some such plan as the Pamphlet suggests. I give my best prayers, such as they are, that some means of drawing to us so many good people, who are now shivering at our gates, may be discovered.'[2] Just over 150 years later, in July 1980, the president of the National Conference of Catholic Bishops in the United States, Archbishop John Quinn, received a letter from Cardinal Franjo Šeper, prefect of the Congregation for the Doctrine of the Faith. Pope St John Paul II had decided to make a special 'Pastoral Provision' for the reception of Anglican[3] or former Anglican clergy into full communion with the Catholic Church. Many individuals, of course, in the meantime, had followed Newman in becoming Catholics.

In 1951, under Pope Pius XII, married Protestant clergy – initially German Lutherans – began to gain dispensations to be ordained priest and by the late 1960s

---

[1] Pope Benedict XVI, Apostolic Constitution on Providing for Personal Ordinariates for Anglicans Entering into Full Communion with the Catholic Church *Anglicanorum Coetibus* (4 November 2009), art. III.

[2] Bl. John Henry Newman in a letter to Ambrose Phillipps de Lisle (27 January 1876), in *The Letters and Diaries of John Henry Newman, vol. XXVIII: Fellow of Trinity, January 1876 to December 1878*, ed. Charles Stephen Dessain and Thomas Gornall SJ (Oxford: Clarendon Press, 1975), 20.

[3] Usually referred to in the United States and Scotland as 'Episcopalians'.

similar dispensations were being given by Pope Paul VI. But it was the admission of *groups (coetūs)* of faithful into the Catholic Church, together with their pastors, which was now happening in North America, given impetus by the ordination of women to the Anglican presbyterate in the 1970s.[4] When the Church of England also began to ordain women to the presbyterate, in 1994, those who jumped ship were mainly individual clergy, taken on by Catholic dioceses. There were a couple of congregations that initially sought reconciliation with the Catholic Church but this route was neither encouraged nor fostered.[5] This historical background is an important key to understanding how it came about that the lead liturgical book of the Ordinariates was the *Book of Divine Worship*, derived from the American tradition of Anglican liturgy, the *Book of Common Prayer* of 1979, rather than a liturgical book from the English tradition. However, as we shall see, the work of archbishop of Canterbury, Thomas Cranmer,[6] compiler of the Prayer Books of 1549 and 1552, is seminal to the whole Anglican liturgical enterprise.

1 *The Book of Divine Worship*

The *Book of Divine Worship*, published in 2003,[7] essentially a version of the *Book of Common Prayer* of 1979 'according to the use of the Episcopal Church' (of America)[8] and containing liturgical forms for the 'Pastoral Provision', was formally discontinued on 1 January 2016. Meanwhile, on 29 November 2015, Advent Sunday, *Divine Worship: The Missal*, had come into use.[9] Neither the 'Pastoral Provision' of North America, which was inaugurated in 1980, nor the Ordinariates in Britain, North America and Australia, which were erected in 2011 and 2012, following the promulgation of the Apostolic Constitution *Anglicanorum Coetibus* by Pope Benedict XVI on 4 November 2009, amounted to the Uniate concept, discussed by Newman and de Lisle, and

---

[4] This phenomenon in the United States was not the first instance of women's presbyteral ordination in the Anglican Communion but it was the catalyst for group, as distinct from individual, movements. Seven parishes of this kind formed the Pastoral Provision. They were in four states: Massachusetts, Pennsylvania, Missouri and several in Texas.

[5] The London groups that were received into full communion were notably from St Stephen's, Gloucester Road, and St Matthew's, Bethnal Green.

[6] Thomas Cranmer (1489–1556) was archbishop of Canterbury during the reigns of Henry VIII, Edward VI and, briefly, Mary I, under whom he was burnt as a heretic. He supported the annulment of Henry's marriage to Catherine of Aragon, the catalyst for the separation of the Church from union with the Holy See.

[7] *The Book of Divine Worship: Being Elements of the Book of Common Prayer Revised and Adapted According to the Roman Rite for Use by Roman Catholics Coming from the Anglican Tradition,* Approved by the National Conference of Catholic Bishops of the United States of America and Confirmed by the Apostolic See (Mt Pocono: Newman House Press, 2003). Now out of print, it continues to be available on http://church.atonementonline.com/wp-content/uploads/Book-Of-Divine-Worship.pdf (accessed 15 December 2016).

[8] *The Book of Common Prayer and Administration of the Sacraments and Other Rites and Ceremonies of the Church Together with the Psalter or Psalms of David according to the Use of the Episcopal Church* (New York: Church Hymnal Corp., 1979).

[9] *Divine Worship: The Missal in Accordance with the Roman Rite,* The Celebration of Holy Mass for Use in the Personal Ordinariates established under the Apostolic Constitution *Anglicanorum Coetibus* (London: Catholic Truth Society, 2015).

regularly raised thereafter in ecumenical dialogue. Nonetheless the *Book of Divine Worship* fulfilled the criterion of a liturgical book 'proper to the Anglican tradition' and 'approved by the Holy See'. It remains of interest both for what it included – broadly much of the Prayer Book of the Episcopal Church as used in 1980 – and for what it omitted and excluded. It omitted, for obvious reasons, 'Episcopal Services', the reconciliation of penitents and the anointing of the sick; since, in form, manner and underlying sacramental theology, the understanding of the Episcopal Church differed from that of the Catholic Church.

2 Calendar and Lectionary

Before compiling *Divine Worship: The Missal,* the Interdicasterial commission set up by the Holy See *Anglicanae Traditiones,*[10] produced a calendar, since included in the missal. The calendar adjusts the ranking of feasts, as does the calendar of any particular church or diocese. In the Ordinariate of Our Lady of Walsingham, 24 September became a solemnity, Blessed John Henry Newman (9 October) a feast. In addition to the emphasis given to the English spiritual tradition, immeasurably enhanced by Fr Aidan Nichols' collection of post-biblical readings in the *Customary of Our Lady of Walsingham,*[11] the most striking feature is the restoration of much of the language of older calendars: the Sundays after Epiphany and the *-gesima* Sundays, the Pentecost Octave, Sundays after Trinity, Ember Days and Rogation Days. Though the minor propers and collects for Sundays *per annum* reflect the shape of the *usus antiquior,* there is a disconnect with the readings for the weeks of the year which, as in the *Revised Common Lectionary*[12] and in modern Anglican books, American and British, are arranged by date.[13] The lectionary for use in the Ordinariates is the Second Typical Edition of the Roman Lectionary, using the inimitable Revised Standard Version of the Bible, Second Catholic Edition.[14] The RSV is not only very much in the English Bible tradition – which, for all its ingenuity, the Jerusalem Bible is not – but avoids the opaqueness of the Authorized Version, especially in the Pauline epistles. Consonant with the instruction *Liturgiam Authenticam* (2001)[15] greater accuracy and clarity

---

[10] 'Interdicasterial', that is including representatives and nominees of both the Congregation for the Doctrine of the Faith, and the Congregation for Divine Worship and the Disciple of the Sacraments.

[11] *The Customary of Our Lady of Walsingham: Daily Prayer for the Ordinariate,* ed. Andrew Burnham and Aidan Nichols (Norwich: Canterbury Press, 2012).

[12] The *Revised Common Lectionary,* published in 1994, is essentially a revision of the Roman Lectionary. The Church of England's *Common Worship* further adapted the *Revised Common Lectionary.*

[13] Thus, for example, the readings for Sunday 10 July 2016, Seventh Sunday after Trinity, are those of the 15th Sunday *per annum,* Year C.

[14] *Lectionary: Revised Standard Version Second Catholic Edition with Grail Psalms,* For Use of the Holy See and the Dioceses of the Bishops' Conferences of Botswana, Ghana, Kenya, Lesotho, Nigeria, South Africa, Swaziland, Zimbabwe and of those countries where the Bishops have given approval, 3 vols. (San Francisco: Ignatius Press, 2012).

[15] Congregation for Divine Worship and the Discipline of the Sacraments, Fifth Instruction for the Right Implementation of the Constitution on the Sacred Liturgy *Liturgiam Authenticam* (28 March 2001).

is achieved without too much loss of beauty and poetry. Meanwhile the audacious brilliance and dangerous fallibility of dynamic equivalence are largely avoided.

3 Occasional Services

Divine Worship: Occasional Services,[16] containing the Order of Holy Baptism, the Order of Reception into Full Communion with the Celebration of Confirmation, the Solemnisation of Holy Matrimony, and the Order of Funerals, published in 2014, follows the original Anglican texts closely, especially as regards weddings and funerals. The American *Book of Common Prayer* 1979 had not provided traditional language versions of Baptism, Confirmation or Marriage and, for these, the *Book of Divine Worship* had been resourced by the American 1928 *Book of Common Prayer*. This is the family of texts, clearly Cranmerian in origin, which form the basis of the Baptism and Confirmation rites in *Divine Worship: Occasional Services*.

Detailed comparison is not possible here: suffice to say that the principal change is conforming the rites to the Catholic pattern and enriching the Catholic structure with the rich theological language of Cranmer.[17] An example of the theological gravitas of the baptismal rite is the introduction, a revision of the words of the American 1928 Prayer Book:

> Dearly beloved, seeing that God willeth all men to be saved from the sinful nature which they inherit, as well as from the actual sins which they commit, and that our Saviour Christ saith, None can enter into the kingdom of God, except he be regenerate and born anew of Water and of the Holy Spirit; I beseech you to call upon God the Father, through our Lord Jesus Christ, that of his bounteous mercy he will grant to this man (*or* woman *or* child) that which by nature he (she) cannot have; that he (she) may be baptised with Water and the Holy Spirit, and received into Christ's holy Church and be made a living member of the same.[18]

Conforming Anglican tradition with Catholic practice, the signing with the sign of the cross – which in the English Prayer Books and in the American 1928 Prayer Book had taken place after the Baptism – happens now before the Liturgy of the Word. Similarly, observing the Catholic order, the anointing with Chrism – discontinued in 1552 and reappearing in twentieth-century Anglican practice, first informally, then in liturgical revisions[19] – occurs on the crown of the head after Baptism but, in the adult rite, the post-baptismal chrismation is administered on the forehead as the sacrament

---

[16] *Divine Worship: Occasional Services*, For Use by the Ordinariates erected under the Auspices of the Apostolic Constitution *Anglicanorum Coetibus* (London: Catholic Truth Society, 2014).

[17] For further exploration, see Edward Maxfield, '*Unum Baptisma*: *Divine Worship* and The Order of Holy Baptism for Infants', *Antiphon* 19 (2015): 155–72.

[18] *Divine Worship: Occasional Services*, 17.

[19] For example the rubrics of the American *Book of Common Prayer* 1979, 298 mention the Chrism as an option. The English *Alternative Service Book 1980*, Services Authorised for Use in the Church of England in Conjunction with the *Book of Common Prayer*, together with the Liturgical Psalter (London: Hodder & Stoughton, 1980), 225, 226, 241 and 252 states that 'the sign of the Cross may be made in oil blessed for this purpose'.

of Confirmation and accompanied by the words of the modern Roman rite, 'N., be sealed with the Gift of the Holy Spirit'.

There is also, as in the older *Rituale Romanum*, but now optionally, the placing of salt in the mouth of the baptizand, and an appendix gives a formula for the blessing of salt. Except in emergency, Chrism on the crown of the head, the white vesture and the lighted candle are all required. 'The white vesture, commonly called the Chrysom'[20] may be omitted in the adult rite. *Divine Worship: Occasional Services* also has rites for 'The Order of Reception into Full Communion with the Celebration of Confirmation', and other necessary rites of initiation.[21]

The Marriage and Funeral rites in *Divine Worship: Occasional Services* are arranged as one would expect in the Roman rite. Nuptial Mass is the norm for Marriage, with texts also for 'Holy Matrimony outside Mass' and 'Holy Matrimony between a Catholic and a Non-baptised Person'. Similarly, though the Funeral Mass is the norm, there is 'The Order for Funerals outside Mass'. There is also 'The Order for a Vigil for the Deceased with Reception in Church'. What is significantly different about these rites is that, unlike other pastoral services, they are forms familiar within the British culture. Whereas the Orders for Baptism and Confirmation are from a different cultural milieu – Cranmerian words seldom used in the UK since 1970 and largely as found in the American 1928 Prayer Book – the Orders for Marriages and Funerals are still within the British cultural memory. These are largely the words used, for example, in royal marriages, watched on television by millions, and found under *Common Worship*[22] as 'Alternative Services, Series One: The Form of Solemnization of Matrimony', with the rubric 'This service is virtually identical with the service in the [English] Prayer Book proposed in 1928'.[23] The same is true of The Order of Funerals, which is based on the Series One Burial Services. There is of course much other material, as would be expected in Catholic rites, and though there is no space here for detailed analysis, the sources for this material – for example the responsory, *Libera me*, used at the absolution at the bier – include texts common to the Sarum use[24] and the pre-conciliar Roman rite.

---

[20] *Divine Worship: Occasional Services*, 37.

[21] 'Conditional Baptism', 'Emergency Baptism', 'Baptism of One in Imminent Danger of Death', and 'The Public Receiving of One who has been privately baptised'. There is also available, though not in the liturgical book *Divine Worship: Occasional Services*, a version of Confirmation for older candidates, to be used by the bishop, the ordinary or one to whom the faculty has been given. At the time of writing (2016) this text, for the use of the Ordinaries, was otherwise unpublished.

[22] *Common Worship* is the generic name of Church of England liturgical resources compiled since the beginning of the third millennium and authorized for use in the Church of England.

[23] On the 1928 Prayer Book, see https://www.churchofengland.org/prayer-worship/worship/texts/1928.aspx (accessed 20 December 2016): 'In July 1929 the Archbishop of Canterbury moved a resolution in the Upper House of the Convocation of Canterbury which stated that "in the present emergency and until other order be taken," in view of the approval given by the Convocations to "the proposals for deviations from and additions to the Book of 1662, as set forth in the Book of 1928," the bishops could not "regard as inconsistent with loyalty to the principles of the Church of England the use of such additions or deviations as fall within the limits of these proposals." The resolution was passed by 23 votes to 4. In 1966 most of the 1928 services were legally authorized for use in public worship – some in amended form – as the First Series of Alternative Services'.

[24] Conveniently accessible through *The Sarum Missal in English*, trans. A. Harford Pearson (Eugene, OR: Wipf & Stock, [1868] 2004).

4 Sources for the *Divine Worship* Missal

4.1 *The Book of Divine Worship*

Turning to the Mass, we need to begin with the *Book of Divine Worship*. In its 'Holy Eucharist: Rite One', we find a rite based on that found in the *Book of Common Prayer* 1979, albeit substituting for the offertory and 'The Great Thanksgiving' the Liturgy of the Eucharist, more or less as found in the ICEL 1973 English translation of *Missale Romanum*. In this transitional book, even for Rite One (the traditional language version of the Holy Eucharist) the Preparation of the Altar and the Gifts, together with the *super oblata*, had to be in contemporary language. Though the Eucharistic prayer was the Roman Canon, in the translation ascribed to Myles Coverdale, the use of the Eucharistic prayers of Rite Two (not those of the 1979 Episcopalian Book but the ICEL 1973 contemporary language translations in the *Roman Missal*) was also permitted. When the Ordinariates were created in 2011, the Holy See made clear that use of the Rite Two (contemporary language) Episcopalian material in the *Book of Divine Worship*, together with other texts in contemporary language, such as the contemporary, inclusive-language psalter,[25] was to be discontinued forthwith. Five years later the time of transition is largely over and the *Book of Divine Worship*, as a whole, is no longer authorized.

4.2 Cranmer's Texts

Though the *Book of Divine Worship* was the lead book for the work of *Anglicanae Traditiones*, it is but one of three secondary sources, each drawing upon the distinctive primary source – liturgical texts of the English Reformation. Chief among these Reformation texts is the work of Archbishop Thomas Cranmer, compiler of the Prayer Books of 1549 and 1552, whom we have already encountered. Scarcely less important is the psalter of Myles Coverdale from his Bible translation of 1535. And then there is the organic evolution of the English Bible, with the work of William Tyndale[26] and Myles Coverdale[27] in the sixteenth century leading to that of Lancelot Andrewes[28] and his committee, which produced the King James Version in the early seventeenth century. The Personal Ordinariates continue to make use of the public offices of the Anglican Prayer Book tradition – Mattins and Evensong (Morning and Evening

---

[25] That is, in inclusive language as regards human beings. This psalter, being in the public domain from its inception, was very influential. The experimental office book *Celebrating Common Prayer: A Version of the Daily Office, Society of Saint Francis* (London: Mowbray, 1992) had it as its psalter.

[26] William Tyndale (c. 1494 to 1536) was an English Reformer, famous for translating much of the Bible into English. A substantial proportion of the King James Version is attributable to Tyndale.

[27] Myles Coverdale (1458 to 1569) translated the Bible into English, principally from German, paying particular attention to those parts not completed by Tyndale. Coverdale's psalter was used for the sixteenth-century editions of the *Book of Common Prayer* and, not supplanted in 1662 by the King James Version, remains the psalter of the English *Book of Common Prayer* to the present day.

[28] Lancelot Andrewes (1555 to 1626) was in turn bishop of Chichester, Ely, and Winchester.

Prayer), and the Holy See has issued guidelines for doing so but, to date, no official liturgical book has been issued.[29]

Cranmer's work, consolidated in the Elizabethan revision of 1559, was given permanence in the 1662 *Book of Common Prayer*, following the restoration of the monarchy (1660).[30] It remains the main authorized liturgical text of the Church of England.[31] In the meantime, attempting to bring Episcopalianism to Scotland, King Charles I had authorized the Scottish Prayer Book of 1637, which reflected the spirituality of Lancelot Andrewes and the early Caroline divines, before Oliver Cromwell's Commonwealth and the temporary triumph of Puritanism. The Scottish Episcopal Church, benefitting from disestablishment in 1689, was able to produce a new book in 1764 and it was this book, rather than the English books, which was the basis of Samuel Seabury's 'Communion Office', published in New London, Connecticut, in 1786.[32]

Given this brief history, it is not hard to see how, in *Divine Worship: The Missal*, we arrive at a book whose distillation of Cranmerian material owes much to the American Prayer Book tradition, classically expressed in the US's *Book of Common Prayer* of 1928, and maintained and developed in the traditional language versions of the 1979 Prayer Book. It follows from that that, for Americans, the *Book of Divine Worship* and the transition to the Ordinariate rites has been an experience of continuity, whereas former Anglicans in the UK – those belonging to the Ordinariate of Our Lady of Walsingham, and Catholics with an Anglican personal history looking on at the Ordinariate liturgy – have been wrestling with liturgical rupture. More likely than not, their experience of Eucharistic worship since 1970 had been of a liturgy in modern English – often something similar to, or even identical with, the Roman *Novus Ordo*. Even when they have stayed within a traditional language culture – which has remained extant among a minority – they have found that the editing of texts in the *Book of Divine Worship* and *Divine Worship: The Missal* is normally American. A couple of simple examples: English Anglicans, following Cranmer, say 'For thine is the kingdom, the power, and the glory' after the Lord's Prayer. The American Episcopalian tradition has 'For thine is the kingdom, *and* the power, and the glory': '*and* the power' goes back to Samuel Seabury's 'Communion Office'.[33] Similarly, in the Prayer of Thanksgiving, after Communion, Cranmer has 'we most heartily thank thee, for that thou dost *vouchsafe to* feed us, *who have duly received* these holy mysteries'. This wording persists in the English Prayer Book texts as repackaged in *Common Worship* 2000, but it was changed in the 1979 American Prayer Book to 'we most heartily

---

[29] Guidelines are necessary because, for example, 1662 Prayer Book Evensong otherwise could be celebrated using *Cantate Domino* (Ps 98) in place of the *Magnificat* and *Deus misereatur* (Ps 67) in place of the *Nunc Dimittis*. The *Magnificat* is an invariable feature of Vespers (Evensong) in the Latin rite. The Personal Ordinariates each maintain their own conventions: the British Ordinariate uses the *Customary of Our Lady of Walsingham*.

[30] During the Commonwealth (from 1649 to 1660) the monarchy, episcopal ministry and the Prayer Book were suppressed. Meanwhile Charles II was in exile in France.

[31] With the odd result that services most commonly encountered in the Church of England are technically 'alternative services'; alternatives, that is, to the *Book of Common Prayer* 1662.

[32] Samuel Seabury was the first bishop in the Protestant Episcopal Church of the United States. He derived his orders from the Scottish Episcopal Church because, following American independence, he was unable to be appointed by, or swear allegiance to, the British crown.

[33] *Divine Worship: The Missal*, The Order of Holy Mass, The Communion Rite.

thank thee, for that thou dost feed us, *in* these holy mysteries', and that is the wording in *Divine Worship: The Missal*.[34] There are many such instances in the editing of the orations and it seems entirely equitable that the foundational texts and translations – and the spelling in the liturgical books – are from the English Anglican tradition but the editorial redaction is predominantly American. The third continent in which there is an Ordinariate, Australia, looks gratefully to both of these contexts and, anyway, the expertise of the Australian liturgist, Bishop Peter Elliott, was evident throughout the work of *Anglicanae Traditiones*.

4.3 *The Anglican Missal*

If we see all of this – the English Prayer Book material, its redaction within the American Prayer Book tradition and its scrutiny by Professor Clinton Allen Brand, associate professor of English at the University of St Thomas, Houston, Texas, and an expert on literary English of the sixteenth and seventeenth centuries[35] – as giving us the first of our three secondary sources, we need to look beyond the official Anglican liturgical books for the other two. Our second and third sources are less well known but they are sufficiently important to our understanding to justify us spending a little time considering them. They are two sacramentaries, broadly speaking translations of the pre-conciliar Roman Mass. Neither the *English Missal* nor the *Anglican Missal* was ever authorized for use in any of the countries where an Ordinariate has been erected under the aegis of *Anglicanorum Coetibus*. In that sense, they are not 'liturgical books proper to the Anglican tradition', as defined by *Anglicanorum Coetibus*, art. III. Both were products of the Anglo-Catholic ritualist movement, which followed logically from nineteenth-century Tractarianism.[36] Though they originated in England, both went on to have American editions,[37] and the missals were so constructed that the priest could celebrate anything from an apparently Anglican rite, complete with the familiar prayers of the Cranmerian liturgy, to what was to all intents and purposes the Tridentine Mass in English.

These liturgical books, unofficial though they were, were used in abundance. Much of the missionary work carried out by Anglicans was undertaken by societies with a particular churchmanship, and versions of what was really the Roman rite were adapted for places as far apart as Zanzibar, with its famous missionary bishop Frank Weston, and Korea. In these more monolithic ecclesiastical cultures, such liturgies as the 1919 Swahili Mass could be authorized. It is amusing to look through the *Anglican Missal* at some of the headings: 'from the Scottish Rite', 'from the American Rite', 'from the South

---

[34] Ibid.

[35] See Clinton A. Brand, 'Very Members Incorporate: Reflections on the Sacral Language of Divine Worship', *Antiphon* 19 (2015): 132–54.

[36] For background, see John Shelton Reed, *Glorious Battle: The Cultural Politics of Victorian Anglo-Catholicism* (Tennessee and London: Vanderbilt University Press, 1996).

[37] *The Anglican Missal in the American Edition*, Containing the Liturgy from the Book of Common Prayer According to the Use of the Church in the United States of America together with Other Devotions and with Liturgical and Ceremonial Directions Proper to the Same (Mount Sinai, NY: Frank Gavin Liturgical Foundation, 1943). Subsequently rights were sold to the Anglican Parishes Association. There was also a Spanish edition in use in the Caribbean.

African Rite'. Using the *Anglican Missal* was clearly quite an adventure. The text of Cranmer's Communion Service is presented imaginatively: the Ten Commandments or Summary of the Law may be used, the *Gloria in excelsis* happens either near the beginning (as in the Roman Mass) or near the end (the position to which Cranmer moved it in 1552), the private prayers of priest and deacon from the Roman Mass are inserted, there is more than one text for the offertory, some prefaces are accompanied by proper *infra actionem* inserts, and the *Communicantes* are given also in Latin. There is a Last Gospel and there are several versions of the Canon. From the 1921 English edition one can infer the debate that was raging in the Church of England about how to deal with the unsatisfactory shape of Cranmer's Prayer of Consecration, as the 1662 Prayer Book called it.[38] Thus the *Anglican Missal* has the Canon as laid out in the 1549 Prayer Book – in which Cranmer presented a prayer deceptively evocative of the Roman Canon, using its language but changing its theological freight. It also has a translation of the Roman Canon – which is different from both the version in the *English Missal* (see below) and the translation attributed to Myles Coverdale. It also has the Roman Canon in Latin. It has what it calls 'the Canon of the Scottish Mass', 'the Canon of the American Mass' and 'the Canon of the South African Mass' – reflecting more advanced churchmanship and more exotic practices in provinces not in thrall to English Evangelicalism, and the constraints of the law brought to bear on ritualists. Finally it has what has been subsequently referred to as 'the interim rite' – that is, the Eucharistic prayer with which 'Prayer Book Catholics', as they called themselves, maintained their doctrinal integrity throughout the twentieth century. Interestingly, 'the interim rite', that is, the combination – linked by a 'wherefore' – of Cranmer's Prayer of Consecration and his Prayer of Oblation, having been informally sanctioned by the bishops in the meantime,[39] was authorized for use in the *Alternative Service Book* 1980,[40] and in *Common Worship* 2000. Deliciously, the *Anglican Missal* also gives us Latin headings. *Ad mensam dulcissimi convivii tui* is the heading given to the Prayer of Humble Access, not, as one might expect *Non accedimus ad hanc mensam tuam*, the wording of the 1560 Latin version of the 1559 Elizabethan Prayer Book. The American edition similarly has a collection of Eucharistic prayers, including that of the American Prayer Book of 1928 (related to Eucharistic Prayer I in the 1979 *Book of Common Prayer* of the Episcopal Church in the United States of America).

---

[38] *The Anglican Missal* (London: Society of SS. Peter and Paul, 1921). The English Church Union, more recently the Church Union, is an Anglo-Catholic group in the Church of England, founded in 1859. It produced what was known as 'The Green Book' as a response to the *Draft Proposed Book of Common Prayer* of 1923, adopted by the Church of England's National Assembly: *A Suggested Prayer Book, Being the Text of the English Rite, Altered and Enlarged in Accordance with the Prayer Book Revision Proposals* made by the English Church Union (London: Humphrey Milford – Oxford University Press, 1923).

[39] Acting arguably in an *ultra vires* fashion: Parliament retained control over worship until it was delegated in the Church of England (Worship and Doctrine) Measure 1974. A 'measure' is a piece of legislation duly processed by the Church of England's General Synod which, after ratification by Parliament, receives the royal assent and passes into law like any other Act of Parliament.

[40] The collection of Alternative Services, that is, alternative to the *Book of Common Prayer* 1662, resulting from fifteen years' liturgical experimentation in the Church of England.

4.4 *The English Missal*

The other secondary source was the *English Missal*, published in five editions from 1912 to 1958.[41] The first three looked to the *Roman Missal* of Pope St Pius V as revised until the time of Pope St Pius X. The last two editions include the revised Holy Week rites of 1958. The American edition *mutatis mutandis* substitutes for 1662 Prayer Book material texts that conform to the American 1928 *Book of Common Prayer*. Though, as already said, this missal too was never authorized for use in any of the countries where we now find Ordinariates, it was immensely influential, being used in differing ways, by many Anglo-Catholic parishes. Ingeniously, by including the Sarum as well as the Roman lections,[42] and the main prayers of the *Book of Common Prayer*, it could be celebrated ostensibly as a somewhat decorative Prayer Book rite, with offertory prayers and Canon in Latin or English said 'silently' (i.e. in a low voice). Many a priest, in the midst of the Canon said quietly, would interpolate in place of the *Qui pridie*[43] Cranmer's Prayer of Consecration aloud – the whole prayer or just the Institution Narrative. Meanwhile, as in any polyphonic High Mass, the choir would sing *Sanctus* and *Benedictus*, to one of a few English choral settings.

The compilers and translators of these missals, the *Anglican Missal* and the *English Missal*, were liturgists and scholars. They were Anglo-Papalists, that is to say, they regarded the break with Rome in the sixteenth century as an unfortunate intrusion of national politics, and wanted to see Catholicism restored and flourishing in the ancient Provinces of Canterbury and York. They could see the case for using the vernacular in the liturgy – except, perhaps, for the most sacred moments – and, while disagreeing with his theology and his radical reordering of the Eucharist, they recognized that, though heretic and schismatic, Cranmer, was a great translator and an accomplished wordsmith.[44] His translations of medieval Latin collects are truly peerless, even when he subtly modifies the theology, and his original compositions – the Prayer of Humble Access, the Prayer of Thanksgiving – are serene and spiritually spacious prose. Cradle Catholics, coming across these prayers in the context of an Ordinariate-use Mass have been known to be grateful for the discovery of these treasures. Anglicans, used to the *Book of Common Prayer* Communion Service, would notice some differences and changes in the ordering of things but, even so, there is still much to recognize.

---

[41] *Missale Anglicanum: The English Missal* (London: W. Knott, 1912). The fifth edition of the altar missal was published by W. Knott & Son in 1958 and was reissued in 2001 by Canterbury Press, Norwich.

[42] The Sarum (Salisbury) use was the pre-eminent use of pre-Reformation England. The Salisbury propers were similar to but not identical with those of the pre-conciliar Roman Mass. A detailed list of sources is available in *Liturgy and Worship: A Companion to the Prayer Books of the Anglican Communion*, ed. W. K. Lowther Clarke and Charles Harris (London: S.P.C.K., 1932), 380–402.

[43] The Public Worship Regulation Act 1874 prescribed imprisonment for priests using ritualist liturgical practices. When enforcement of the Public Worship Regulation Act ended in 1906, the custom of Canon said 'silently' in Latin with the official texts of the *Book of Common Prayer* said aloud continued.

[44] See Andrew Burnham, 'The Contribution of English Liturgical Patrimony to Continuing Renewal in the Roman Rite', in *Sacred Liturgy: The Source and Summit of the Life and Mission of the Church*, ed. Alcuin Reid (San Francisco: Ignatius Press, 2014), 315–33. The volume contains the proceedings of the *Sacra Liturgia* conference held in Rome in 2013.

5 The Sarum Use and Anglo-Catholicism

At the beginning of the work of *Anglicanae Traditiones*, there was discussion about whether the Sarum use, the prevalent use in pre-Reformation England, should be revived. Like the Dominican use, to which it bears some resemblance, the Sarum use is not so very different from the Roman rite. However that was not to be the way forward preferred by either dicastery – the Congregation for the Doctrine of the Faith, and the Congregation for Divine Worship and the Disciple of the Sacraments – on the grounds that, while up to the Reformation the Sarum (Salisbury) use met the criterion of tradition established by Pope St Pius V,[45] it could not be said that it had been current in any meaningful sense in the period of 1549[46] to the present day.[47] A former Anglican, Fr Anthony Symondson SJ, took the same view:

> The historical reality of maintaining the Sarum Use among English recusant Catholics after the passing of the Act of Uniformity in 1559 and the excommunication of Queen Elizabeth I in 1570 is that it quickly became superseded by the arrival of Cardinal Allen's English Mission in 1580. The Douai priests and Jesuits brought with them the Missal of St Pius V and none, as far as we know, celebrated the Sarum Use in recusant households. Effectively it became extinct among recusant Catholics.[48]

Symondson's account of the Sarum revival in the last 150 years is as accurate as it is sharp:

> It is well known that in the 1870s and 1880s there were attempts in some prominent English Anglo-Catholic parishes to revive Sarum ceremonial adapted to the *Book of Common Prayer*, but nowhere was the Sarum Missal revived. These attempts at ritualistic Englishness were sabotaged by Percy Dearmer in 1899 when he published *The Parson's Handbook*, a directory aimed at adapting Sarum rubrics to the Prayer Book. For a period of forty years this volume was influential in medievalizing Anglican worship irrespective of doctrinal clarity and certitude. In effect it led to doctrinal dilution and the introduction of mere pageantry. For that reason the mainstream Anglo-Catholic movement became Roman in its liturgical

---

[45] The bull *Quo primum* of Pope St Pius V allowed only those rites that were at least 200 years old to survive the promulgation of the 1570 missal.

[46] When the First Prayer Book of King Edward VI was imposed.

[47] There is a persistent rumour, for which it is thought that no evidence has ever been found, that reviving the Sarum use was briefly considered at the restoration of the hierarchy in 1850, but abandoned in what were Ultramontane days. In 1852 Wiseman ordered the use of Roman chant books in Westminster, and Manning made the Pustet editions of chant (which had the papal publishing monopoly before the Vatican/Solesmes editions came out) compulsory in 1876. Meanwhile, although Pugin had pursued the Gothic shape of church, with rood screen dividing nave and chancel, later churches tended to be in the Italianiate auditorium style. In short there are few signs, in the Catholic obedience, of the pursuit of Sarum conventions.

[48] Anthony Symondson SJ commenting on 'Liturgical Considerations for Future Ordinariates', an essay posted online by *New Liturgical Movement*, 20 May 2010, under the heading *The Future Liturgy of an Anglican Ordinariate*; available online: http://www.newliturgicalmovement.org/2010/05/future-liturgy-of-anglican-ordinariate_20.html (accessed 18 December 2016), with typos corrected.

life and the Dearmerised version of Sarum became a despised and ridiculed source. British Museum religion, as it was called.[49]

Anglo-Catholic derision is no rare commodity and soft targets such as the 'Sarumism' of much English cathedral culture and of publications such as *New English Hymnal* (1986)[50] is lampooned by Anglo-Catholics; as is the whole *Common Worship* enterprise, most of which took place, appropriately enough, under the chairmanship of the then bishop of Salisbury.[51] Some of the biting comment is typical of how the British rub along together (a prominent evangelical, for example, referred to *Common Worship* as 'a Laudian takeover')[52] but it is the stock-in-trade of the Anglo-Catholic movement.[53] Meanwhile, scholars will continue to uncover distinctly Sarum traces in the *Divine Worship* missal, not least, in an appendix, the Sarum tones for greetings, orations and preface, as still used by English Anglicans.[54]

6 Grafting Anglican Shoots on the Roman Trunk

The work of *Anglicanae Traditiones*, in the words of its co-chairman, Archbishop J. Augustine di Noia OP, was 'the Holy See's prudent grafting of proven Anglican shoots on the rooted, living trunk of the Roman Rite to promote healthier growth'.[55] The deep roots of *Divine Worship: The Missal* are not, therefore, its Anglican material, as might be supposed from the phrase 'liturgical books proper to the Anglican tradition' (*Anglicanorum Coetibus*, art. III) but the Roman rite, of which it is an authentic and properly traditional expression. Since the Prayer Books of the English Reformation had set out to replace the medieval Mass with a Reformed Communion Service,

---

[49] Ibid.

[50] There was some disappointment that, under the chairmanship of Prebendary George Timms, the *New English Hymnal* appeared to disregard some of the emergent conventions of recent (Roman) Catholic liturgical reform. It retained *Ubi caritas* for the *Pedilavium*, Psalm 22 for the Stripping of the Altars, and several medieval sequences. By including *O Virgo virginum* as an eighth Advent antiphon, it appeared to endorse the Sarum dating (*O Sapientia* on 16 December, etc.) rather than the Roman dating (17 December onwards). However, *Divine Worship: The Missal* has the Roman dating (17 December onwards), making each of the Evening Prayer *Magnificat* antiphons also the Alleluia verse for the day and allocating *O Virgo virginum* to the morning Mass of Christmas Eve. This provision differs from the *Graduale Romanum* 1974.

[51] Bishop David Stancliffe, bishop of Salisbury, 1993 to 2010, and chairman of the Church of England Liturgical Commission, 1993 to 2005. *Common Worship* attracts such affectionate references as 'Uncommon Worship'.

[52] After Archbishop William Laud (1573–1645), high church Caroline divine and archbishop of Canterbury from 1633 until he was arrested in 1640 and executed in 1645. The 'Laudian take-over' comment was made by the prominent evangelical liturgist, the late Michael Vasey. See Michael Perham's Vasey Memorial Lecture 2001, 'Benedict, William Laud and Michael Vasey: How Distinctive should Anglican Worship be?', which is available on https://biblicalstudies.org.uk/pdf/anvil/19-1_033.pdf (accessed 12 December 2016).

[53] See Reed, *Glorious Battle*, xxiv: 'Eventually I had to conclude that the offensiveness was not just accidental … that many were drawn to the movement precisely because it offended those whom they wished to offend.'

[54] *Divine Worship: The Missal*, Appendix 12.

[55] J. Augustine di Noia, '*Divine Worship* and the Liturgical Vitality of the Church', *Antiphon* 19 (2015): 109–15.

Anglican Eucharistic material, set in a new framework, had to be adapted and reordered carefully.

The genius of the Cranmerian Communion Service lay not only in its tonal qualities but in what might be called its ministry to those who came inadequately prepared. They had to listen to the Ten Commandments[56] and Sacred Scripture, a long exhortation or two (seldom now heard) and an invitation to confession. Having made a heartfelt general confession, they heard the Absolution and the Comfortable Words. There are magisterial contrasts: 'manifold sins and wickedness', 'grievously committed' against the 'Divine Majesty' of the 'Judge of all men', are acknowledged and bewailed. These are sins 'provoking most justly (God's) wrath and indignation'. 'The burden of them is intolerable.' The assurance of forgiveness, pronounced by the priest, is that of 'our heavenly Father, who of his great mercy hath promised forgiveness of sins'. The Prayer of Humble Access – 'we are not worthy so much as to gather up the crumbs' – was still to come. And the Prayer of Consecration too speaks of 'our heavenly Father' and 'his tender mercy' and the death of Jesus Christ 'upon the Cross for our redemption … one oblation of himself once offered, a full, perfect, and sufficient sacrifice, oblation, and satisfaction, for the sins of the whole world'. If the *Divine Worship* missal has managed to draw out the riches of this theology of forgiveness and mercy and transplant it from the soil of Reformation polemic into the Catholic garden of the soul, it has achieved a great deal.

If the Sarum use were not to be a way forward, nor were recent liturgical expressions of Anglicanism. Interesting experiments, such as the *super oblata* of the Anglican Church of Canada[57] and the post-communion prayers of *Common Worship*, were not pursued. It was not the provenance of these texts that was the problem: after all nothing could need more careful doctrinal handling than the texts of Thomas Cranmer on which we drew. Cranmer was a master of refashioning Catholic-sounding texts and imbuing them with the insights of Protestant theology.[58] The Congregation for Divine Worship was clear, however, that there should not be a text in modern English which would compete with the 2010 English translation of the *Roman Missal*. That said, it has not been unproblematic in England, not least ecumenically, that the *Divine Worship* project has neither sprung from, nor really been attentive to, the distinguished work of the Church of England Liturgical Commission in the period 1965 to the present day.[59] This is a topic for exploration on another occasion.

An article by Steven J. Lopes gives an account of the unpublished *Ratio* that guided the commission, as the missal was prepared.[60] As well as the contributory sources, which

---

[56] *Divine Worship: The Missal*, Appendix 3.
[57] *The Book of Alternative Services of the Anglican Church of Canada* (Toronto: Anglican Book Centre, 1985).
[58] See Burnham, 'The Contribution of English Liturgical Patrimony'.
[59] The ecumenical consensus texts of the English Language Liturgical Consultation (ELLC) were not adopted in the *Roman Missal* 2010. With regard to *Divine Worship: The Missal*, according to the *Ratio*, *Common Worship* (2000) was consulted only when the *Book of Divine Worship*, the classic Prayer Book heritage, the *English Missal* and the *Anglican Missal* 'did not provide the necessary material'. See Steven J. Lopes, 'A Missal for the Ordinariates: The Work of the Anglicanæ Traditiones Interdicasterial Commission', *Antiphon* 19 (2015): 116–31, at 121.
[60] See Lopes, 'A Missal for the Ordinariates'. Mgr Steven Lopes, Co-ordinating Secretary of *Anglicanae Traditiones*, became bishop (and ordinary) of the Ordinariate of the Chair of St Peter in February 2016.

we have noted, and the attention to Anglican liturgical patrimony these represent, there is also mention of the texts of the chants (introit, gradual, etc.) which 'are taken from the existing translations of the *Graduale Romanum*, as common to the *English Missal*, the *Anglican Missal*, and the *Anglican Use Gradual*'.[61] In the English context one would want to add the *English Gradual*[62] and the *English Hymnal*,[63] the sources for the *Anglican Use Gradual*. Though the lectionary provides a responsorial psalm and Alleluia specific to the Sunday or weekday *per annum*, the *Divine Worship* missal also provides gradual and tract or Alleluia specific to the Sunday according to its calendar. It is worth noting that, like the Last Gospel at Mass,[64] those texts of the gradual which are not from the Coverdale psalter are either from the *Anglican Missal* or *English Missal* translations of non-Scriptural passages (e.g. the *Offertorium* of the Requiem Mass) or, where they are Scriptural, from the King James Version. There was a view that here too translations of the RSV should have prevailed but that route was not taken.

Though much of the detailed prescription of the General Instruction of the Roman Missal, printed at the beginning of the *Divine Worship* missal, for example regarding the use of the four Eucharistic prayers, appears out of place in the context of a missal that has only two Eucharistic prayers, it serves to make the point that this is truly the Roman rite. There follows a detailed article on what is and what is not distinctive about the celebration of Mass according to the *Divine Worship* missal.

> The rubrics of the *Divine Worship* Order of Mass aim to preserve traditional customs of Anglican Eucharistic worship with respect to orientation, postures, gestures, gestures, and manual acts, while also permitting the celebration of Mass in a manner similar to that of the *Roman Missal*, Third Typical Edition. This rubrical flexibility provides for the variety of liturgical traditions and experiences among the parishes and communities of the Personal Ordinariates.[65]

The next paragraph proceeds to say that 'Mass celebrated more solemnly … should also include the ministrations of one or more Deacons. … In the absence of a second Deacon, another cleric or even an Instituted Acolyte may serve the subdiaconal ministry and read the Epistle.'[66] There are other references to an earlier way of proceeding. The Alleluia is not to be sung in 'Pre-Lent' (the '-*gesima* Sundays') and the sequence, which arose musically from an elaboration of the *jubilus* at the end of the Alleluia verse, may

---

[61] Adapted in *The Anglican Use Gradual*, ed. C. David Burt (Mansfield, MA: Partridge Hill Press, 2006).
[62] *The English Gradual. Part II: The Plainchant of the Proper*, ed. Francis Burgess, 7th edn (London: Plainchant Publications Committee, 1961).
[63] *The English Hymnal* (London: Oxford University Press, [1906] 1933), 'Introits and Other Anthems', nos. 657–733. Even in the Full Music Edition of the *English Hymnal* the texts appear without music. The purpose is to equip congregations to follow what is being sung from the Wantage Graduals, whether the elaborate version of the propers is being sung or the simple version.
[64] *Divine Worship: The Missal*, Appendix 6.
[65] Ibid., Rubrical Directory, no. 10.
[66] Ibid., no. 11. A footnote refers us to Pope Paul VI, Motu proprio *Ministeria quaedam* (15 August 1972). Slightly surprisingly the position would seem to be that a priest may be a substitute for the second deacon but not for the first.

once more follow the Alleluia.[67] The distinctive rubrics for Masses for the Dead are restored.[68]

The Mass according to *Divine Worship* may feel very similar to the pre-conciliar Mass,[69] particularly if it is celebrated *versus Dominum*, begins with Prayers at the Foot of the Altar,[70] or *Asperges*,[71] moves between the Epistle side of the altar and to the Gospel side, and concludes with the Last Gospel – but none of these features is obligatory. Similarly, the offertory normatively takes the form found in the Tridentine Mass, but the *Novus Ordo* rite remains an alternative – with 'thou-thee-thy' forms of the *Berakhot*. It is clear that the Roman Canon is to be the usual form. It is expressed in sacral language,[72] with the dominical words in the Institution Narrative conformed to the version in other Eucharistic prayers, as agreed in 1968.[73] As an alternative, the pseudo-Hippolytan Eucharistic prayer, slightly antiqued, is available for weekdays and for Masses attended mainly by children.

The ceremonial is more complex than that of the Ordinary Form of the Roman rite: there are signs of the cross at the end of *Gloria* and Creed, a genuflection during the *Et incarnatus est*, as well as genuflections before and after each elevation, and after the concluding doxology of the Eucharistic prayer, but Mass may begin at the chair and the Liturgy of the Eucharist may be celebrated *versus populum*.

7 *Divine Worship:* The Missal and the Evolution of the Roman Rite

Speaking of the *Missale Romanum*, Cardinal Robert Sarah, prefect of the Congregation for Divine Worship, has said:

> It would ... be desirable that the Penitential Rite and the Offertory of the *usus antiquior* be inserted as an appendix in a future edition of the Missal in order to underline that the two liturgical forms illuminate one another, in continuity and without opposition.[74]

---

[67] Ibid., no. 24. In the Ordinary Form the sequence (of which there are fewer) precedes the Alleluia.

[68] Ibid., no. 45. This means no Psalm 43, no incense until the offertory, no Alleluia, a simpler ceremonial at the Gospel without acolytes' candles, no blessing of water at the offertory, no *Gloria Patri* after the *Lavabo* psalm, different responses at the *Agnus Dei* and 'May they rest in peace' in place of the blessing and dismissal.

[69] See also Andrew Burnham, 'The Liturgy of the Ordinariates: Ordinary, Extraordinary, or *Tertium Quid?*', a paper given at a conference of CIEL UK in London on 24 November 2012. 'Pre-conciliar' here means the Mass as it would have been celebrated optimally in 1958, not the 1962 form.

[70] *Divine Worship: The Missal*, Appendix 1.

[71] Ibid., Appendix 2.

[72] The canon, as we have seen, is in the translation attributed to Myles Coverdale.

[73] See Annibale Bugnini, *The Reform of the Liturgy 1948-1975*, trans. M. J. O'Connell (Collegeville: The Liturgical Press, 1990), 382.

[74] Robert Cardinal Sarah, 'Silenziosa azione del cuore', *L'Osservatore Romano*, 12 June 2015, 6. The English translation is taken, with some modifications, from http://www.catholicworldreport.com/Item/3947/silent_action_of_the_heart.aspx (accessed 27 December 2016).

The flexibility in the *Ritus servandus* of *Divine Worship: The Missal* will surely play a part of the planned evolution of the Roman rite, the emergence of the Fourth Typical Edition. In *Divine Worship* we have a well-ordered laboratory in which different ways of celebration, different texts, can be explored in a complementary way. Certainly there are weaknesses and inconsistencies, as with any human endeavour, but, to date, few have become apparent.[75] Experiencing the missal, imaginatively used, might lead one to conclude that, throughout the Roman rite, the Roman Canon should be used invariably at a solemn Mass, the Alternative Eucharistic Prayer at a simple weekday Mass; the full offertory rite at a sung Mass, the simpler form at a low Mass; *versus Dominum* at sung Mass, *versus populum* on a more informal occasion. More daring is the juxtaposing of traditional propers (for example, after Trinity) and the three-year lectionary. And perhaps we could see further experiments: at present the restoration of the one-year Eucharistic lectionary has been thought a step too far, but, for all but the most assiduous Mass attender, it is arguable how successful the three-year Sunday lectionary has been. Annual repetition of collects, epistles and gospels, a feature of traditional Anglican patrimony, builds liturgical memory. As does the use of whole psalms, or sections of psalms, rather than the strange patchwork of responsorial psalmody, whose abbreviations and discontinuities often militate against memorability. Perhaps, in the wake of *Divine Worship: The Missal*, the minor propers of the *Graduale Romanum* and even the one-year Eucharistic lectionary might be fully reintegrated into the *Missale Romanum*.

It may be that the greatest contribution of the *Divine Worship* missal to the evolution of the Roman rite is its making available a liturgical reform which, in several ways, is the closest thing we have to the reform which *Sacrosanctum Concilium* had in mind. Though this form will remain, for many years, a comparatively recent addition to the Roman rite, it has deep roots. Time will tell how influential the missal, and the other liturgical books of the Personal Ordinariates, will prove to be, but it is possible that what has come to pass, through the foresight and generosity of the Holy See, and particularly of Pope Benedict XVI, will be out of all proportion to the actual size of the Ordinariates, which remain numerically small. Liturgists will not be fazed, of course, by discrepancies between the importance of the use and the numbers for whom the use is directly relevant: the Ambrosian rite of Milan and the Mozarabic rite of Toledo and the Iberian peninsula are served by only a handful of congregations but they remain extant,[76] seedbeds for future growth of 'the One True Fold of the Redeemer'.[77]

---

75 To give one example, whereas the missal's introduction to the Comfortable Words (from the 1662 Prayer Book) suggests that they are the words of 'our Saviour Christ', there is an option to use just one or two of them, which could be the words not of Christ but of St Paul and St John. The *Book of Divine Worship* (following the 1979 American Book) avoids this by using the introduction 'Hear the Word of God to all who truly turn to him'. A revision would choose between the 1662 form (that is, requiring all of them) and the 1979 form (that is, requiring only one or two, but with an appropriate introduction).

76 See Hans-Jürgen Feulner, 'Anglican Use of the Roman Rite? The Unity of the Liturgy in the Diversity of Its Rites and Forms', *Antiphon* 17 (2013): 31–72, at 34–40. Professor Feulner, a liturgist with a particular interest in Anglican liturgy, was a member of the *Anglicanae Traditiones* Commission.

77 Bl. John Henry Newman used this phrase in a letter to Henry Wilberforce from Littlemore (7 October 1845), see John Henry Newman to Henry Wilberforce (Littlemore, 7 October 1845), in *The Letters and Diaries of John Henry Newman, vol. XI: Littlemore to Rome, October 1845 to December 1846*, ed. Charles Stephen Dessain (Oxford: Oxford University Press, 1961), 3.

The Vicissitudes of Liturgy and Architecture Shown at the Example of Berlin's Cathedral of St Hedwig

Peter Stephan

1 The Tension Between Form and Function in St Hedwig's Cathedral

1.1 The History of the Exterior

The history of St Hedwig's Cathedral goes back to the eighteenth century. After coming into power, the Prussian king Frederick the Great planned to build a pantheist cult edifice in the south-east corner of the so-called *Forum Fridericianum* in Berlin (today known as *Bebelplatz*; fig. 3). Its original intention was for it to be used by various religious faiths – for this reason he chose the Pantheon in Rome, consecrated to 'all the gods', as its reference.[1] After the conquest of Silesia in 1742, the need for a sacred space arose for the new Prussian inhabitants who were of Catholic denomination. The king allocated the site of the Berlin municipality for this space, with the guideline that the typology must still be Pantheon-oriented. The designs were entrusted to the royal court architect Georg Wenzelaus von Knobelsdorff (fig. 1). To make St Hedwig's Cathedral more distinguishable as a Christian place of worship, Knobelsdorff added a lantern to the Pantheon-dome. He encircled the cylinder of the dome with twelve columns, which were supposed to surround Christ present in the cross on top of the vertex; in addition to that, the statue of an apostle was placed on every column.

After the death of Knobelsdorff, Jan Bouman was entrusted with the project and completed it between 1753 and 1773 by reducing the design to the simple Pantheon-dome (fig. 4). Economy would have played a similar role as the wishes of

[1] See Christine Goetz and Victor H. Elbern, *Die St.-Hedwigs-Kathedrale zu Berlin* (Regensburg: Schnell & Steiner, 2000); Sibylle Badstübner-Gröger, *Die St.-Hedwigs-Kathedrale zu Berlin* (Regensburg: Schnell & Steiner, 1991); Jürgen Boeckh, *Alt-Berliner Stadtkirchen. Bd. 2: Von der Dorotheenstädtischen Kirche bis zur St.-Hedwigs-Kathedrale*, Berlinische Reminiszenzen, 58 (Berlin: Haude & Spener, 1986); Marianne Tosetti and Heinz Nixdorf, *Die St. Hedwigs-Kathedrale zu Berlin* (Leipzig: Schmiedicke Verlag, 1973).

the enlightened king to reduce the specifically church-like character of the design. Nevertheless, St Hedwig's Cathedral possessed an important urban function. With its slanted placement it must have acted as a visual focus for the boulevard *Unter den Linden*, as well as from the main courtyard of Prince Heinrich Palace. At that time the roofs of the neighbouring houses would not have been higher than the dome, therefore allowing it to find complete expression.

Still, Bouman's decision to waive the lantern created a contradiction between the architectural form on the one hand and the sacred and urban function of the church, on the other. To overcome this contradiction between form and function, Max Hasak added a lantern with a cross to the exterior during 1884 and 1887, with explicit reference to Knobelsdorff (fig. 5). The church could now be distinctly recognized as a place of worship. Furthermore, the urban presence was strengthened. The importance of this increased when the neighbouring houses grew in height (a new stage-house for the Opera House and the addition of stories to the Dresdner Bank building). Moreover, the dome itself had become an urban leitmotif. Thanks to Hasak, St Hedwig's Cathedral corresponded to the two churches of the *Gendarmenmarkt* and the Royal Palace. Shortly afterwards, the domes of the Bode Museum, the *Stadthaus*, the *Neuer Dom* (New Cathedral) and the *Oranienburger Strasse* Synagogue were added.

1.2 The Weakening of Urban Presence

After the church had completely been burnt out during the Second World War and became part of East Berlin, the capital of the German Democratic Republic, in 1949, it received a new dome construction in the 1950s, made of 84 reinforced concrete segments (figs. 3 and 13). The idea of reconstructing the lantern was discarded. This led to a profanation in appearance; today there is nothing to help identify the building as a place of worship, if we disregard the inconspicuous cross on the roof. Furthermore, the church can barely compete with the neighbouring buildings; it also only plays a secondary role in the urban concert of domes of the area.

1.3 The History of the Interior

When Knobelsdorff planned St Hedwig, he replaced the cassettes of the Pantheon-dome with ceiling paintings that represented the heavenly glory (fig. 1). Bouman built the dome with vertically oriented vault ribs, in which the sacred light that fell from heaven could cast a solid radiance (fig. 6). As in the iconography of the Hagia Sophia in Constantinople, St Mark's Basilica in Venice or the Roman university church Sant'Ivo alla Sapienza, the light of the Holy Spirit falling from above was cleaving to the stone. Like the Temple of Solomon, St Hedwig seemed to be the house that was built by holy wisdom itself (Prov. 9).

To express this emanation of Pentecost, Bouman placed figures of the apostles next to the twelve column pairs (which Knobelsdorff had already included in his designs of the dome lantern; fig. 1 and 6). Thereby, Bouman fell back on the traditional meaning of the apostles as 'pillars of the Church (*columnae ecclesiae*)' (see fig. 9). As the columns are directly connected to the vault ribs of the (heavenly) dome, it indicates that the Eternal Jerusalem is founded on the apostles (Rev. 19.4) like in the high choirs of Gothic cathedrals. In reverse reading, the church that was built transcends the earthly architecture to become a heavenly architecture. At the end of the nineteenth century, the heavenly sky was figuratively implied: with twelve picture-medallions, which hover between the (painted) ribs (fig. 8). In 1930 Berlin was elevated to the status of a diocese. Now the Austrian architect Clemens Holzmeister was commissioned to modernize the interior of St Hedwig's (fig. 10–11). Holzmeister rearranged the presbytery and seating according to liturgical viewpoints. However, his special attention was focused on the dome. With expressionist vocabulary he strengthened the intended meaning as 'the heavenly glory moulded in stone'. The many small rods evoked a Pentecostal rain of fire, which first hit the illustrated saints in the picture-medallions and then fell on the apostles envisioned as pillars. With these alterations, Knobelsdorff's idea of showing a divine foundation built upon the apostles (Acts 2.2-3) was developed to the next level.

1.4 Loss of Transcendence

The redesigning of the inside in 1950 was completed under the principle of reduction just as the rebuilding of the outside (fig. 12–13). An inner vaulting shell, which would have hidden the concrete ribs, was waived – justified with reference to purist material aesthetics. Because of this reduction, the interior space lost even more sacred dignity than the outside. The grey and dark radial ribs, which converge in an oculus, do simulate light rays, yet this semantic content only becomes valid with the help of artificial illumination. But even then, the evocation of heavenly glory and the miracle of Pentecost can barely be understood.

Furthermore, the columns have lost their symbolism. Through the knocking off of the stucco capitals, fluting and bases, they have been transformed into bare supports. As such they are no longer recognizable as the 'pillars' of the church. In addition, they can no longer manifest their supporting role properly; as the new dome, which is set higher, jumps back considerably and is organized completely differently. They stand in no harmonious relation, structurally or intellectually. In the end, they have been degraded to meaningless accessories.

1.5 Loss of Architectural Meaning

Architecturally, St Hedwig's Cathedral belonged to the most significant baroque sacred buildings in northern Europe. Knobelsdorff's idea to not just copy the Pantheon but to 'improve' it was the decisive factor (fig. 2 and 7). The order of columns, which in the ancient prototype is connected with the wall shell in a non-classical way, was set free – in the form of a circle of columns that were not purely decorative but had a load-bearing function. In a certain way, Knobelsdorff turned the architecture of the *tholos* (a round temple with an outer circle of columns), which he had also planned for his lantern, inside out – a solution Schinkel then used just a few hundred yards away in his rotunda for the *Altes Museum*, also to create an 'improved' version of the Pantheon. The only Catholic Church in a Protestant city had become a benchmark of good architecture.

This tectonic principle was intensified theologically by Knobelsdorff, Bouman, Hasak and especially Holzmeister (fig. 1, 6, 8–11), by taking reference to the symbolism of the Temple of Solomon, built by divine wisdom, and the Heavenly Jerusalem. The building style of massive walls from the Roman Pantheon was therefore sublimated by classical Greek tectonics and the metaphysics of Jewish-Christian iconography. In the combination of the Roman rotunda, the Greek *tholos* and Solomonic wisdom architecture, a synthesis of Rome, Athens and Jerusalem became manifested in the middle of Berlin for the Western intellectual world. This synthesis can also no longer be experienced today.

1.6 Obstruction of the Liturgy

Towards the end of the 1950s, the architect Hans Schwippert decided – against the resistance of campaigners for the protection of historic monuments – to excavate the core of the old crypt to create space for a lower sanctuary, which he connected with the upper sanctuary by means of a wide double-flight stairwell generating one large shared space (fig. 12–15).[2] Furthermore, he combined the lower and upper altars through a marble slab to an upright standing stele. With his in-depth alterations, Schwippert added elements to the church that are completely foreign to the original building concept.

The lower sanctuary fulfils important functions, as a space for baptisms and weekday Masses, and as a burial vault for the bishops of the diocese as well as for Bl. Bernhard Lichtenberg, a martyr of the Nazi regime who was dean of the cathedral. Nevertheless the over-dimensioned staging of the entrance immediately in front of both altars significantly affects the liturgy in a devastating fashion. The result is a gap between the priest and the congregation, which not only contradicts the concept of a Eucharistic congregation but also impedes the liturgical entrance at Mass and makes festive processions impossible. Furthermore there is not enough space for all the faithful; some of them must sidestep (or rather step down) into the lower sanctuary. Additionally, the view of a person entering the church is steered away from the altar to the area below. In place of a joint congregational 'Sursum corda' ('Lift up your hearts' in the Eucharistic liturgy), there is now a movement pulling downwards. The same can be said about the celebration of Holy Mass in the lower sanctuary, where one can literally watch over the priest's shoulders from behind the railings; and one looks to the Holy of Holies, which is kept within the tabernacle on the lower altar, again not upwards but downwards. The paradigms of worship are literally turned upside down. Schwippert's architecture acts contrary to the liturgical regulations of the Second Vatican Council in every respect. Schwippert's interventions are also problematic as his floor opening of eight metres' width is almost a quarter of the diameter of the entire church. As a result, the spatial effect, intended by Knobelsdorff and Bouman, is almost completely cancelled. It is obvious that Schwippert must have been inspired by the *confessio* of the major basilicas in Rome, but here the relation between openings and the overall space is by far more harmonious. Moreover, in those basilicas a ciborium leads the onlooker's

---

[2]   See Heinz Endres, *Die St. Hedwigs-Kathedrale in Berlin: Baugeschichte und Wiederaufbau* (Berlin: Morus-Verlag, 1963).

view from the *confessio* upwards, connecting it visually as well as symbolically with the dome or roof above.

1.7 The Lost Reference to the Historical Location

St Hedwig's Cathedral has been shaped by post-war modernism with the exception of the outer walls. Consequently, many historical (building) details were phased out during the reconstruction after 1950. Consequently, the typological characteristics of the church were removed and its fundamental idea distorted. Knobelsdorff had designed the so-called *Forum Fridericianum* as a conceptual whole and additionally set it in relation to the area of the royal palace (fig. 3). In this sense it was part of the fundamental concept that the outer visual identity and spiritual purpose of the church was to be in a dialogue with the other buildings. As a Christian sacred place, it corresponded with the Opera House, which was a sanctuary of the muses. As a residence of the heavenly kingdom, it corresponded with the ruling-class architecture of the Prince Heinrich Palace and the City Palace. As a seat of divine wisdom, it corresponded with the academic architecture of the Royal Library, the State Library and Humboldt University. As a house of peace, it corresponded with the military architecture of the *Zeughaus* (Arsenal) and the New Guardhouse. And, last but not least, as a Catholic Church it corresponded with the Protestant cathedral.

The strong focus on the 1950s and 1960s, which characterizes the image of the current church, negated these historical relations. The compositional and iconographic reduction together with this negation of history prevents the church from expressing the references that are associated with its highly symbolic location.

1.8 St Hedwig's Cathedral in Changing Times

The visual appearance of St Hedwig's Cathedral has always reflected the situation of Catholicism in Prussia and in Germany. In the beginning, Berlin's Catholic diaspora was only tolerated. Consequently, St Hedwig's was rather modest in appearance (fig. 4). Although the church stood on prominent building ground, it was barely recognizable as a sacred edifice, having literally been pushed into the furthest corner of the square. This 'marginalization' only changed in society with the emancipation of Catholicism in the nineteenth century; the *Kulturkampf* led to a moral and political strengthening of German Catholicism, despite Bismarck's intentions. The step-by-step modifications of St Hedwig's Cathedral administered by Hasak and Holzmeister are an impressive testimony of this development (fig. 5, 8, 10-11). The fact that the church was rebuilt after the Second World War is owed to the willingness of East Berlin's congregation to make sacrifices, and the ready help of West German sponsors. Still, the cathedral had to step down a rank in urban planning during the communist dictatorship, as before in the times of Frederick the Great. From within it even received traits of an underground church with Schwippert's open lower sanctuary (fig. 12, 14-15). Today, this architectural modesty gives off the wrong vibe. Unlike in the communist German Democratic Republic, Catholicism now has a strong place in Germany's federal society.

To have such a place in society means that the church has the opportunity to witness to God's presence in the world.

This form of making present is paraphrased by the Latin word '*repraesentatio*'. A house of worship does not need any splendour but needs to be 'representative' with regard to appearance as well as programme. This is especially the case for a cathedral located in the capital and cosmopolitan city Berlin. Here, the church has to show a structural presence – on the same level as its dialogue partners in politics and society.

2 Renovatio Ecclesiae

2.1 The Competition

In 2013 the Archdiocese of Berlin launched an architectural competition for the reordering of St Hedwig's Cathedral in Berlin (fig. 16). The aim was to close the open crypt constructed by Hans Schwippert. For this competition the author of this essay developed a design in cooperation with the Berlin architect Professor Bernd Albers. The main focus of our project, which entered the competition, was to give back St Hedwig's its original force of expression, open up more free space and strengthen the urban value of the church by applying precisely selected improvements. In the future the church should be, more than it has been until now:

1. A '*house of God among the people*' with a significant vocabulary of sacred architecture and iconography that makes God's presence tangible;
2. The face of Catholicism, with the building taking position in the urban context as *the Cathedral of the Roman Catholic Archdiocese of Berlin* in a prominent location in the capital city;
3. A *historic monument*, which is capable of responding to the references resulting from its location steeped in history;
4. Adequate in fulfilling the cognitive and aesthetical standards, defined by Knobelsdorff, as a *heritage building*;

In order to achieve these aims, we considered four points important:

1. A reformulation of the dome shell;
2. The addition of a (modern) lantern;
3. A restitution of the columns;
4. An extension and intensification of the iconography through corresponding furnishing.

Our architectural draft, with the approach of a comprehensive renewal, went beyond the intended goals of the competition's instructions, which is why it was not considered in the proceedings. Nevertheless, it is meant as a contribution to the debate as to how sacred spaces can be designed today. We still believe that the conversion project only makes sense and is justified if the current provisional character of the building is overcome, and is brought back to a holistic solution. This unique opportunity should be used with determination and conviction to make the redesigned St Hedwig's Cathedral into a sign of integral, intellectual and architectonic innovation – on the basis of Knobelsdorff's concept. We should have the courage to think of history, develop traditional forms and bring religious elements to the forefront.

2.2 Opening up New Spaces for the Liturgy

The entanglement of upper and lower sanctuaries, created by Schwippert, is eliminated (fig. 18); the church floor is closed again. As a reminiscence, but also as a new independent symbol, a (much smaller) panel of glass with the nimbus of Christ is placed *in the very centre* where the opening was. It guides the falling light from above to below. At the same time it allows a view of the dome from the lower sanctuary. Upper and lower sanctuaries still stay connected in this way.

The upper sanctuary serves the celebrations of Mass on Sundays and solemnities with almost 450 seats. The choir stalls, congregational seating and the newly created central aisle for the entrance procession can now be oriented quite naturally towards the altar. Behind the choir stalls there is space for a choir and medium-sized orchestra, while the organ can stay in its place. As the seating is mobile, the entire altar island can be used for large-scale concerts (concerts with the renowned cathedral choir are an important feature in the life of the parish).

The round head-end is increased in significance by housing the Blessed Sacrament as it had done in the pre-war period (fig. 20). This chapel can be reached through the passage behind the altar island and through the outer stairs located in the entrance to the building from the *Hedwigskirchgasse*. The lower level of the chapel can be used as a bishops' crypt. The sacristy is outsourced to an additional building with two levels that can thus serve both the upper and the lower sanctuaries. Its placement in the northeastern pendentive of the main rotunda and head-end allows the clergy to enter the church from the side – instead of from behind the altar island. Furthermore, the great rotunda and head-end are enhanced with a third building volume. This volume integrates itself harmoniously into the ensemble but like the other redesigned elements, adopts a modern aesthetic language.

The lower sanctuary receives its own midpoint with a central baptismal font surrounded by four columns, based on early Christian baptisteries (fig. 19). Equipped with about 170 seats the space is separated from a circular crypt through a circular wall. This allows weekday Masses to be celebrated at another altar undisturbed, while the chapel and prayer rooms can still be used by visitors. The lower sanctuary can be entered through two stairwells, which can be accessed from the sides of the entrance area of the upper sanctuary.

2.3 Creating an Architecture that Serves

The upper sanctuary receives a clear orientation with the reuse of Schwippert's furnishing (mensa and stele of St Peter with tabernacle; fig. 15, 18). The focal point is the altar, which has been kept at its old place by purpose – although the spatial volume would suggest a placement in the centre if considered from a purely architectural standpoint.

The decision to leave the altar in its place contains a programmatic message: the liturgy is not subordinated to the architecture but the architecture serves the liturgy. The altar, as a liturgical place, does not form the geometric but the spiritual centre of the church. The altar expresses, especially because of its off-centre positioning, the pilgrimage of God's people through space and time towards Christ. The idea that the faithful surround the altar as '*circumstantes*' finds a concrete shape not in the stiffness of a circular concentric composition (see fig. 16), but in a suspenseful dynamic anticipation of the Parousia. In this regard, a horizontal axis leads through the whole church from the entrance to the Blessed Sacrament chapel. Furthermore, the stele of St Peter with the tabernacle and the carpet evoke associations with the former high altar (fig. 18).

2.4 Giving the Space a Sacred Dignity and Spiritual Depth

To strengthen the orientation towards Christ, the bishop's *cathedra* is moved slightly to the side, as Cardinal Rainer Woelki, the former archbishop of Berlin, wished. As a symmetrical pendant it receives the *sedilia* for non-pontifical celebrants. A longitudinal axis, which leads from the centre aisle to and beyond the altar of the Holy of Holies and then peaks in the Blessed Sacrament chapel, is created in-between.

Furthermore, the central aisle, altar island and Blessed Sacrament chapel form a chalice and paten in their composition of the floor plan (fig. 20-21). The Heavenly Jerusalem is evoked by the modern twelve-pieced wheel chandelier above the altar (fig. 19). In addition to the existing stele of the Blessed Virgin Mary, the statue of St Hedwig, which had been in the lower level, is placed in the upper sanctuary, so that the female saints form a triad together with the stele of St Peter (fig. 18). The horizontal symbolism and spatial dramaturgy are complemented by a meaningful axis. The new projected inner dome shell and lantern enhance the effect of the building's height. As in the original version, this proposal envisages twelve pairs of pillars for the twelve apostles, on whom Christ built his Church.

2.5 Renewing the Church As a Sign of Pentecost

The theme of Christ building the Church on his disciples receives a thematic exaltation: the birth of the Church at Pentecost (fig. 17). In this sense, the dome, which follows the example of the Hagia Sophia, floating above a circle of windows, portrays God's wisdom which 'has built herself a house' in the form of a church (see Prov. 9.1 and Acts 2.2-3). The lantern symbolizes the heavens, God's dwelling place (fig. 19). While the architecture moves upwards, the Spirit of God pours forth in the opposite direction. The light is first manifested in a star, which is made up of twelve stylized fiery tongues. These continue as ribs formed as rays, which pass through the dome portraying the universe. Holzmeister's image of Pentecostal glory (fig. 10-11) is transformed into a load-bearing architectural structure. The symbolism of the dome, which dates back to the Pantheon (fig. 7), as a likeness of the vault of heaven, is expanded through references to Byzantine, medieval and baroque examples (Church of the Holy Sepulchre in Torres del Rio, San Lorenzo in Turin, Hagia Sophia, St Jacques in Liege, St Mark's Basilica in Venice, Sant'Ivo alla Sapienza). A visualization of God's new creation is offered in place of just images of the cosmos (see Rev. 21.5). Moreover, the iconography of the dome refers to the Roman tradition, to visualize the shedding of the Holy Spirit by rose petals falling from the oculus of the Pantheon. And like in the Roman university church Sant'Ivo alla Sapienza, the light of the Holy Spirit is concentrated in the architecture of the dome and goes over into the architecture of the church on earth.

2.6 Making God Present

Furthermore, a light axis is created from the lantern, through the glass base slab, to the baptismal font (fig. 19). This envisions the persons of the Holy Trinity: the Father in the steel circle of the lantern, the Holy Spirit in the materialized light of the dome and the Son in the altar, the tabernacle and cross nimbus of the base slab. In addition, it reminds us of the presence of Christ in the sacraments: in Confirmation (dome), in the Eucharist (altar area) and in Baptism (lower sanctuary).

2.7 Giving Beauty and Inner Logic Back to Architecture

Along with the expanded theological statement comes appropriate architectural meaning – the goal is to develop the classical domed building in every aspect. To begin with, the bare supports (fig. 12) become Corinthian columns again (fig. 18). This brings back the classical tectonic texture. Furthermore, the fine-particled framing construction can once again create a dialectic relation with the smooth wall shell. At the same time the metaphor of the apostles as '*columnae ecclesiae*' is reactivated (see fig. 9).

On the one hand, the new dome shell with the lantern improves the spatial proportions. The dome ribs on the other hand guide the circle of columns and dome to a union: they take up the vertical orientation of the columns and continue it in a logical manner until they meet at the lantern. During the process they experience synthesis from wall to framing architecture.

The good proportions of the historic floor plans reach an even higher degree of harmony. Moreover, the ribs give the space an additional dynamic, by combining horizontal and vertical, resting and swinging elements.

2.8 Understanding St Hedwig's Church as Concept Architecture

According to the prevailing criteria for the protection of historic monuments, a removal of Schwippert's floor opening would be an objectionable encroachment of the (existing) building stock (fig. 14-15). Still, this encroachment is justified, even advisable. In Western thought, material substance has been enhanced since the time of Plato, Aristotle and Thomas Aquinas with an intellectual spiritual substance, which describes the actual nature, the fundamental idea of things: form is the result of the idea.

Knobelsdorff's plan for St Hedwig's gave this thought an especially strong expression with his thematization of the miracle of Pentecost: the church as an edifice transcends into the heavenly church because the designs were of heavenly origin and the reason for its founding, the celebration of Holy Mass, represents heaven (fig. 1). It is not a coincidence that the copper etching, which documents the laying of the foundation stone, shows a model of the church descending, floating on clouds escorted by angels (fig. 2). The root idea of St Hedwig's church, its message, is completely embodied in Knobelsdorff's ingenious design. And this design is inspired by heaven; Bouman was only able to realize this design in simplified form due to financial difficulties (fig. 6). Yet he kept the concept of his predecessor – he even elaborated on certain aspects.

After the *Kulturkampf* and elevation of Berlin to a diocese, Hasak and Holzmeister were able to take Knobelsdorff's idea and congenially (re-)interpret it in the architectural vocabulary of their time (fig. 8, 10). In contrast stood the post-war reconstruction, under the theme of discontinuity (fig. 12-15). In contrast with Bouman, Schwippert did not connect the formal reduction with the reformulation of the basic statement. Today, the cathedral's appearance is robbed of its actual idea and shape.

2.9　Continuity in Change: Elaborating on History and Developing it Further

To preserve St Hedwig's Cathedral does not mean forcing an outdated condition on future generations, but rather the restoration of its liturgical functions and message as an important sacred building – in the sense of preserving its spiritual substance. This includes healing fractures that have distorted its character significantly. In the sense of continuity, our project transfers the existing concrete dome and supports of the 1950s onto new forms, which tie in with the underlying concept. In the process the material substance is not destroyed but newly coated.

The coating of the older building substance is a metaphor of the Jewish and Christian history of salvation, which dates back thousands of years. In the Old Testament, salvation is symbolized by the festive garment, with which Jerusalem decorates itself for its divine Creator, like a bride for her husband (Isa. 52.1; 61.10 and 62.4-5). In the New Testament this relationship becomes a metaphor for the church, which awaits Christ as '*sponsa ornata*' (Rev. 21.2). Furthermore the festive garment is a common symbol of '*renovatio ecclesiae*' since the early Middle Ages.

In the case of St Hedwig's Cathedral, '*renovatio ecclesiae*' includes both uncovering of existing but concealed layers of meaning and developing new ones. In this process, a contemporary sacred typology is created, which employs a universal language capable of speaking to all Christian denominations as well as visitors from diverse spiritual and cultural backgrounds (fig. 17).

2.10　Strengthening the Urban Presence and Taking Position

Another significant element of our proposal is the crowning of the dome with a lantern and the replacement of the actual roof cross by a larger one. Even at the end of the nineteenth century art historian Richard Borrmann lamented that Bouman had not built the lantern intended by Knobelsdorff: 'The lanterns originally planned for the church were never built. In this state of makeshift design of the exterior ... the church has remained until this day.'[3] When Hasak constructed the lantern he added a large cross on the top, for which he provided the following justification: 'I took it for granted that a Christian church should be crowned with a cross, and that it should form its main final chord rather than disappear like a small, coy flicker in the heights.'[4]

The spiritual substance of the St Hedwig's church should radiate outwards. Thanks to the lantern, the level of recognition as a sacred building is strongly improved and its iconographic presence next to its somewhat dominating neighbours is strengthened (fig. 22). Dome and lantern become part of Berlin's well-known urban concert of dome constructions. Hence it becomes clear that the church has 'its place in society'.

Moreover, the Pentecostal theme of the interior allows the church to enter into a complex dialogue with other edifices – as a house of God's wisdom, St Hedwig's Cathedral responds to the monuments of human knowledge: Humboldt University and the State Library; as a work of religious art it communicates with the representative buildings of profane art, like the Opera House and the nearby museums; as a manifestation of divine freedom it stands next to the New Guardhouse; and as a memorial for victims of war and tyranny, it positions itself against former military buildings such as the *Zeughaus* (arsenal) and *Kommandantur*.

2.11 Setting an Example

From a historical perspective, the Pentecostal theme sets the divine light of reason (fig. 17) against the fire of ignorance and hate, which raged throughout the entire city during the burning of the books at the *Bebelplatz* in 1933, during the *Kristallnacht* in the *Oranienburger Strasse* in 1938 and during air warfare.

Thus the church makes fruitful for the future the legacy of clergy like Cardinal Konrad Graf von Preysing and Bl. Bernhard Lichtenberg, but also of its ordinary faithful, such as the Catholic resistance fighter Josef Wirmer. This future is brought about in the union of peoples at Pentecost (Acts 2.4-11). In the centre of the unified capital Berlin and in a Europe growing ever closer, St Hedwig's church sets an example of coexistence and reconciliation.

Finally, a phrase by Pope Benedict XVI may serve as the motto for our project of the '*renovatio*' of St Hedwig's: 'Let us hope that the Lord will help us to contemplate his beauty, both in nature and in works of art, so that we, moved by the light that shines from his face, may be a light for our neighbour.'[5]

---

[3] Richard Borrmann, *Die Bau- und Kunstdenkmäler von Berlin: Im Auftrage des Magistrats der Stadt Berlin* (Berlin: J. Springer, 1893), 173.

[4] Max Hasak, *Die Hedwigskirche in Berlin und ihr Erbauer Friedrich der Große* (Berlin: C. Heymann, 1932), 226.

[5] Pope Benedict XVI, General Audience (31 August 2011).

List of Figures

Figure 1 J. L. Legeay: Copper etching of Georg Wenzeslaus von Knobelsdorff's design of St Hedwig's church. Kunstgeschichtliches Institut, Universität Freiburg.

Figure 2 J. L. Legeay: Copper etching of the laying of the foundation stone of St Hedwig's church, 1747. Kunstgeschichtliches Institut, Universität Freiburg.

Figure 3 St Hedwig's Cathedral today on the *Bebelplatz* with the Opera House (left), Hotel de Rome (former Deutsche Bank) and the former Royal Library (right). Peter Stephan, Berlin.

Figure 4 St Hedwig's Cathedral without lantern around 1860. Kunstgeschichtliches Institut, Universität Freiburg.

Figure 5 St Hedwig's Cathedral around 1920 with lantern and taller buildings nearby. Kunstgeschichtliches Institut, Universität Freiburg.

Figure 6 The inside of St Hedwig's, built by J. Bouman. Watercolour painting about 1800. Kunstgeschichtliches Institut, Universität Freiburg.

Figure 7 The Pantheon in Rome. Kunstgeschichtliches Institut, Universität Freiburg

Figure 8 M. Hasak's version of the dome of the St Hedwig's Cathedral with the illustration of the heavenly glory. Kunstgeschichtliches Institut, Universität Freiburg.

Figure 9 The apostles as the pillars of the church in Freiburg Cathedral. Kunstgeschichtliches Institut, Universität Freiburg.

Figure 10 C. Holzmeister's version of St Hedwig's Cathedral. Kunstgeschichtliches Institut, Universität Freiburg.

Figure 11 The glory of the Holy Trinity in Holzmeister's dome. Kunstgeschichtliches Institut, Universität Freiburg.

Figure 12 The interior of St Hedwig's Cathedral today. Kunstgeschichtliches Institut, Universität Freiburg.

Figure 13 The oculus of the dome at present. Peter Stephan, Berlin

Figure 14 Interior of St Hedwig's during Holy Mass. Kunstgeschichtliches Institut, Universität Freiburg.

Figure 15 The stairs leading to the lower sanctuary with the stele of St Peter, which connects the main altar (above) and the altar with the tabernacle (below). Kunstgeschichtliches Institut, Universität Freiburg

Figure 16 The project that won the 2013 competition by Sichau & Walter Architekten GmbH und Leo Zogmayer (© www.erzbistumberlin.de). Peter Stephan, Berlin.

Figure 17 Design of a new dome shell (Albers/Stephan). The gilded top of the lantern represents the glory of the Holy Spirit. It is the centre of the star covering the whole shell below. The 12 red rhombi serve as allegories of the flames of Pentecost. The rays of heavenly light get transformed into the restored columns of the church representing the twelve apostles. Bernd Albers, Berlin.

Figure 18 Design of the interior with restored columns, a new altar island and the stele of St Peter as part of the new tabernacle. The centre of the church is marked by a glass slab with cross nimbus in the centre, which illuminates the baptismal font in the lower sanctuary below (Albers/Stephan). Bernd Albers, Berlin.

Figure 19 Transverse section with allusions to the Holy Trinity and the sacraments of Baptism, Eucharist and Confirmation (Albers/Stephan). Bernd Albers, Berlin.

Figure 20 Floor plan (Albers/Stephan): central aisle, altar island and Blessed Sacrament chapel form a chalice and paten in their composition of the floor plan. Bernd Albers, Berlin.

Figure 21 From the cathedral treasure of St Hedwig: paten (c. 1980) and chalice (c. 1928). Bernd Albers, Berlin.

Figure 22 Exterior of St Hedwig's Cathedral with a new lantern (Albers/Stephan). Bernd Albers, Berlin.

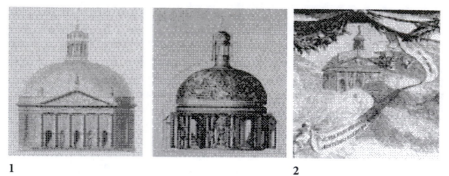

1

2

3

4

5

6

7

8

9

10

11

12

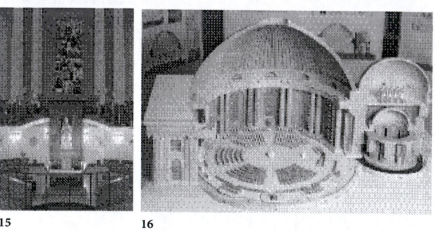

13

14

15   16

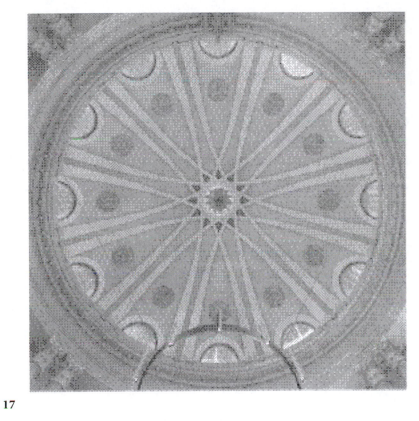

17

18

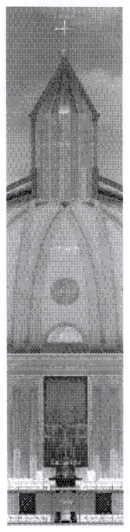

19

20

21

22

Homily at the Votive Mass of Saints Peter and Paul, Apostles

Robert Cardinal Sarah

'Jesus made the disciples get into the boat and precede him to the other side, while he dismissed the crowds. After doing so, he went up on the mountain by himself to pray' (Mt. 14.22-23). The times when Jesus is separated from His disciples are the times when He dedicates Himself to prayer. The disciples find themselves far out in the lake, and added to this separation from Jesus is the distress of battling for their lives with a heavy sea and struggling against a headwind all alone. They had departed while it was daylight but now they find themselves at night, in fact, 'it was the fourth watch' (Mt. 14.25).

This is a common human experience that we may often find ourselves in moments of our life when Jesus seems distant from us and the relentless waves and persistent winds of difficulties and suffering hit us from all sides. Indeed, this is an image of the Church in the storms of history and the life of every believer trying to navigate through the waters of struggles and hardships. To the degree that we do not perceive the presence of God, fears increase, shadows stubbornly linger and the storms of life become more terrifying.

Yet, it is in such moments that our Lord manifests Himself. 'And in the fourth watch of the night, He came toward them, walking on the sea' (Mt. 14.25). The fact that Jesus came is no surprise, for in truth, He never left His disciples. What is surprising is the way in which He came – walking on the sea. Jesus comes to His disciples treading on the very waters that threaten to capsize their boat and destroy their lives. In doing so, Jesus showed them that He is Lord even of the sea and wind. His mere presence in the boat causes the waters to calm.

'Take courage, it is I; do not be afraid' (Mt. 14.27). In making His presence known to them with these words, our Lord presents them with a choice: focus on the storm or focus on Him. He did not just simply say to them, 'Do not be afraid,' but He says, 'It is I; do not be afraid.' In other words, if they fix their focus on Him they will not be afraid. If they experience His assuring presence, many of their fears will dissipate. These three words – 'It is I' – help us to recall when God revealed Himself to Moses as the 'I AM', during a time of great suffering for the people of Israel. 'It is I' – these three words are also the answer to all our questions. Indeed, it is Jesus! The one who sets prisoners free, the one who feeds the hungry, cures the leper, gives sight to the blind, hearing to the deaf; He who calms the sea; He who raises the dead.

One of the disciples, Peter, accepts the Lord's offer to focus on Him rather than the storm. 'Lord, if it is you, command me to come to you on the water' (Mt. 14.28). By shifting his focus on the Lord, Peter's fear dissipates and with great courage, he walks on water, ignoring the storm. The fact that Peter is walking on water towards Jesus testifies that his focus is in the right direction. But when he feels the strong wind; when he hears it howling and when he senses the waves around him seem to get bigger, he takes his eyes off Jesus to look at them. Peter has shifted his focus back to the storm. And as soon as he does that, Peter, true to his name, starts to sink like a rock. Peter's dilemma teaches us an important lesson for our spiritual life: only by focusing on Christ we will stay afloat through the storms and challenges of life. Peter did not learn this lesson right away, but learned it, he did. Recalling this singular event years later, he wrote, 'Cast all your anxieties on him, for he cares about you' (1 Pet. 5.7). Jesus wishes to be our peace, our strength and the solution to life's many troubles.

'Take courage, it is I; do not be afraid.' Through the dimension of time, our Lord also extends this choice to each of us: either we focus on the storms in our life or we focus on the Lord. If we focus on the storm, we will always live in increasing fear. However, if we focus on the Lord, we will grow in confidence and trust. In the absence of God, fears and anxieties increase and darkness lingers. But in seeking and abiding in his presence, there is courage and the assurance of victory with his grace. In this light, Thomas à Kempis in the *Imitation of Christ* reiterates the importance of our personal relationship with Jesus: 'When Jesus is near, all is well and nothing seems difficult. When He is absent, all is hard. ... How foolish and vain if you desire anything but Him! Is it not a greater loss than losing the whole world? For what, without Jesus, can the world give you? ... If Jesus be with you, no enemy can harm you.'[1]

How can we, then, keep our focus on Jesus? We can keep our focus on Jesus through prayer. For in prayer it is essentially God who speaks and we who listen attentively to his will. At the beginning of the Gospel, Jesus gives us this example of dedication to prayer. St Matthew tells us that Jesus went up into the hills by himself to pray. Similar to this moment, there are Gospel passages describing that Jesus would frequently go off alone to pray. He revealed to us a God who was a trinity of persons, a communion of love between Father, Son and Holy Spirit. He lived this communion with His Father, especially through prayer. The most beautiful thing is that we are called to this intimate communion with God. 'As You, Father, are in Me and I am in You, may they also be in Us' (Jn 17.21). We are called to enjoy the same intimacy with him that He shares with His Father. Of course, prayer can be hard work because it requires perseverance and effort. But it is an exercise that can transform our lives. The more we pray, the more we will know God's will, the more we will love Him and ever more focused on Him. For in fact, prayer is keeping the eyes of our heart focused on Jesus, so that his grace can bring us safely through life's storms. As long as our prayer life is strong, the waves can surge and pound all around us, Jesus will keep us safe.

---

[1]   Thomas à Kempis, *The Imitation of Christ*, II, 8, trans. Aloysius Croft and Harold Bolton (Mineola, NY: Dover Publications, 2003), 35.

With this in mind, let us continue this Eucharistic celebration, which is the highest form of prayer and a real focal point for our life. Our Lord has made Himself really present, Body, Blood, Soul and Divinity, in the Sacrament of the Eucharist. As we look upon Jesus in the Eucharist, as we kneel in adoration and receive Him with love and devotion, we are doing what Peter did as he stepped out of the boat, fixing our gaze on Jesus Christ the Lord, whose love and grace can give us stability and support among life's storms.

15

Set Free at the Source of Our Demise Homily at the Votive Mass of Our Lord Jesus Christ, Eternal High Priest

Salvatore J. Cordileone

In the long pontificate of St John Paul II it would be difficult to pick one moment to define as the most moving of all, but certainly in the running would have to be his visit to his would-be assassin, Ali Ağca, in prison, and forgiving him for attempting to take his life. St John Paul goes back to the point of the pain, the origin of this attempted assassination, to heal the pain at its root, to forgive, for forgiveness brings healing.

As I reflect on this, it is not unlike those who undergo therapy for some sort of trauma they suffered early in life. They, too, have to go back, so to speak – go back to the source of the pain, to address it right there, confront it and address it, in order to find healing and freedom. This is a reality of our human nature; if we are to find healing, we must go back to the source of where it all started – not just psychological healing, though, but spiritual as well. Not just personal spiritual suffering, but the spiritual demise of our whole human race.

And so in this votive Mass of our Lord Jesus Christ, the Eternal High Priest, we pray in the preface to God the Father, 'who didst establish the salvation of mankind on the tree of the cross. That, whence death came, that also light might rise again. And that he who overcame by the tree, by the tree also might be overcome,' a reference to the deception of our first parents. They were deceived from a tree, which was placed in a garden.

That is how the evil one overcame and seduced us, and took us away from the happiness for which God created us. God undoes the damage by going back to where it all started, the tree of the cross. The tree of the cross undoes the damage of the tree in the Garden of Eden. Our Lord dies on that cross, and he is buried in a garden outside of the city. As our first parents were deceived in a garden and cast out, out of paradise, our Lord is buried outside of Jerusalem, a symbol of paradise.

It was by means of our flesh that the devil corrupted us, capitalizing on our flesh. And so our flesh will corrupt after death. Therefore, the eternal Son of God takes on a body, he takes on our human flesh, so that he may offer to his Father a perfect priestly sacrifice; so that in our flesh, which was the source of our demise, he might redeem our flesh, bestowing on the redeemed a glorified eternal body, which will not corrupt but will allow the elect to behold God face-to-face for all eternity.

Our Lord makes this offering in his body, which he assumed from our nature, an eternal offering. He continues to offer himself for us in our own space and time, through the offering of his Body and Blood in the Most Holy Sacrament of the Altar, all the way until the consummation of all history. He broke the bread, leaving us this memorial just as his body would be broken for us. He offered his blood under the appearance of wine, just as he would pour out his blood for us on the cross, and does so for us at every Mass.

It corresponds to us, then, in our flesh, to allow him to touch us at the source of our separation from him that he might forgive, heal and free us. He emptied himself for us in order to assume a body, and in that body to offer the perfect sacrifice for our salvation; so we, too, must empty ourselves of ourselves so that he might fill us with himself. We must then pursue the path of humility, allowing the Lord to bring us low, through our acts of penance and fasting, through our prayer and through our works of charity.

During these days that we are together God has abundantly blessed us with experiences of prayer and fellowship that lift our souls to Him as we behold a glimpse of His beauty. Through this He has increased in us our love of Him, and our desire for Him. He touches us at the depths of our being; let us then allow Him to heal us there so that we may be filled with His light and beauty, that the whole world may know this forgiveness and healing, and enjoy the peace and freedom that only He can give.

16

Homily at the Votive Mass of Blessed John Henry Newman

Keith Newton

As for you, always be steady, endure suffering, do the work of an evangelist, fulfil your ministry (2 Tim. 4.5).

I am delighted to welcome you all here to this beautiful church at the end of the *Sacra Liturgia* Conference. The archbishop of Westminster generously handed this building over to us in 2013 to be dedicated to the life of the Ordinariate of Our Lady of Walsingham. It is especially significant for us that it is dedicated to Our Lady and St Gregory who sent St Augustine to evangelize England. It is also the first Catholic Church Blessed John Henry Newman, our patron, attended with his father as a child, as mentioned in his *Apologia*, and there is evidence that he came here on numerous occasions following his conversion in 1845. That same year he wrote a letter to a A. J. Hanmer about the authenticity and continuity of the Catholic Church in which he said: 'To my mind the overbearingly convincing proof is this – that were St Athanasius or St Ambrose in London now, they would go to worship, not at St Pauls Cathedral, but to Warwick Street and Moor Fields.'[1]

In 1879 Newman was in Rome and on the morning of 12 May he was in the house of Cardinal Howard when he received a letter directly from the Secretary of State informing him that Pope Leo XIII had made him a cardinal. On receiving the news he spoke to the English and American Catholics as well as Church dignitaries who had assembled with him. What he said has come to be known as the *Biglietto Speech*.

As with so much of his writing this speech has an immediacy that speaks to us in the twenty-first century and especially to those of us in the Ordinariate who like him have made the journey from Anglicanism to the Catholic Church. He alludes to the fact that he had undergone many trials for advocating the kind of progressive views which one day would be fully vindicated by the Second Vatican Council, which has been called by some 'Newman's council'. He was accused by some of having liberal views but as he made clear in his speech, he had opposed this for over fifty years:

---

[1] To A. J. Hanmer, 18 November 1849, in *The Letters and Diaries of John Henry Newman, Vol. 13: Birmingham and London: January 1849 to June 1850*, ed. Charles Stephen Dessain (Oxford: Oxford University Press, 1963), 295–6.

Liberalism in religion is the doctrine that there is no positive truth in religion, but that one creed is as good as another, and this is the teaching which is gaining substance and force daily. It is inconsistent with any recognition of any religion, as true. It teaches that all are to be tolerated, for all are matters of opinion. Revealed religion is not a truth, but a sentiment and a taste; not an objective fact, not miraculous; and it is the right of each individual to make it say just what strikes his fancy.[2]

You would think he was speaking of today, not the end of the nineteenth century. How appropriate then to have the first reading today set for the Feast of Blessed John Henry Newman in which St Paul writing to Timothy (2 Tim. 4.1-5) describes those who refuse to listen to sound teaching but instead listen to those who say things people want to hear; and those who find arguments for men and women to justify themselves for doing what they want to do instead of challenging them to be faithful to the truth as it has been revealed through our Lord Jesus Christ: 'For the time is coming when people will not endure sound teaching, but having itching ears they will accumulate for themselves teachers to suit their own likings, and will turn away from listening to the truth and wander into myths' (2 Tim. 4.3-4).

It was because of the uncertainty of teaching of doctrine and morals that many of us accepted Pope Benedict's generous, open-armed invitation to enter into the full communion of the Catholic Church through the Ordinariate of Our Lady of Walsingham.

We have come to a place Newman would describe as 'sure and safe'. Another convert, Robert Hugh Benson, who was the son of an archbishop of Canterbury – you can imagine the media interest of his day – and also a former Anglican religious, wrote in his book *Confessions of a Convert* that to return to the Anglican Church 'would be the exchange of certitude for doubt, of faith for agnosticism, of substance for shadow, of brilliant light for sombre gloom, of historical world-wide fact for unhistorical provincial theory'.[3]

But of course it is not enough to rejoice in the sound and orthodox teaching of the Catholic Church – none of us can be complacent. Many of the issues that beset the Anglican Communion are surfacing in the Catholic Church today – challenges to her teaching so wonderfully set out in the *Catechism of the Catholic Church*. There has been a crisis of catechesis in the Church over recent decades and so many people are ignorant or even dismissive of her teaching.

There can be few passages in the New Testament where the duties of the Christian teacher are set out more clearly than the fourth chapter of St Paul's Second Letter to Timothy. We are to teach with urgency because it is a not a matter of interesting opinion but about eternal salvation. We are not to miss an opportunity in proclaiming the faith wherever we are, we are to make people aware of what is sinful behaviour, we should rebuke when necessary but with patience and love and encourage all to follow in the way of Christ.

---

[2] *Addresses to Cardinal Newman with His Replies, etc., 1879-81*, ed. William P. Neville (London: Longmans, Green, and Co., 1905), 64.
[3] Robert Hugh Benson, *Confessions of a Convert* (London: Longmans, Green, and Co., 1913), 142.

This is an urgent matter. We cannot be the evangelists, as St Paul calls us to be and the Church requires us to be, unless we are convinced of the truths of the faith and live them out in our daily discipleship. We are all called, clergy and lay faithful, to hand on the faith intact to future generations.

'It is the truth revealed through Scripture and Tradition and articulated by the Church's Magisterium that sets us free,' said Pope Benedict XVI when he addressed the English and Welsh bishops in 2010. He continued: 'Cardinal Newman realized this, and he left us an outstanding example of faithfulness to revealed truth by following that "kindly light" wherever it led him, even at considerable personal cost.'[4]

St Paul ends this passage by describing the way the faithful Christian should behave: 'As for you, always be steady, endure suffering, do the work of an Evangelist, fulfil your ministry' (2 Tim. 4.5). There have been and there will continue to be times of trial for us – grace is not cheap. We need to hold fast, accept the sufferings and perhaps misunderstandings, which are slight, for Christ's sake. We do this as bringers of 'Good News'. The New Evangelisation is not simply to attract lapsed Catholics back to the Church but to those in this country who have never really heard or understood the Good News in Jesus Christ. In doing this we have only one ambition, which, like Blessed John Henry Newman's, is to serve Christ and his Church.

---

[4] Benedict XVI, *Address to the Bishops of the Episcopal Conference of England and Wales on their 'Ad Limina' Visit* (1 February 2010).

CPSIA information can be obtained
at www.ICGtesting.com
Printed in the USA
LVOW08*1118020817

543428LV00010BB/230/P

9 780567 678430